Working With Groups

SECOND EDITION

Trevor Tyson

School of Business
Swinburne University of Technology

First published 1989 (reprinted 6 times)
Second edition published 1998 by
MACMILLAN PUBLISHERS AUSTRALIA PTY LTD
627 Chapel Street, South Yarra 3141
Reprinted 1998, 1999 (twice), 2000, 2001, 2002

Associated companies and representatives
throughout the world

Visit our website at www.macmillan.com.au
E-mail us at academic@macmillan.com.au

National Library of Australia
cataloguing in publication data

Tyson, Trevor.
    Working with groups.

    2nd ed.
    Includes index.
    ISBN 0 7329 4563 1.
    ISBN 0 7329 4564 X.

    1. Group problem solving. 2. Decision making, Group. 3.
    Working Groups. I. Title.

302.34

Typeset in Times by
J&M Typesetting Pty Ltd, Blackburn North

Printed in Hong Kong

Cover design by Raul Diche
Cover photograph by Trevor Tyson

CONTENTS

LIST OF FIGURES

PREFACE TO THE SECOND EDITION

In a postscript to the first edition, I pointed out that its predominantly rational-analytical approach needed to be balanced by an awareness and acknowledgment of the nonrational, largely unpredictable and 'sometimes awesome' unconscious processes that also occur in groups. This second edition attempts to bring about this balance by including other approaches that may be helpful in revealing and understanding more of the hidden forces that drive individual and group behaviour. A greater emphasis has been placed on systems thinking applied to the individual, the group, and the contextual components of groupwork, and to the way systems theory complements other approaches to the study of unconscious processes. Two such approaches – drawn from the traditions of Gestalt Psychology and Psychoanalysis – have been included by way of an introduction to the influence of the unconscious on group dynamics. Further new material has also been included on self-managing teams and managing diversity. All the references and recommendations for further reading have been extensively revised and updated.

Because the concepts set out in this book are closely interrelated, and an appreciation of the whole is as important as the detailed understanding of the parts, a 'scan and dip' approach is likely to be just as useful as a solid reading from front to back. However the book is used, the reader will soon discover the inevitability of certain significant aspects turning up for discussion in multiple locations.

The scope of the book

The type of group that is the subject of this book is the work group, a term used in its broadest sense, that is, one which comes together with a defined purpose. The purpose might be to make decisions, solve problems, formulate policy, or produce a plan or a design for any end-product. Such groups may be formal or informal, and are found in most organisations (committees, project groups, etc.), in educational settings (syndicate groups, research teams, etc.) and in the community at large (pressure groups, interest groups, social groups, etc.). They meet more or less regularly in face-to-face interaction, have a specified primary task, and may last days, months or years. Most of these work groups start their life as a mere collection of individuals – an aggregate – with little to connect them other than the stated purpose for which they have been brought together. It is from this point onwards that they embark on a process of social and technical organisation as they seek simultaneously to satisfy personal needs and organisational demands.

Any meeting of a committee, work team, study group or community group usually sees the members engaged in familiar activities such as setting objectives, planning, and making decisions. As member commitment to an involvement in the life and purpose of the group deepens, members are inevitably confronted with the more difficult tasks of problem-solving, conflict management, and team-building. Most peoples' experience of groupwork will include a familiarity with both ends of the effectiveness spectrum: from a rewarding sense of being in a well-run and efficient team on the one hand, to a sense of frustration or despair at lack of progress on the other.

Many groups 'click' spontaneously with the right mix of personalities, skills and resources in a positive and reinforcing environment; others have to spend time and energy on 'troubleshooting' as well as working hard to develop into a team. A little theory and a few guidelines can go a long way towards easing the struggle of team-building. 'Shoulds', 'oughts', and 'do's and don'ts' in the form of prescriptions for effective behaviour can accelerate the development of a group towards maturity and excellence. In the first four parts of this book, thirteen key concepts are presented in summary form, distilled from a wide range of literature sources spanning more than fifty years of research. The summaries are intended to serve first of all as definitions and aide-memoires for students and beginners in the field of group dynamics, for lay people involved in community groups and associations, and for novice leaders who want to increase their personal and professional effectiveness in work groups. For the more expert practitioner in the management, education, health, psychology, social work, and planning professions, some new ideas and a host of references should make this book a valuable resource and guide. The key concepts are supplemented by four case studies which help to integrate theory and experience by providing opportunities to apply the concepts and language used throughout the book.

The structure of the book

Part 1 presents a number of theoretical frameworks, progressing from simple to complex, for the study of groups. Key Concept 1 (Group Development) provides an overall context in its presentation of different models for describing the way groups evolve (or fail to evolve) over time after their formation. Key Concept 2 (Systems Thinking) sets out a basic systems approach that views groups as organisms constantly involved in input-transformation-output processes. Key Concept 3 (Psychodynamic Approaches) moves on to investigate the complexities of the influence of the unconscious on both individual and group behaviour.

This initial conceptualisation sets the stage for Part 2 (Organisation), in which the inseparable concepts of structure and process are examined in Key Concepts 4 and 5. As dynamic social systems, groups cannot evolve without interaction, and Part 3 (Work), consisting of Key Concepts 6 to 11, looks at the bread-and-butter operations typical of most work groups in the public, private or voluntary sector: communicating, leading, planning, decision-making, and managing conflict and diversity. The aspects covered in this part are not necessarily sequential in practice, and are certainly not mutually exclusive categories. To set goals for the group requires the members to plan, manage conflicts, and come to decisions. Dealing with problems may entail modifying goals, unmaking decisions, altering plans. The behaviours and interventions examined in these six key concepts are seen as the basic inputs influencing a group's efforts to work on its task and to develop into an effective team.

Part 4 (Learning) presents first in Key Concept 12 (Group Effectiveness) some models of the highly-developed/well-organised group or team, and explores the relationship between group development and organisational learning. This part concludes with Key Concept 13 (Team-building) and puts forward a brief argument for the benefits of planned rather than ad hoc change (team-building by conscious choice) closing with a brief look at self-managing teams.

Part 5 consists of four case-studies each set in a different context. Case Study 1 describes a series of meetings of a newly-formed management coordination committee. The analysis forges links between the life-cycle concept presented in Key Concept 1 (Group Development) and concrete experience of the group as they come together for their first few meetings. Case Study 2 examines two contrasting structure/process combinations which occurred in an organisational behaviour class for management students. The analysis focusses on some of the important structural and process variables discussed in Key Concepts 4 and 5, and on the way the interplay between structure and process created constantly shifting patterns. The situations described will be familiar to practising managers and group leaders at any level who have had experiences in work groups faced with choices involving values and conflicts of interest.

Case Study 3 recounts the experiences of the manager of a small business concern as she deals with an impending crisis in her work system. It illustrates something of the way the Key Concepts covered in Parts 2 and 3 (structure, process, communication and leadership in particular) are in practice closely interdependent. The analysis of this case explores those attributes of a small work system that underlie an emerging problem between two leaders at different levels of management. Case Study 4 examines an incident involving a team of two: a pair of experienced co-leaders who are confronted with a minor crisis and work together to deal with it by employing some creative problem-solving techniques. These four case studies also present the reader with opportunities to re-analyse the stories in their own way using the Gestalt and Psychodynamic approaches set out in Key Concept 3. This, to use the language of those approaches, will provide closure for the use of the book-as-a-whole!

Trevor Tyson
Melbourne
August 1997

COVER STORY

The two symbols on the cover photograph are intended to represent the conscious and unconscious processes which are present in all human groups. In the forefront is the metronome, standing for the conscious aspects of behaviour: rational, intellectual, sequential, time-bounded, measurable. In the background, harder to discern yet possibly of even greater importance is the gong, standing for the unconscious aspects of behaviour: irrational, sensuous, simultaneous, spatial, mystical. In other frameworks, these two aspects have been identified as left brain/right brain, masculine/feminine, or Yang/Yin. People who work in and with groups are called to explore and recognise the existence of both aspects, and then constantly to seek ways to connect and integrate them, for they are indeed but two aspects of the one reality: the group.

ACKNOWLEDGMENTS

My colleagues and students in the School of Business at Swinburne University of Technology have provided me with a rich and supportive environment in which to teach and learn over the past seven years. All have been instrumental in providing learning opportunities and teaching challenges that revitalised my interest in the Gestalt and Psychodynamic perspectives on organisational dynamics. In these two areas, my theoretical understanding has been significantly extended by critical feedback, reflections and discussions with John Batros, Lyn Willshire, Sue Long and mentor-extraordinary John Newton. In putting these approaches into practice in the classroom, Cathy Papalia and Wendy Harding have challenged and extended me.

For their involvement with me over a long period of time in developing innovative experiential programs for undergraduate programs, I particularly extend my thanks to Liz Gomm, Heather Russell, Barbara Lasky, Duncan Smith and Marg Robbins. All my other colleagues have been generous friends in sharing their time, energy and expertise.

DEDICATIONS

To my extended family and the many friends who have contributed to my learning in countless ways.

To my immediate family, to whom and for whom I give thanks: my wife Anita and our children Danielle, Matthew, Meaghan, Ben and Rebecca. They continue to be my most challenging and rewarding learning group.

PART 1

APPROACHES TO THE STUDY OF GROUPS

There is nothing so practical as a good theory
Kurt Lewin

Learn your theories as well as you can,
but put them aside when you touch
the miracle of the living soul
Carl Jung

Key Concept

1

GROUP DEVELOPMENT

Groups and Teams

Key words: *aggregate group team life-cycle stages themes*

Being 'in a group' is an experience that is repeated many times over in an adult lifetime, with large amounts of energy being channelled into the often difficult struggle of coping with demands of membership. For most of us, the family is the first and primary group, but we also seek membership in many others as we socialise, work, play, study, worship, seek support or give expression to our creative talents. Some of these groups co-exist or overlap, and at any one time we may be a contributing member of several, while attempting to join or move out of others. Over time, each of us grows to recognise intuitively what a group is, gradually building up an image or concept of what constitutes 'a group' as opposed to a mere aggregate or collection of individuals.

Groups come into being or are created for a purpose: for individuals, the work or social group may serve to satisfy their needs for fellowship and affiliation, to offer support and stimulation, or to provide the additional assistance and resources necessary to achieve personal goals. In organisations, groups come into existence to bring together the skills and talents needed to do work that requires many hands or heads: collection and processing of information; liaison and coordination; planning, decision-making and problem-solving; negotiation and conflict resolution; enquiry and research.

Numerous definitions of 'group' are to be found in the literature, ranging from the casual to the comprehensive:

> *'Any collection of people that perceive themselves to be a group'.*
> (Handy, 1976, p. 145)

> *'Two or more persons who are interacting with one another in such a manner that each person influences and is influenced by each other person'.*
> (Shaw, 1981, p.8)

> *'A group is a dynamic social entity composed of two or more individuals, interacting interdependently in relation to one or more common goals that are valued by its members, so that each member influences and is influenced by every other member, to some degree, through face-to-face communication. Over time, if the individuals who comprise the group continue to assemble, they tend to develop means for determining who is and who is not a member, statuses and roles for members, and values and norms that regulate behavior of consequence to the group.'*
> (Bertcher, 1979, p. 14).

Bertcher's definition may be regarded as either exhaustive or exhausting, but at least it embraces a number of central concepts essential to an understanding of group behaviour. One of these is the idea that groups change over time in an evolutionary process whereby an *aggregate* or gathering of individuals may become transformed by organisation first into a *group* (as defined by social scientists), and eventually into a *team:* a group with an established structure and an acknowledged capability to be effective. This evolution can be portrayed as a continuum (Figure 1.1) on which a group can be located at any moment in time.

Aggregate	Group	Team
Unorganised	*Organising*	*Highly organised*

Figure 1.1   The group development continuum.

Examples of an aggregate would be a crowd, or a number of people sitting in a doctor's waiting-room: usually they interact very little, have developed no social structure, and are unlikely to meet again in the same combination. They differ substantially from a partly or well-organised group, which social psychologists generally agree share the following characteristics:

- members interact with one another;

- members have an awareness of group identity and 'boundary';

- members have at least a minimum set of values, roles and norms which regulate their interaction and differentiate them from other groups;

- members have a common task or a more or less clear group goal which gives direction and limits to their activities;

- members have established and identifiable patterns of communication, status, influence and interpersonal attraction.

Task and Maintenance

The processes that underlie group development fall into two realms that continuously seek to co-exist with as little conflict as possible: the group engages in some goal-oriented activity (*task*) while also striving for good social relations and a general state of well-being (*maintenance*). Although concern for task quite rightly predominates in work groups, an over-emphasis on one realm at the expense of the other will inevitably produce frustration, discontent or withdrawal, and if the group is to be effective an appropriate balance must be achieved (Figure 1.2).

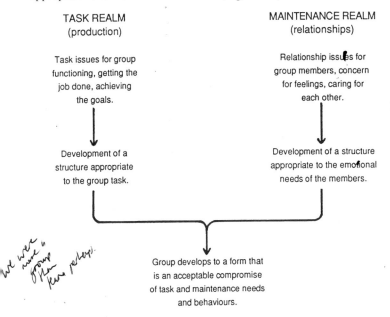

TASK REALM
(production)

MAINTENANCE REALM
(relationships)

Task issues for group
functioning, getting the
job done, achieving
the goals.

Relationship issues for
group members, concern
for feelings, caring for
each other.

Development of a
structure appropriate
to the group task.

Development of a structure
appropriate to the emotional
needs of the members.

Group develops to a form that
is an acceptable compromise
of task and maintenance needs
and behaviours.

Figure 1.2   The task and maintenance realms (Crawley, 1978).

When a group has developed to a level characterised by effective work procedures and high productivity coupled with a sense of cohesion and satisfying relations among members, it may be said to be a team. In colloquial use, the words 'group' and 'team' are often used as if synonymous, but in the light of the above definitions, 'team' implies at least a mature role structure and an advanced level of performance.

The Life-Cycle of the Group

Groups can be viewed as living organisms: like the human life-cycle (birth, infancy, childhood, adolescence, adulthood, old age, death) they have a beginning, a middle and an end. The development of a group is not simply in a straight line, but tends to go in a series of forward movements interspersed with regressive interludes. The general movement, if the group is healthy, is towards its avowed goal despite the backward periods.

The way groups first come into existence, then develop, mature and eventually die has come to be known as the life-cycle of the group. This term seems to be an extension of the idea that as individuals we progress from birth to death through clearly identifiable phases such as those postulated by Erikson (1963). Each of his stages is characterised by a core *psychosocial crisis* which has to be resolved in order to move on into the next phase without personality disorders of some kind:

Birth–1st year	Trust *v* mistrust
2nd year	Autonomy *v* shame & doubt
3rd–5th year	Initiative *v* guilt
6th year–puberty	Industry *v* inferiority
Adolescence	Identity *v* role confusion
Early adulthood	Intimacy *v* isolation
Middle adulthood	Generativity *v* stagnation
Late adulthood	Integrity *v* despair

Levinson (1978) proposed a different set of categories that are even more analogous to the way groups tend to develop. He saw the life-cycle of western men as a succession of relatively stable eras separated by transitional periods of change. These transitions are times of instability (or at worst, serious crisis) as the individual experiences the end of the outgoing era and prepares for the incoming one. In each era there are distinctive developmental tasks to be undertaken and challenges to be faced. Levinson's transitions and eras are:

0–3 yrs	Early childhood transition
3–17	Childhood and adolescence
17–22	Early adult transition
22–40	Early adulthood
40–45	Mid-life transition
45–60	Middle adulthood
60–65	Late adulthood transition
65–	Late adulthood

The idea that groups have discernible developmental stages found wide popularity in the 1950s and 60s. Tuckman (1965) synthesised the findings of several dozen theorists into his popular 'Forming-Storming-Norming-Performing' model. Later, fifty models were summarised in a book by

Category	Tuckman 1965, 1977	Northen 1969	Charrier 1972	Hartford 1972	Schutz 1972	Stanford & Roark 1974	Neilson 1978	Gersick 1988
EARLY	Forming	Planning & intake	Polite	Pre-group	Inclusion (in/out)	Beginning	Safety v. anxiety	1st meeting
		Orientation		Convening				Phase 1
			Why we're here	Formation		Norm development	Similarity v. dissimilarity	
	Storming	Exploring and testing	Bid for power	Integration; disintegration and conflict; reintegration	Control (up/down)	Conflict	Support v. panic	Transition
MIDDLE	Norming	Problem solving	Constructive	Group functioning and maintenance		Transition	Concern v. isolation	Phase 2
						Production		
LATE	Performing		Esprit		Affection (near/far)	Affection	Interdependence v. withdrawal	
						Actualisation		
	Adjourning	Termination		Pre-termination	Control			Completion
				Termination	Inclusion			
				Post-termination				

Figure 1.3　Group development stages.

Lacoursiere (1980) devoted entirely to the concept of group developmental stages. Figure 1.3 shows a smaller selection, arranged chronologically; all of these, and many others unlisted, are formulated from different perspectives or biassed towards different aspects of group life, yet they bear obvious similarities overall.

Tuckman's model was formulated from the findings in articles from the research literature on therapy groups, 'T' (training) groups, and natural- and laboratory-group studies. Schutz's model was formulated around social-emotional issues and concerns, and grew out of the author's research and experience with sensitivity training and encounter groups. He sees three principal interpersonal concerns: *inclusion* (who is in and who is out) *control* (who is dominant, who is submissive) and *affection* (who is intimate and who is distant); each concern tends to predominate in the early, middle and late stages of the group life-cycle respectively.

If the group is facing the end of its life, Schutz contends that the concerns will re-surface in reverse order as the members regress to cope with the impending termination of the group and their separation from each other. Hartford, a social worker, is one of the few who gave consideration to the processes that occur before a group meets for the first time as well as those that occur after a group finally disbands. The former are of particular importance in shaping the members' prior expectations of the group and the mood in which they will arrive at the first meeting.

To illustrate the patterns of group behaviour in the various stages of a group life-cycle, a synthesis of a number of the works shown in Figure 1.3 is presented below.

Pre-group: Prior to the first meeting of the group, members may or may not have information about who else will be involved, who the leader will be, what resources will be available, and what the task will be. Interaction may or may not take place, but for the most part each individual in what is at this stage just a 'nominal' group will be concerned with building his or her own private fantasies about what it will be like, or what they hope it will be like. Decisions might be made about the extent to which they will be a part of the group, whether they will arrive on time or not, how they will behave if others do this or that, and so forth.

Forming: As the group members come together for the first time, they are dependent (looking for support and guidance) and tentative (testing to discover what behaviours are acceptable in the group). The issue of *inclusion/exclusion* is paramount as they explore how they will fit in, their ambivalence about being a member, and how they can relate to the leader. Conversation is largely superficial 'cocktail party' chatting as they try to orientate to each other and to the task. Questions about the task seem to be: what are we here for? how can we get started? will we be able to do this? There is a searching for a sense of direction and a strong leader. The

forming stage enables the group to begin to define its boundary and to
establish the beginnings of its unique culture (McCollom, 1990).

Storming: Often, things begin to bog down a little after the forming
stage. Some issues of inclusion/exclusion may still not be entirely
resolved before the first conflict occurs as personal agendas are revealed
and members start to assert or defend their individuality. Interactions are
uneven, there is usually some in-fighting (a rebellion against the leader or
dominant members) and a 'pecking order' begins to emerge. Sometimes
the conflicts are kept under the surface and result in a sense of hopeless-
ness, then apathy as doubts arise about their ability to cope with the task,
even about the worth of the whole enterprise. This *fight/flight dynamic* is
characteristic in all conflict situations.

Norming: If the group weathers the storming phase and successfully
handles conflict and hostility, a sense of renewed hope may emerge.
Members begin to be tolerant of each others' differences and accept the
group, cohesion increases, norms are established, harmony becomes
important. More detailed procedures and roles are established, and
although leaders are still needed for guidance and reassurance, members
are by now far less dependent on them.

Performing: With the group structure and identity formed, the members
'get on with the job', fulfilling roles that enable them to achieve an appropriate balance between productivity and interpersonal affection (i.e.
between task and maintenance). Problems still crop up from time to time,
but these are minor setbacks rather than major disruptions. The leader is
now seen more as a peer and resource person, and there is a consolidation
of a status hierarchy based on members' skills and resources as they are
relevant to the purpose and functioning of the group.

Termination: Termination behaviours include checking out goal
achievement, coping with ending, disbandment and departure, and making
plans for the future. There may also be some regression to patterns of control or inclusion/exclusion by some members as a denial of the end particularly if the group had been emotionally significant to those members.
Sadness is often expressed; some form of ritual may be called for to facil-
itate this expression or to suppress it. Re-unions may be earnestly planned.
There may be feelings of excitement about using the fruits of the experience or applying the lessons learnt.

It is important to recognise that the stages of group development are
not like watertight compartments, and although the above models *appear*
to be linear, all the authors acknowledge two important qualifications: (i)
progression is likely to be irregular with intermittent regressive interludes
or periods of stagnation: a stage might last an hour in one group, a month
in another; and (ii) transition from one stage to another is usually gradual

rather than sharp. In addition, some groups may skip a stage entirely, others may remain stuck and make little or no progress at all.

Incremental Development

As in the case of the companion term 'organisation development' (OD), group development may also be based on team-building: planned change towards greater maturity *via* a series of interventions, exercises or programmes which analyse group performance and provide feedback and training for improved effectiveness. Using group development in the

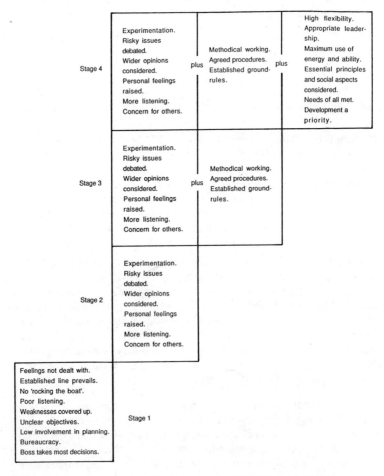

Figure 1.4   An incremental model of group maturation (Woodcock, 1979)

team-building sense, Woodcock (1979) proposed a 4-stage model of the maturing process (Figure 1.4). The model is a simple one, yet neatly marries the idea of the task/maintenance realms to the idea of incremental growth as groups move through successive stages towards maturity and teamhood.

Woodcock called Stage 1 an 'undeveloped team' rather than an aggregate, and said it is found *'wherever people have come together to complete a task but have devoted little or no time to considering how they should or do operate'*. Stage 2 he called the 'experimenting team': the move from Stage 1 to 2 comes when the members decide to review their operating methods and show a willingness to engage in team-building activities. Further competencies are added incrementally as the group revisits the earlier task and emotional issues worked on in the first two stages and decides to establish more mature procedures and ground-rules to see them into Stage 3 (the 'consolidating team'). Task and relationship improvements consolidated in the previous two stages are supplemented by a deeper concern for flexibility and cooperation that finally takes them into Stage 4 ('the mature team').

Punctuated Development

In contrast to the above, Gersick (1988) presents a model of group development based on a study of eight task groups of varying size (3 to 12), duration (7 days to 6 months), and context (university students and administrators, bank executives, hospital administrators, social workers, community fundraisers). Two surprising consistencies were found across all eight groups. First, they shared a pattern of development that Gersick labelled 'punctuated equilibrium' – two lengthy phases of inertia punctuated by a concentrated revolutionary period of change. Second, this moment of change or transition from Phase 1 to Phase 2 occurred in each group at the same point in its life-cycle: precisely halfway between its initial meeting and its deadline for completion of the task. It was as if a 'deadline awareness' suddenly occurred, and Gersick noted the similarity here with sports matches and the significance of the half-time break, or a human lifetime and the significance of the mid-life crisis.

In Phase 1, Gersick claims (p. 22) that groups rush to define the parameters of their situation, then examine them no further, and work in a largely unstructured way on trial and rejection of possibilities. Little attempt is made to look at longer term goals or to make contact with their environment. The mid-point revolution 'appears to work like an alarm clock, heightening members' awareness that their time is limited, stimulating them to compare where they are with where they need to be and to adjust their progress accordingly' (p. 34). Contact is made at this time with the environment, but diminishes again as Phase 2 gets under way. In this phase, their behaviour is substantially different: plans made during the transitional period are implemented, often mechanically and with a return of inertia that lasts until the deadline draws close enough to generate both the 'putting it all together work' to complete the product, and a renewed interest in the external customer.

Gersick's findings indicate the importance of the first and last meetings: the initial one which sets the direction and characteristics for Phase 1, and the final one in which the groups display a burst of energy as they concentrate on finishing off the task by completing the work set in train in Phase 2. Finally, and in contrast to Tuckman's and similar models, Gersick takes note of the contrasts in attitude to outside influences, particularly at the transition point, when all the groups suddenly decided to open themselves up to such influential people in their organisational context as task delegators (e.g. professors, departmental heads) or helpers (e.g. facilitators, consultants).

Thematic Development

Rather than viewing group development as linear, with or without regressive cycles, some researchers contend that major themes are discernible that are recurrent and non-linear, and which emerge continuously over the group's lifetime. Any or several of these can arise at any time, and must be successfully dealt with; if not, the group will not learn, develop, or increase its effectiveness. In these theories, groups are seen to focus serially on critical themes and issues that arise in no particular order and drain the members' energy away from the primary task and plunge them into more primitive or regressed behaviours 'Once a theme is surfaced...it will develop in a fairly predictable pattern, from its surface aspect to its deepest level of significance' (Banet, 1976). After a theme has been explored and worked through to the satisfaction of the group, members will revert to working on the primary task.

Erikson (1963) and Neilson (1978), referring to human and group life-cycles respectively, described critical themes in terms of polarities that need to be resolved if the person or group is to move on. Although a sequential order is seldom followed in the case of a work group, some of these crises have obvious parallels in groups that may be struggling with difficult internal relationships (for example, issues of trust *v.* mistrust, interdependence *v.* withdrawal), or are unclear about their group's primary task or corporate responsibility (group identity *v* role confusion), or have run out of creative ideas or energy for the primary task (generativity *v* stagnation).

In contrast, Whitaker and Lieberman (1964) focussed on singular themes, believing that groups begin with a 'first round' of certain basic themes, which differs from later recurrences of the same themes. The authors, being concerned mainly with therapy groups, identified only socio-emotional themes which recur and must be dealt with repeatedly: angry impulses towards the leader, sexual feelings towards each other, competition, revenge, etc. Cohen and Smith (1976) also described group development in terms of themes rather than sequential stages. The themes they identified are: anxiety, power, norms, interpersonal relations and personal growth.

The distinction between linear and thematic models is not always clear-cut. Balgopal and Vassil (1983), in referring to five 'recurrent patterns': exploration, involvement, conflict, cohesion and work, acknowledge that these tend to be grouped into the beginning, middle and late phases of group life. Themes are certainly harder to discern, and their identification depends to a large degree on the observer's idiosyncratic view of what has been occurring.

The usefulness of the developmental models is considerable, particularly if the user has a working knowledge of several. What is important is what each model can offer by way of understanding and insight into groups, not whether any particular model is right or wrong. Having a repertoire rather than relying on a single model will assist in a better understanding of the behaviours, needs and concerns being manifested in a particular group situation, and at the same time will clarify what leadership action would be most appropriate in that situation. All group members should at least be aware of the general characteristics of the group development process, while leaders in particular would also benefit from a more detailed knowledge of a model which focusses on emotional content such as Schutz (1972).

For detailed reading on group development, see Gersick, 1988; Kormanski, 1985; Lacoursiere, 1980; Neilsen, 1978; Banet, 1976; Schutz, 1972; Tuckman, 1965, 1977.

2

SYSTEMS THINKING

Whenever we observe a group in session, our sensors (principally eyes and ears) perceive only that which is directly recordable: appearances, movement, expressions, gestures, talk, noise, messages exchanged. Our cognitive processes discriminate and select that which is meaningful, and then combine it with memory and past experiences to interpret, conceptualise or predict. Our viewpoint or preferred *representational approach* will determine whether we 'see' parts or wholes, (i.e. individuals or groups). Systems thinking can be applied to both.

Systems Theory

Key words: *system   boundary   environment
input   output   feedback*

First, some definitions: *a system is a set of elements that are actively interrelated and operate interdependently as a total entity.* The 'set' consists of all those parts that the observer decides are in or of the system, everything else being part of that system's *environment.* The line created by the observer around the system distinguishes it from its environment, and is the system *boundary.* Boundaries that are relatively impermeable (i.e. allow little or no exchanges of energy or matter to cross between the system and its environment) define a relatively *closed system*; conversely, boundaries that do permit such exchanges to occur define an *open system* (Figure 2.1).

The environment may also be regarded as a *suprasystem*: a larger surrounding system of which the system under observation is itself a part or *subsystem.* Subsystem/system/suprasystem together form the concept of a *hierarchy* of systems (Figure 2.2).

ENVIRONMENT

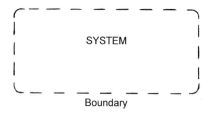

Figure 2.1   An open system in its environment.

It is possible, in the simple example of John Smith, Chairman of the School Council's Executive Sub-Committee portrayed in Figure 2.2, to examine the Council, the Sub-Committee and John Smith *collectively* (as a hierarchy) or any of the three *separately* (each as a system in its own right). The observer decides on the perspective, and hence on the boundaries and nomenclature according to the purpose of the observation. The determination of what is and what is not the system is therefore somewhat arbitrary and dependent on each observer's bias; this may cause problems when two or more group members are in dialogue about such matters as membership, autonomy or intergroup relations but do not, for example, share the same view of where the boundaries have been drawn.

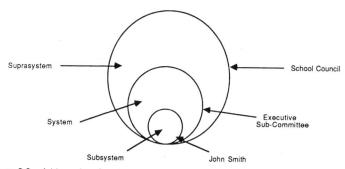

Figure 2.2   A hierarchy of systems.

Matter or energy in the form of people, materials, instructions, interruptions, noise, information and so on that enter the system from its environment are examples of *inputs*. Manufactured goods, knowledge, services, decisions, and waste products passing across the boundary from the system to its environment are examples of *outputs*. Through the activity processes within the system, inputs undergo a *transformation* into outputs (Figure 2.3).

ENVIRONMENT

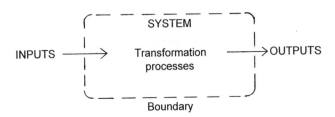

Figure 2.3   Input-transformation-output process.

For a social system to function properly, it must retain a steady state of homeostasis, which is to say it must remain in dynamic equilibrium through appropriate inputs, processes and outputs. The environment may furnish information about the group, particularly about its outputs, that is fed back to the group as new input (Figure 2.4). Such *feedback* about performance is essential to detect and rectify deviations from the desired state of equilibrium, and to mitigate unwanted impacts on the environment.

ENVIRONMENT

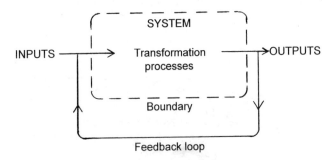

Figure 2.4   Feedback.

The new information provided by feedback can lead to changes that will improve the processes and/or the outputs, but when it is delayed or distorted, it may contribute towards further instability. In this case, or in the total absence of feedback, the system will proceed towards a state of disorganisation, and eventually disintegrate, according to the natural law of *entropy*. The reverse process is *negative entropy*, which results from any force, influence, or feedback that re-stabilises the system, corrects its faults, or enhances its growth towards maturity and wholeness.

Groups as Open Systems

The language used above is that of General Systems Theory (Von Bertalanffy, 1968). The original theory and its derivatives (e.g. Emery, 1981) provide us with a consistent set of concepts that are particularly helpful when trying to understand group behaviour at the level of the total group, i.e. when focussing on the group-as-a-whole as an *intact social system* openly exchanging energies with its environment. Systems thinking can equally well be employed to explore the intrapsychic behaviour of the individual, the interpersonal behaviour of a pair or a subgroup, the behaviour of the group as a complete entity, or intergroup and inter-organisational relationships. The observations and interpretations that arise from any such explorations may ultimately be expected to be put to practical use by informing any action (contributions or interventions) that an observer, member or leader might be preparing to take. Figure 2.5 brings the theory to life in its portrayal of a typical work group as an open system exchanging materials with its environment.

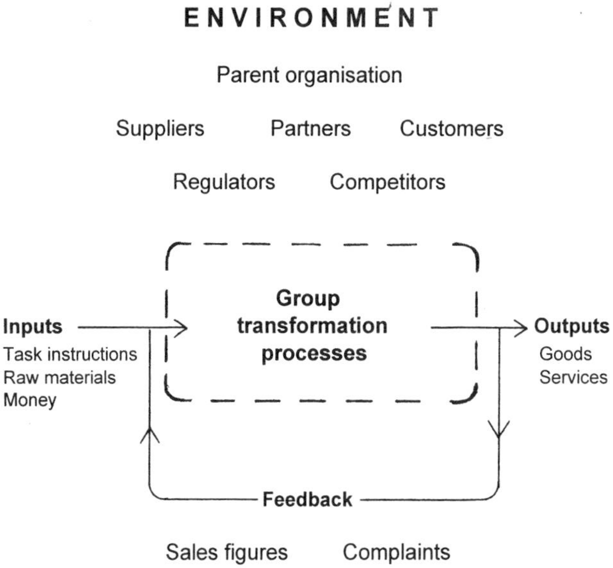

ENVIRONMENT

Parent organisation

Suppliers   Partners   Customers

Regulators   Competitors

Inputs → **Group transformation processes** → **Outputs**

Inputs
Task instructions
Raw materials
Money

Outputs
Goods
Services

Feedback

Sales figures   Complaints

Figure 2.5   A work group in its task environment.

A work group is defined by a boundary around its activities that simultaneously separates it from and connects it to its external environment. As an open system, the group depends on a continuous process of being able to import and export across its boundary whatever it needs to ensure its survival and carry out its primary task. Adequate resources coming in and quality products going out are prerequisites for this survival, and so are effective human and technological processes within the group itself.

The task of the group leader or manager is largely that of a *boundary manager,* with special responsibility for regulating the transactions across the boundary to ensure the successful completion of the primary task. An equally important responsibility is constantly to scan the external environment for changes, threats, and opportunities that could affect the group. Environmental influences originate from sources that range from immediate and frequent to distant and occasional. They produce effects that may be momentary or prolonged, slight or profound, depending on the multiplicity of forces that pertain within and outside the system at a given time.

Influences originating in the immediate social environment of a work group include nearby individuals and other groups. By demonstrating their own values, norms, expectations and demands through external roles such as supplier, client, customer, competitor, observer or critic, they can bring powerful influences to bear on the group, often supported by incentives, rewards or punishments. Smith (1977, pp. 359–72) also emphasises the importance of the influence on individual behaviour that is exerted by the dynamics between the member's group and others with which it interacts in its immediate task environment.

Social influence, if negative, can result in fatigue, boredom, reduced motivation and performance, loss of concentration, accidents and a host of other stress-related outcomes. A perceived hostile threat from an external group can result in an immediate increase in group cohesion; a compliment can raise flagging morale; a harsh indictment could result in disintegration or dramatic restructuring of the group.

More distant influences originate in the wider political, legal and socio-economic milieu: policies, technology, incentive programmes, financial support, and markets. More distant still are the cultural values, norms, ethics, attitudes and taboos of society in general. All of these will initially impinge on the parent organisation in complex and often unpredictable ways. The responses of an organisation to different environmental conditions in turn impinge on its internal work groups. Mintzberg (1979), in discussing environmental effects on organisational structure in particular, classified environments on four dimensions: stable/turbulent; simple/complex; integrated/diversified; munificent/hostile. He hypothesised that, in general:

- stable environments favour formal, standardised organisations and work groups;

- dynamic or turbulent environments tend to produce organic, flexible, less formalised organisations;

- the more complex the environment, the more decentralised will be the organisational structure;

- the more hostile the environment, the more the organisation will centralise its structure, at least temporarily.

Largely ignored in the literature on organisations, is the external physical environment, both natural and man-made. Nearby buildings, the natural landscape, weather conditions and geographical location are physical determinants acknowledged by environmental designers, architects and psychologists as having at least some impact on work groups in either positive or negative ways. Crowded city offices compared with rural conference centres offer groups markedly different experiences, as do prolonged heatwaves and freeze-ups.

Finally, the external environment must be clearly distinguished from the space in which a work group operates. Often referred to inaccurately as the 'internal environment' (a contradiction in terms) this is better described as the *work-space* or *group territory*. Influences on member behaviour that originate in the work-space include the room (size, aesthetics and comfort); furnishings (particularly seating); equipment and tools; natural and artificial lighting; temperature, air quality and noise. Steele (1973) gives a useful overview of the relationships between immediate physical setting, job satisfaction, and group development.

Groups as Sociotechnical Systems

During the 1950s and 60s in Britain, investigations into industrial work methods carried out by action researchers from London's Tavistock Institute of Human Relations saw the importance of treating the *social system* (management and workers) and the *technical system* (machinery, instruments, methods and skills) as a single interwoven work system rather than as two separate ones. The whole organisation as well as its work groups, when viewed in this way, takes into account the importance of acquiring and using technology with the workforce in mind, and selecting and developing the workforce with the technology in mind – a matter of 'the best match' between the two. Also included is consideration of the match between each work group and others, as well as the reciprocal relations continously occurring between the whole organisation and its external environment.

Out of the continuing work on the sociotechnical design through the 1970s and 80s, a major focus emerged on the importance of using self-managing (or semi-autonomous) work groups as an antidote to technocratic structures and autocratic leadership styles which were becoming increasingly out of place in a rapidly modernising and diversifying workforce. In promoting a sociotechnical approach, it was considered that work groups that were allowed to be self-managing were best able to integrate their membership and work methods with the selection and use of appropriate technology so as to operate as a whole. The expectation that this would maximise performance and job satisfaction as well as increase productivity and quality was not always met, but there were sufficient success stories to ensure that self-managed teams became a feature of many organisations by the 1990s. (The nature of self-managing teams is further examined in Key Concept 13.) The following table shows the main characteristics of work groups in classical and sociotechnical organisations:

The classical approach:	The sociotechnical approach:
External controls, through strict supervision.	Internal controls through self-regulation.
The person as an extension of the machine, an expendable spare part.	The person as complementary to the machine, a resource to be developed.
Division of labour, narrowly-skilled members.	Optimum task groupings, multi-skilled members.
Competition, alienation and low risk-taking.	Cooperation, involvement, and innovation.

For detailed reading on systems thinking, see Oshry, 1995; Emery, 1981; de Board, 1978, Chap. 8; Von Bertalanffy, 1968.

For detailed reading on sociotechnical systems, see Vaverek, 1987; Zobrist and Enggist, 1984; Trist, 1981; Pasmore and Sherwood, 1978; Emery and Trist, 1969; Trist et al., 1963.

Key Concept

3

PSYCHODYNAMIC APPROACHES

Traditional psychologies subscribe to the concept that within each of us is a 'dynamic psyche': that busy mind or internal world that is constantly processing incoming data from the immediate surroundings, connecting these to internally stored data, and responding as appropriately as possible with actions, feelings and thoughts. In its broadest sense, the phrase 'a psychodynamic approach to the study of group behaviour' refers to the use of established psychological theories such as Freudian psychoanalysis, Jungian analytical psychology, Gestalt therapy, Transactional Analysis, and so on. The term has also come to be used more specifically to refer to a particular orientation pioneered at the Tavistock Institute of Human Relations in London during the 1950s and based on an integration of systems theory and psychoanalytic theory. The term 'psychodynamic approach' will be used here in the broad rather than the narrow sense.

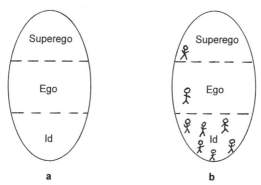

Figure 3.1 Individual psyche and group psyche.

Psychodynamic approaches (a) use psychological constructs to examine the internal processes of individuals behaving as a group, and (b) apply psychological constructs to the analysis of the behaviour of the *group-as-a-whole,* as if this social entity had its own distinctive or 'collective psyche'. Figure 3.1, as an example, uses Freud's structure of the psyche with its divisions into the Superego, Ego and Id (Freud, 1923) to hypothesise the existence of such a 'group psyche'.

The Superego is equivalent to the conscience – it incorporates moral standards and prohibitions inherited from authority figures, particularly the parents. The Id is inward-looking, concerned only with the body and gratifying its animalistic impulses, and constantly acting to defend the Ego against anxiety or shame by mobilising the defence mechanisms (see also Key Concept 5). The Ego is the mature part of the person, in touch with reality, and able to make decisions based on rational thought and planning. The Ego is constantly striving to mediate between the urges of the Id and the Superego.

The same framework can be used to view a group as if it had a 'group psyche' driving its behaviour as a whole entity (Figure 3.1b). In different group situations, members will have different predispositions for one or another of the psychic responses: 'behaviour is the product of the situational facts and the structure of the person' (Adams, 1993, p. 167). Through their individual behaviour when in interaction with others, each member will influence group-as-a-whole behaviour and ultimately the type of group culture that emerges. At any specific moment in time, a group-as-a-whole response to a stimulus or critical incident may be determined by the proportion of members who are triggered into one or another of the psychic responses. Figure 3.1b might be a depiction of a violently aggressive group, a critical mass of the members being in 'Id response' at that moment. The 'Ego types' may be too few to moderate the Id behaviour of the majority or to channel their energy into productive work on the task. Other interpretations are equally feasible: perhaps the Id types are simply up to mischief, with an ineffective 'group conscience' available in the sole Superego type. Eric Berne's 'Parent-Adult-Child' construct from Transactional Analysis (see Key Concept 6) could provide a similar interpretative framework.

Many contemporary psychologies provide a rich store of conceptual material that could help to understand individual and group behaviour at both the conscious and unconscious levels. As a full treatment of a whole psychological tradition is beyond the scope of this book, a limited set of psychodynamic principles have been selected for discussion in this section, each preceded by a synopsis of the tradition that produced them. Inevitably, such a brief treatment suffers from generalisation and simplification, but it is hoped that as the terminology introduced is reinforced throughout the rest of the book, it will suffice to whet the appetite for more advanced reading and reflection.

The two approaches described below — Gestalt Psychology and the Bion/Tavistock approach — have been selected because each stems from a long tradition of research and application, because they are compatible and share a common underpinning in systems thinking, and because together they offer complementary yet distinctive contributions to the understanding of the unconscious forces that underlie and drive individual and group behaviour.

The Gestalt Tradition

Key words: *wholes   parts   polarities   synergy*
             figure-and-ground   closure   insight

The German word 'gestalt' has no exact equivalent in English, but is generally taken to mean 'a completed whole'. The concept was developed by a group of German psychologists working in Berlin in the 1910s and 20s in the field of human perception (Koffka, 1922, 1925; Kohler, 1929; Wertheimer, 1945). Their work was focussed primarily on observing and describing perceptual and learning processes, both in animals and in humans. They showed that we do not just perceive things in our 'sensory field' as unrelated isolated elements, but strive to organise them in the perceptual process into meaningful wholes. Figure 3.2 illustrates how even a set of disconnected and quite diverse parts (the black and white dots) can be organised in such a way that we suddenly perceive them as a whole (turn the page upside down and hold it at arm's length).

Gestalt theory has been applied in many fields over the past seventy years, most notably in psychology, psychotherapy, education, and human relations training. It is closely allied to systems theory, with which it shares many key principles. For many years the Gestalt approach was focussed almost exclusively on the behaviour of the individual. In early experiments on animals conducted by Kohler (1925) and later by Birch (1945) chimpanzees learned to use boxes or sticks to access food initially placed out of their reach. In each experiment, the moment arrived when the chimpanzees perceived the Gestalt: how they could combine themselves and the implements so as to reach and draw in the food. This was the moment of 'insight learning' as the parts were integrated into a meaningful whole, and a new behaviour became available to that animal for future use in similar situations.

Kurt Lewin, the 'father of group dynamics', was closely associated with the Gestalt school in the 1920s, but was more interested in the practical application of the principles to human behaviour in groups. After emigrating to the United States in 1933, Lewin devoted his time and prodigious energy to establishing group leadership training and developing his empirically-based theory of group dynamics (Lewin et al., 1939; Lewin, 1944, 1947, 1948, 1951). His contributions to the field included the formulation

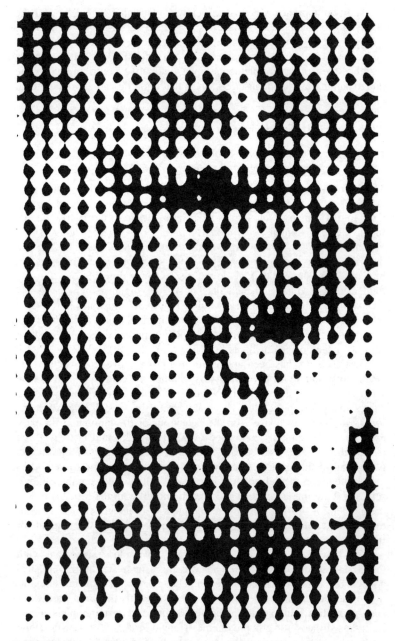

Figure 3.2   Perception of a whole (Gestalt) from parts.

of an original model for experiential learning in organisational behaviour (see Key Concept 12), and a theory of organisational change based on Force Field Analysis (see Appendix C).

In the 1950s, psychoanalyst Fritz Perls pioneered Gestalt Therapy (Perls et al., 1951), a one-to-one dialogue between client and psychotherapist which focusses on feelings, thoughts, and actions of the client in the immediate here-and-now presence of the therapist. Symptoms are thought to be created and maintained by unawareness of how parts of the self are denied or split off and therefore cannot be owned and integrated into the whole self. Change happens only when our denied parts are re-owned, when we acknowledge that we are capable of hating as well as loving, destroying as well as building, being frightened as well as being brave. Every time we reconcile one of the many polarities inherent in each of us we move further along the path towards health and wholeness. Many of the principles of Gestalt Therapy have direct application to the analysis of language in interpersonal dialogue (see Key Concept 6, and the work of Perls, 1969, 1973; Passons, 1975; Clarkson and Mackewn, 1993).

In the 1970s the application of Gestalt principles to organisational development began to emerge but was still mainly focussed on the individual or on interpersonal communication (see for example Herman, 1974; Karp, 1976, 1980; Herman and Korenich, 1977). In to-day's literature on group behaviour it is rarely mentioned, yet the original principles that produced powerful insights when applied to individuals, can readily be used to examine the behaviour of the group-as-a-whole, behaving as if it were an entity with a 'group psyche'. The emphasis in both cases is on perception and the way that it contributes to the reciprocal influencing of one party by another.

Eight principles drawn from the Gestalt Psychology tradition and most readily applicable to the analysis of individual as well as group behaviour are described below.

1. **Synergy:** Synergy occurs when the whole is greater than the sum of the parts. Only when a collection of notes on a piano are played in a certain way do they suddenly form a whole that we recognise as a particular melody – the melody is that recognisable 'extra'. Some of the parts or relationships can be altered (e.g. flute instead of piano, played more slowly or quickly, changed to a different key) without destroying the recognisable whole. Parts that are not perceived to form a whole do not give satisfaction or attract our attention as readily as those that do (see Figure 3.3).

In Figure 3.3a, each shape is a whole figure in itself, and each is the opposite of the other, yet they are placed in a spatial relationship that does not form a single dimension or meaningful whole. In Figure 3.3b they are positioned in a relationship that allows a whole to form in our mind (perhaps a rotary fan blade?) while simultaneously seeing the separateness of the original two parts. In Figure 3.3c, a more immediately obvious whole

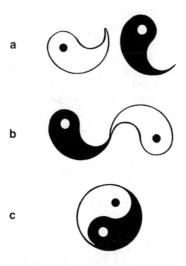

Figure 3.3   Parts, opposites and wholes.

occurs with the total merging of the two parts to form something greater than the sum of the parts: a circle, in this case one that is even more meaningful being the ancient Chinese symbol of wholeness, the integration of the opposites Yin and Yang. Separate the parts, and the circle disappears, yet we are left with two intact parts that are each, paradoxically, also whole.

As with the above parts and wholes, so with the individuals that comprise a group. An individual is energised and able to be creative to the extent that all his/her parts physical, psychological, emotional and spiritual are in harmony. What energy is to the individual, synergy is to the group (Karp, 1980). It is that state sometimes achieved by a pair or group of people where their whole-ness is perceived and felt to be greater than the sum of the parts: a powerfully experienced 'we' feeling. The converse, negative synergy, can also occur if the group lacks coordination or performs poorly *because* they are a group and cannot 'get their act together'.

Only when a group of people function in a coordinated way will they achieve something more than the mere sum of their separate efforts. Being together and co-operating effectively can add that something extra that we recognise as the group's unique 'greatness' where 1+1+1+1+1=7 ! Ideally, such moments would occur fairly frequently during a group's life-cycle.

For leaders as well as followers, the art of good group membership is to know about and to act in ways that will move the group towards wholeness, towards the live experiencing of its unique synergy. These states of enjoyable and above-normal performance that are intrinsically rewarding, marked by spontaneity and effortlessness, and a sense of group integration and power are what Maslow (1968) called 'peak experiences' and Csikszentmihalyi (1975) called the state of 'flow'. (See Privette, 1983, for a description of the interrelationship between peak experience, flow, and superior performance).

2. **Polarity:** Individuals and groups alike are characterised by polarities: competent/incompetent, dependent/autonomous, courageous/fearful, caring/hating, and so on. In most instances there is a pervasive, usually unconscious, desire to ignore or deny the negative aspect. From Gestalt psychology comes the notion that dualistic language and thinking separates what are two parts of the same whole, two extremes of a single dimension present to some degree in all people and in all groups. Such dichotomising can lead to distorted contact with the real self and the external world, or the real group and its external environment. Where the goal of self development through Gestalt therapy is to reintegrate the denied or split off negative parts of the self, group development similarly demands the acceptance and resolution of its opposites: both the good and bad aspects of the group, both its strengths and its weaknesses. The key phrase is 'both/and', not 'either/or'.

The Yin/Yang symbol (Figure 3.3c) can be taken as a representation of a group that is integrated, yet aware of its polarities. It is also the symbol of cyclic movement between opposite poles. As each grows to its maximum it gives way to the beginning of its opposite, a continuous fluctuation of energies that have distinct parallels in group behaviour. Morgan (1997, pp. 283–97) describes in detail these opposing forces in organisations, how they drive change, and how the apparent contradictions and paradoxes need to be managed.

The Gestalt concept of wholeness through reconciliation of the opposites even takes us beyond seeing the group as a system in an environment by arguing that group and environment are indivisible – each forms and is formed by the other in a continuous dance of exchanges and transformations. In this sense, 'boundary' is a mere convenience – a mental and often arbitrary construct in the mind, most usefully seen as that which both connects and separates.

3. **Figure and ground:** Out of the whole 'sensory field' which is internal to and surrounds an individual or a group at any given moment, attention is constantly being drawn to one aspect or another that emerges from the background and captures our attention – a sound, an object, something spoken, an idea, a goal, an anticipated reward or response. The process of recognising any object or pattern first involves distinguishing it from its surroundings, that is, it must be seen as an emerging 'figure' against a background. As an object or pattern begins to take form and stand out from the background, a Gestalt is beginning to form. The Gestalt in Figure 3.2

probably formed very quickly once the page was turned upside down! A rising need usually triggers what is to become 'figural' in the individual's field. At other times some figure emerges from the background unbidden, and may then create a need, for example a need to complete something unfinished. Miscommunication between people can often be attributed to one not understanding what is figural for the other in their discussion. When a need is satiated by appropriate behaviour, or when a figure is fully understood or attended to, it recedes to make way for the next one to emerge. This is the Gestalt cycle of action (Figure 3.4).

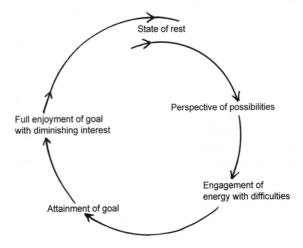

Figure 3.4   A Gestalt cycle of action (after Adams, 1993).

4. **Closure:**   Adams (1993) gives three examples of closure: completion of an attempt to organise parts into a meaningful whole or 'gestalt'; the satiation or full satisfaction of a need to the point where it changes; the successful completion of a cycle of action (Figure 3.4). People in work groups are strongly motivated to seek closure of cycles of action, or of stages of development, by the successful achievement of goals, completion of tasks, or resolution of conflicts. In this way, the psychological tension that is set up whenever a group is created to perform a task is reduced to manageable proportions and eventually resolved.

5. **Potential:**   Potential is 'power-in-waiting', and resides within the individual or object. It is that which is capable of being activated but is not yet activated. Only when the right internal and external conditions are present and wholistically related can the power be activated. A physical example is that of a battery, two pieces of wire, and a globe – the latter only lights up when the wires are of appropriate thickness, properly connected, and if there is still some energy stored in the battery.

In interpersonal process, one person can assist or obstruct the activation of another's potential, as well as assisting or obstructing the activation of their own potential. In groups, the maximum potential for the whole (the group) can be realised only to the extent to which the maximum potential of the parts (the individuals) is realised.

6. Resistance and difficulty: To generate electrical potential, there must be resistance. According to Adams (1993), life's natural demands and difficulties provide the necessary resistance for the development of a person's potential. Adams relates life's difficulties to resistance and potential in a simple but powerful (!) way when he describes the natural difficulties of the environment as the resistances against which we build up pressure in order to activate our potential (p. 23). In practice for example, this means that the effort we have to make to overcome difficulties encountered in trying to achieve a goal provides the resistance we need to develop our awareness and ability. Conversely, our level of ability determines how well we will cope with difficulty. Self-created or incompletely-understood difficulties constitute obstacles and cause delays (pp. 16–17).

If resistance to change or conflict in groups and organisations is viewed as a positive rather than a negative dynamic, it invites quite different ways of managing it. Acknowledging that resistance to change is both an inevitable *and welcome* aspect of organisational life, traditional responses to it such as breaking it down, discounting it or avoiding it can be replaced by the sort of strategy recommended by Karp (1988) in his 4-step process of Surfacing, Honouring, Exploring and Rechecking. As a basis for this approach, it is crucial that the demander should adopt a respectful attitude towards the resister. Hopefully, an attitude of mutual respect will subsequently develop between them.

7. Contact: A universal feature of the interpersonal process between any two people is the way they engage in a cycle of approach-contact-withdrawal. In this 'towards/away from' dance, the contact phase may be a merging that is superficial or intimate, clear or confused, gentle or violent. One or the other may have difficulty separating, or one may wish to merge at a time when the other is wishing to withdraw. Two parties in relationship have to contend with this dance and with their differences and similarities. When they are in contact but conscious only of their similarities, there is danger of at worst an unhealthy merging occurring or, at best, boredom. In Fritz Perls' dictum 'contact is the appreciation of differences' the word 'appreciation' is to be interpreted as meaning not merely the liking or valuing of what is different about the other, but behaving in ways that actively help to build up or extend those differences.

Perls' dictum is a useful and practical guideline for the management of diversity in groups and organisations, a situation where there is a multiplicity of 'towards/away from' dances going on at the surface and subterranean levels simultaneously. What applies *intra*group also applies *inter*group in the way that two or more groups within the work system may need to make and manage contact and cooperation.

8. **Insight:**   Grasping the meaning of something is the 'aha!' experience: suddenly seeing something in a new way that opens up new possibilities. It is the completion of a Gestalt, the successful closure of a process of seeking understanding or searching for a solution to a problem. For individuals and groups alike, moments of insight can be turning points or quantum leaps in the progression of their work and development.

The principles and definitions described above offer some new ways of thinking about group behaviour. The terminology will be found woven into many of the Key Concepts discussed later in this book.

For detailed reading on Gestalt psychology, see: Adams, 1993; Kohler, 1929; Koffka, 1922.

For detailed reading on Gestalt applications to groups or organisations: Clarkson, 1995; Philippson and Harris, 1992; Batros, 1991; Merry and Brown, 1987; Nevis, 1987; Karp, 1980, 1976; Herman and Korenich, 1977; Banet, 1976; Herman, 1974.

For detailed reading on Gestalt Therapy, see: Clarkson and Mackewn, 1993; Oldham et al., 1978; Passons, 1975; Perls, 1969, 1973; Perls et al., 1951.

The Bion/Tavistock Tradition

Key words: *the group-as-a-whole   work group   basic assumption anxiety   defence mechanism   projective identification*

A major contemporary approach to the study of group behaviour is based on the theory and language of psychoanalysis. The application of psycho-analytic concepts to the group-as-a-whole and anchored in a systems-thinking framework is referred to by practitioners in the Tavistock tradition variously as the psychodynamic approach or socio-analysis, although as pointed out above, these terms could be taken more broadly to include many other frameworks such as Gestalt Psychology and Transactional Analysis.

The most important aspect of work in the Tavistock tradition is the focus on the behaviour of the group-as-a-whole (Wells, 1990). This is analogous to the concept proposed by very early theorists such as Le Bon (1920) and McDougall (1920) of a group mind and its manifestation in the behaviour of crowds. Their research led them to postulate that crowds are often encouraged to behave destructively because of three aspects: the individual's sense of being anonymous, because of contagion, and because of suggestibility. Freud paid close attention to the group mind concept in developing his ideas linking group psychology and the structure of the individual mind (Freud, 1922). Freudian psychoanalysis is only one of a number of personality constructs that can be applied to groups as if they too have a group mind or collective psyche that reacts to situations and interventions from outside in both rational and irrational ways.

Wilfred Bion

The study of collective behaviour using a psychoanalytic framework and applied to the group-as-a-whole became firmly established after World War 2 with the pioneering work of Wilfred Bion before and during the time he was involved in leading groups at the Tavistock Institute.

Bion's work had a major impact on the approach being developed at the Tavistock, and this was extended throughout the 1950s and 60s into a major theoretical perspective by subsequent practitioners, notably Rice (1965, 1969), Turquet (1974, 1975), Miller and Rice (1967), Sofer (1961), Trist and Sofer, (1959) and Rioch (1975a). The tradition continues world-wide to-day through the work of institutions including the Tavistock and Grubb Institutes in London, the A. K. Rice Institute in New York, and the Australian Institute of Socio-Analysis (AISA) in Melbourne.

Bion's theory has its roots in psychoanalytic theory and particularly in its extensions by Melanie Klein (Klein, 1946, 1948, 1959). His work began during his career as a psychiatrist working with the armed forces during and after World War 2 (Bion, 1961). Bion's description of the way groups tend to behave was not one of linear progression through stages of development, rather it was one that differentiates between what he called the Work Group (i.e. the group when it is being effective, working competently on its real task) and the Basic Assumption Group (i.e. the group when it is working on hidden agendas and being apparently irrational, or allowing itself to be diverted from its work). The terms refer not to different groups, but to the one group as it engages in distinctly different modes of behaviour. Lawrence et al. (1996, p. 29) describe Bion's Work Group as follows:

The Work Group: all the participants are engaged with the primary task because they have taken full cognizance of its purpose. They search for knowledge through using their experiences. They probe out realities in a scientific way by hypothesis testing and are aware of the processes that will further learning and development. Essentially, the Work Group mobilises sophisticated mental activity on the part of its members which they demonstrate through their maturity.

Bion's description of his three Basic Assumption Groups are as follows:

The Basic Assumption (Dependency) Group: members collude to act as if they know nothing, are inadequate or immature. Their behaviour implies that the leader is all-powerful, loving and wise, and is supposed to lead them to success with little or no effort on their part. Certainly they do not need to give out adequate information about their concerns and diffi-culties, for the leader knows everything. The leader's process observations are transformed either into reprimands or immutable rules about how they must behave.

The Basic Assumption (Fight/Flight) Group: members collude either to quarrel, rebel or brawl or to withdraw into silence, diversions, day-dreams or apathy as if they have met in order to resist some dire threat by standing together to fight it, or by fleeing from it. Hostility is often directed by the group members towards the leader, while flight is usually from the demands of the task. In either case, the group feels threatened, becomes increasingly anxious, and begins to regress to a primitive defen-sive state.

The Basic Assumption (Pairing) Group: members collude with each other to focus on any two (regardless of gender) who might seem to have formed an attachment to each other. There is an air of hopeful expectancy – never fulfilled, but kept alive nonetheless – that some 'Messiah' might be born from the union to create a new order.

Two other Basic Assumption Groups have been proposed since the publi-cation of Bion's original three, but they have not yet enjoyed the same level of acceptance or application. These are Basic Assumption One-ness (Turquet, 1974) and Basic Assumption Me-ness (Lawrence et al., 1996).

Basic Assumption (One-ness) Group: members collude to seek union with an omnipotent force and surrender themselves to passive participa-tion in order to attain a higher state of consciousness, well-being and wholeness.

Basic Assumption (Me-ness) Group: members collude to behave as if they did not constitute a group at all, but rather that each member was a self-contained group in its own right. The underlying anxiety seems to be that if it was acknowledged that they constitute a group, their individual identity might be submerged or lost completely.

All the states described above (the Work Group and the Basic Assumption groups) are potential states in all groups. Figure 3.5 uses Bion's original construct to illustrate an important point: the terms do not refer to differ-ent groups, but to the same group behaving in significantly different ways. At any one time the group is either in Work Group mode or in one of the Basic Assumption modes. The 'pendulum' moves from one mode to another as the group-as-a-whole fluctuates between the poles of working on the task or avoiding it, between being mature or regressed.

Careful attention to process and content will reveal which state is in the ascendancy at a particular moment. The leader's responsibility is to cooperate with the Work Group, confronting and exposing the Basic

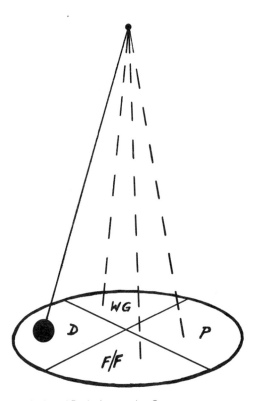

Figure 3.5   Bion's Work and Basic Assumption Groups.

Assumption Group whenever one of them is strongly manifested. As the Basic Assumptions defend the group against rising anxiety, the emerging reactive energy may be mobilised to support the task of the Work Group. Whenever a group's anxiety levels rise to the point where it falls more completely into the grip of a Basic Assumption, work on the task is disrupted, often to the point where the level of anxiety causes the members to become almost completely immobilised.

When in a Basic Assumption mode, the members all think they are behaving rationally, and it is this that makes it difficult for a leader to confront them and move them back to being a Work Group. At one moment, for example, the group may be angrily resisting any such leadership attempts, particularly if the task is threatening or difficult to work on, and will seek indigenous leaders to mobilise their aggressive forces or encourage their flight. If the group leader unconsciously colludes to provide the leadership the Basic Assumption Group expects, then the autonomy and capacity of the group will be seriously diminished.

Projection and projective identification

Central to Bion's theory is the defence mechanism of *projection* and its subsequent extension by Melanie Klein, *projective identification* (Klein, 1946, 1975). Projection is an intrapsychic event whereby a person unconsciously splits off and gets rid of a bad feeling or an unacceptable aspect of their personality by attributing it to another person or, in some cases, to an object. Projection can also involve the splitting off and projecting of positive feelings. In either case, the other is said to be the 'container' for the split-off and projected material. As this process occurs at the unconscious level of fantasy, with both projector and container unaware of the process, it is difficult to detect, yet it may have a profound influence on interpersonal behaviour.

There are numerous potential containers within the membership of the group, but it is usually the leader or a convenient scapegoat that is selected. Sometimes, if enough members of a group are projecting similar feelings at the same time, the group as a whole can be regarded to be engaged in projection. The group may also select an external person or group onto whom they may project their collective fantasy arising from their denied or unwanted feelings about themselves. Projection, then, can be acted out either by a person or by a group, but remains essentially out of awareness: an internally self-serving defence against anxiety.

In contrast, projective identification is an interactive process (interpersonal, group or intergroup) involving exchanges between projector and container. At the interpersonal level, the process starts when unwanted or denied aspects of the self are split off and projected onto a selected person. The next phase is the 'taking on board' by the container of the projected 'material'. The container next begins to behave in one of a number of ways: (i) by simply containing or absorbing the projection without behaviour change, (ii) by enacting the projection and so getting 'hooked' into the projector's fantasy (this is the complementary process of 'introjective identification'), or (iii) by modifying the projection in such a way that the projector is able to reinternalise it in a new and more constructive form and move back into contact with reality.

The third of these responses demands two things of the container: first, an awareness that the process in operation is one of projective identification, and second, the resources and 'ego strength' to modify his or her behaviour in a way that the projector can identify with so that learning and behaviour change can occur. Since the process involves both unconscious and conscious elements of behaviour, this outcome is difficult to achieve. Until some resolution does occur, energy will be drained away from the task and into the interpersonal exchange until such time as one party or the other detects and surfaces the dynamic and names it for what it is. 'What it is', on the part of the projector, is one or all of the following: a defence against internally aroused anxiety, a means of communication, a means of controlling the other, or an attempt to form a closer relationship with the containing person or object.

At the group level, projective identification may occur when a person, typically the group leader or perhaps a convenient scapegoat, is selected by an individual, a subgroup or all the other members as a container for an unconscious collective projection. At the intergroup level, it may occur whenever other groups come to symbolise or represent some unwanted aspect of the group; the dynamics are much the same and can be seen to occur typically between functional departments of an organisation (e.g. Marketing *v.* Sales) or between the organisation and its environment (e.g. management *v.* unions, a company *v.* its competitors). In an educational setting, it can be seen to occur typically between students: (local *v.* overseas, teacher's pets *v.* slackers), or between groups (students *v.* administration, academic staff *v.* technical support services).

Bion believed strongly that projective identification is absolutely central to an understanding of group behaviour, and he built his theory on that foundation. The concept of the Basic Assumption Groups as the direct outcomes of irrational, unrecognised or unresolved projective identification processes was his legacy to the Tavistock Institute, and through them to a worldwide network of institutions and practitioners offering group relations training and conferences based on his seminal ideas.

For detailed reading on the Bion/Tavistock tradition, see: Obholzer and Roberts, 1994; Hirschhorn and Barnett, 1993; Hirschhorn, 1990; Trist and Murray, 1990; Wells, 1990; Colman and Geller, 1985; de Board, 1978; Colman and Bexton, 1975; Bion, 1961.

For detailed reading on projective identification, see: Ogden, 1991; Gilmore and Krantz, 1985; Main, 1985; Horwitz, 1985; Bion, 1961; Klein, 1946.

PART 2

ORGANISATION

He who would learn to fly one day
must first learn to stand and walk
and run and climb and dance:
one cannot fly into flying
Friedrich Nietzsche

Key Concept

4

STRUCTURE

This Key Concept and the next are concerned first with the elements that comprise the *structure* of the group, then with the dynamic aspects of *process*. These two concepts are interdependent in practice and each can cause changes in the other. Nowhere is this seen more clearly than in the case of the formation of subgroups, a clear relationship-building process. Conversely, an established subgroup or clique will affect the rest of the group by the process of further social interaction and influence. For ease of analysis and understanding however, structure and process can be analysed as if separate, providing that it is remembered that they are primary and inseparable aspects of group organisation and development.

Groups as dynamic social systems are constantly adjusting in response to internal as well as external influences. Organising is the process of establishing the structures needed to perform the group's primary task: roles, rules, communication channels, work procedures, and so forth. These make possible the complex activities that members must undertake in order to achieve the group goals. Through this dynamic process, an aggregate becomes a group, a group becomes a team: in short, a sociotechnical system is created and developed.

From time to time, the process of organising may be artificially frozen in order to see the organisation as if it were static: a pattern of interwoven structural elements such as membership, roles, norms, and status hierarchy. An organisational chart (Figure 4.1) is a familiar example of such a frozen picture, and a sociogram (Figure 4.3) a somewhat less common example.

The structure of a group refers to its size, the characteristics of its members and the relationships between them, and the roles, norms and channels of communication as established at a given point in time. While

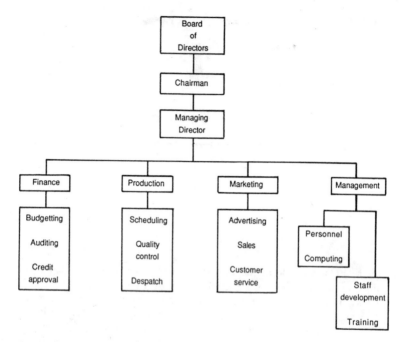

Figure 4.1   An organisational chart.

the structural components are subject to variations that can sometimes be quite sudden, they tend to be relatively stable over time; together they make each group an entity distinct from all others. Parts of the structure are highly visible: the formal positions, committees, working parties etc. Other parts are relatively invisible, such as the power and status relationships, the means of control and influence, the friendship cliques, the grapevine and so on.

The various structural elements are interlocked one with the others, and emerge out of the group formation/group development process. The most important variables are:

Membership variables:	Behavioural variables:	Relationship variables:
Group size	Communication pattern	Status
Personal characteristics	Roles	Power
	Norms	Sociometry
	Culture	Subgroups
	Cohesion	

Group Size

The size of a group determines and is determined by its boundary, which might be conceived as a demarcation line drawn around the group to distinguish it as a unique social system set in an environment. The boundary may or may not separate full-time members from part-time, marginal or aspiring members, and may be relatively open or closed, fixed or changeable. Boundaries may be established physically (by buildings, barricades, etc) or symbolically (by membership lists, uniforms, jargon, etc).

To describe a group's structure properly, the depiction of some sort of changeable boundary is unavoidable, but attempts to do this often open up disputes about membership, status, power and influence. Such conflicts should be confronted and dealt with in the early stages of the group's life-cycle. Uncertainties about who's in and who's out is a common source of anxiety that may interfere with the effective work of the group.

There is unfortunately no simple answer to the two questions 'What is the optimum size of a work group?' and 'Are small groups better or worse than large groups?' Group size depends on many factors, including the group's purpose and the degree of interaction desired; the nature of the task; the time, place and resources available. The question of optimum size can best be dealt with by examining what happens as group size increases, then by reviewing some of the characteristics of small versus large groups. Generally speaking, as groups increase in size, the following tend to occur: *maybe group could have been smaller*

1. an increasing number of members feel threatened and inhibited, resulting in decreased participation;
2. communication difficulties increase as information-sharing becomes more mechanical, the time each member has to talk decreases, decision making becomes more autocratic and a more elaborate or bureaucratic structure begins to arise;
3. the number of potential relationships increases, with the result that there is greater need for a leader to co-ordinate the group activities, achieving agreement and consensus is made more difficult, and subgroups begin to form;
4. when members fall silent, have difficulty being heard, or feel they have little influence in the group, they may create a dissident subgroup which may sabotage progress towards the group's goals;
5. frustration, absenteeism, accidents, disputes and turnover all increase.

On the other hand, as group size increases, the following benefits accrue:

1. the range of available resources, ideas, skills and abilities becomes greater;
2. the work may get done more quickly or more efficiently as tasks are delegated;

3. there is a greater use of checks and balances;
4. with the more elaborate or bureaucratic structure that ensues, certain individuals achieve a greater sense of belonging or security albeit at the cost of becoming more anonymous.

Groups of more than 10 usually start to exhibit most of the disadvantages listed above. Hare (1976) showed that the number of potential relationships in a group is $1/2(n^2 - n)$, where n = the number of members in the group. The addition of one member to a group of four increases the number of potential relationships from 6 to 10; a group of eight has 28, a group of sixteen, 120! If subgroups (coalitions) are taken into account in the first example, the group of five can be seen to have 85 relationships instead of 10! Even-numbered groups can always be stalemated by an even division of opinion or vote. Groups of less than 5 have special characteristics (for example, a group of 2 can only form a majority by agreeing; groups of 3 are susceptible to forming a coalition of two against one).

For detailed reading on group size, see Shaw, 1981 pp. 168–73; Steiner, 1972 Chap. 4.

Personal Characteristics

There are many background influences on group structure that originate in the personal characteristics of the members although the complexity of group situations and the paucity of research data means that only general rather than precise conclusions can be drawn about such variables as age, gender, race, personality and skills.

Age affects behaviour, standards, perceptions and physical abilities, while a long life may be the source either of great wisdom or of dysfunctional cynicism. Members who are homogeneous in terms of chronological age can become united and forceful, or competitive and tunnel-visioned. A group with mixed ages may benefit from the variety of life experiences and perceptions, or may disintegrate from lack of common interest or values. A member whose age is well above or below those of the rest of the group runs the risk of becoming an isolate or a scapegoat. There is no formula for the 'best' mix of ages in a group, as so many other variables are equally important ingredients.

Gender research is aimed at theorising about the differences in behaviour between males and females, and has produced inconsistent results, again probably due to the importance of the totality of situational factors as the prime influence on behaviour. Claims that men are more aggressive than women or that women are more concerned with relationships have not been satisfactorily substantiated. Certainly the gender composition – all-male, all-female, males predominating, females predominating, equal mix – will have a marked effect on behaviour at the interpersonal level, but precise predictions are virtually impossible.

Racially mixed groups have been found, not surprisingly, to experience more tension and conflict than racially homogeneous groups. Race certainly affects communication, status perception, power, conformity and cohesiveness, but it is not clear whether or how it affects productivity or group development.

Temperament, maturity, cognitive style, attitudes (to the world, society, authority figures, the opposite sex), self-concept, sociability, emotional stability all of these personality traits will influence a person's interactions with others. In particular, personality variables affect group mood, cohesiveness, patterns of communication, power and leadership, learning, creativity and productivity.

Each member brings certain abilities (skills, intelligence, perception for example) to the group, and is able to provide at least some additional resources such as information, contacts, or past experiences. The quality and quantity of contributions from the members will be largely determined by their skills and resources, particularly in regard to the roles they take on and the relationships they develop with other members. This in turn affects how others will respond and relate to them, and ultimately whether and how the group develops and achieves its goals. Managing the diversity of personal characteristics of the members of work groups is explored more fully in Key Concept 11.

Communication Pattern

The way a group is structured in terms of formal channels of communication affects the ease and efficiency with which members can exchange accurate information, perform their tasks, and develop relationships and group cohesion. Channels may be one-way or two-way, and flows may be assisted or impeded by various types of barriers.

The most common formal pattern is the hierarchy, where power and status are closely linked to position, and invested in the top ranks. Military, public service, industrial and commercial institutions are almost exclusively of this type, as exemplified in the typical pyramid of the organisational chart shown above in Figure 4.1.

Groups and organisations set up communication structures other than hierarchies based on responsibilities, power or status. Some other common formal or informal patterns are shown in Figure 4.2, and they have markedly different effects on process as well as productivity. Most small work groups adopt the all-channel pattern unless working in a rigid situation such as an assembly-line.

The Chain: represents direct-line relating with no by-passing; vertically this would be authoritarian-hierarchical; horizontally it would be an 'assembly-line' pattern. Pro-task, anti-maintenance.

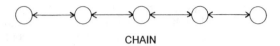

CHAIN

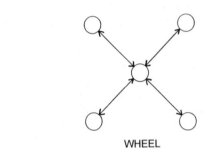

WHEEL

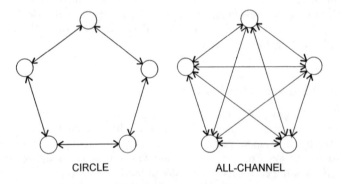

CIRCLE   ALL-CHANNEL

Figure 4.2 Typical communication patterns.

The Wheel: usually a central person (or star) surrounded by subordinates (or admirers) who do not communicate with each other, and may
feel isolated. An advantage is speed in making decisions. Central persons
have a high probability of emerging as a leader if they are not already
holding that office.

The Circle: is nearly always bad, coordination is difficult, flow of ideas
and information is slow.

The All-Channel: is the most likely to produce the best solution to
complex problems; facilitates relationships. A disadvantage is that it can
be slow, or may break down under pressures of time or competition.

The above patterns are rather stylised, and in reality many variations and partial versions will be found. No single one will be appropriate for all tasks, and the structure used should reflect the goals and purpose of the group.

Co-existing with the formal pattern are informal networks such as the 'grapevine' (Kiechel, 1985; Hirschhorn, 1983; Newstrom et al., 1974; Sutton and Porter, 1968). This refers to the network of communication channels through which gossip, rumour, information and misinformation circulate, sometimes with astonishing speed. The grapevine recognises few organisational boundaries, is beyond the control of management, and is fuelled by conditions of uncertainty or anxiety. Material flowing through the grapevine accumulates distortions, simplifications and deletions, and the flow is often blocked or diverted to serve self-interests. In spite of that, it is often given credence over and above official information flows and is valued by upper management levels for its feedback about what is happening 'down below'.

The arrangement of work stations may dictate to a large extent the pattern of communication, as may the nature of the task itself or its related technology. Temporary structures such as seating patterns at group meetings have ramifications for interpersonal communication and process, as well as for the emergence of leadership (Hare and Bales, 1963; Howells and Becker, 1962); some common patterns are shown in Appendix A.

Roles

An organisational role is a pattern of behaviour (thinking, feeling, doing) enacted by a person occupying a particular position or doing a particular job in the organisation. Moreno (1964) defined the term more universally as 'the functioning form the individual assumes in the specific moment he or she reacts to a specific situation in which other persons or objects are involved'. To him, a role is an observable unit of behaviour that consists of three integrated elements:

1. a construct or set of ideas or thoughts;
2. a feeling or set of feelings;
3. a set of actions or behaviours.

Before considering what sort of role relationships and structures occur in groups, some definitions based on classical role theory will help to reveal some of the dynamics that underlie role development:

Expected role: the behaviours which others think appropriate for the position or office; may be prescribed formally, as in a job description.

Sent role: the expected behaviours as conveyed by others to the role actor.

Perceived role: the way the occupant of the position or office thinks he or she *should* behave.

Enacted role: the way the occupant actually does behave.

Role differentiation: the development of a constellation of different roles in the group as it attends to task and maintenance, that is, the development of its role structure.

Role relationships: the way the roles complement each other (or fail to do so), and the vertical difference in rank (superiors, peers, subordinates).

Role cluster: the collection of roles a particular person plays in life, or in the group setting. Peripheral to the cluster are the *emerging* and *fading* roles: the ones the person is beginning to take on or relinquish.

Role set: the 'web' of all the other roles with which an individual interacts as a result of performing his or her own role.

Boundary role: a person in a boundary role interacts both within the group and with other persons and groups external to it, e.g. manager, spokesperson, representative, ambassador etc.

Role ambiguity: confusion about how a role should be performed, or the existence of indeterminate or conflicting expectations.

Role conflict: the experience of distress or uncertainty caused by different or irreconcilable expectations or demands of the role.

Role hunger: an unsatiated yearning to perform a particular role.

Role overload/underload: the degree to which the demands of the role (or the number of roles) exceed or fall short of the amount of time and resources available to the individual.

Role stress: stress due to problems in a role (ambiguity, conflict, overload, etc). This can be reduced if (i) the role structure includes clearly prescribed role expectations (job profiles), (ii) the abilities, motivations and resources of the individual are carefully matched to the demands of the role, (iii) new roles are created or existing ones modified, and (iv) attention is given to stress management, staff development and team-building.

The role structure is the total pattern of different roles identifiable in the group, and the relationships between them. When a group meets for the first time, the role structure may consist only of a leader and a number of members. In formal settings, executive roles described by such titles as President, Treasurer, or Secretary may be established, or responsibilities may be described by less impressive titles such as spokesperson, safety officer, quality controller.

The formal and informal roles a person enacts are determined by a number of factors other than an appointment to a position: self-image and natural predispositions in the personality; the perceived rewards; the impressions the person hopes to make on others; the prestige or power that might accrue; stereotypes and so on. As the group begins to develop a formal structure appropriate to the work to be undertaken, other more personal or informal roles will begin to emerge of the type described in the now classic study by Benne and Sheats (1948). The list below commences with the *'task and maintenance roles'*, acts of leadership that may be performed by any group member.

Task roles are directed to the work being done by the group, maintenance roles to improving group cohesion and fostering good relationships. Group leaders in particular need to be adept at these, although it would be unrealistic to expect any one person to excel in all of them. The responsibility of the leader then, is to encourage an appropriate and balanced use of the following task and maintenance roles among all the group members.

The task roles are:

Starter: initiates action by proposing ways of working, new ways of viewing the problem or organising material.

Information and opinion seeker: asks for information, facts, clarification, and feelings from other members.

Information and opinion giver: offers information and facts, clarifies and expresses feelings and opinions.

Coordinator: draws together the various ideas being expressed; coordinates the activities of various members or subgroups.

Summariser: provides resumes and restates major points discussed, bringing the group together in its thinking.

Energiser: stimulates the group to action and a higher quality of work.

Diagnoser: determines sources of difficulties, analyses barriers to progress.

Reality tester: examines the practicality of ideas, applies them to real-life situations to deduce or pretest their effect.

Consensus tester: asks for a 'straw vote' to determine if the group is nearing consensus on a decision; suggests 'trial balloons'.

Critical evaluator: subjects group decisions or accomplishments to a comparison with group standards and goals.

Technician: helps the group by distributing materials, operating equipment, arranging seating, etc.

Scribe/Recorder: writes down and displays ideas, suggestions and decisions; keeps notes, minutes, records of discussions; acts as the 'group memory'.

Spokesperson: speaks on behalf of the group as announcer, reporter, delegate, ambassador etc.

The maintenance roles are:

Encourager: is warm and understanding, gives recognition and praise for contributions.

Gatekeeper: creates openings for quieter members to have their say; restrains over-vocal members so that everyone has a chance to contribute.

Communication helper: makes sure people hear and understand each other; is receptive, listens and reflects back clearly.

Mediator/Harmoniser: acts as third party to try to resolve conflicts; pours oil on troubled waters; puts tense situations in their wider context.

Trust builder: accepts and respects others' openness; acknowledges risk-taking and encourages individuality; values others.

Process observer: helps examine the group's effectiveness by offering observations on group process; points out examples of constructive behaviours and effective procedures.

In contrast to these facilitating roles, there are the *defensive* and the *dysfunctional* roles. The former are intended to protect the group against anxiety induced by tension, conflict or low self-esteem, or against shame induced by incompetence or failure to make progress. The dysfunctional roles are those which inhibit progress or siphon off the energy of the group towards selfish needs or hidden agendas.

The defensive roles are:

Tension reliever: provides distractions, fills long silences, suggests breaks whenever a difficulty arises. This role may sometimes be more of a facilitating role, or it can be dysfunctional, particularly if the intention is to suppress or avoid an emerging conflict situation that the group may need to confront.

Court jester: helps the group to survive unpleasant situations and difficult problems and crises by clowning, telling jokes, or seeing the funny side of things. The jester gives the group a shared positive experience in the midst of anxiety, thereby providing an opportunity for recovery. Humour, if appropriately used, has great value as a 'social lubricant' (Westcott, 1988, p.139). The topic is more fully discussed in Napier and Gershenfeld (1993, Chap. 8), Duncan and Feisal, (1989), Duncan (1984, 1985), and Wagner and Goldsmith (1981).

Scapegoat: takes on the group's projections of its own bad feelings. Incompetence, failure, guilt, and thoughts that the group does not want to acknowledge within itself are projected onto whichever individual is susceptible to playing the scapegoat; he or she is then isolated and scorned for possessing those attributes. In this way, the group is able to gain relief from anxiety. If the group does not mature or work through the difficult situation, the bad feelings will persist. Some scapegoats react by becoming withdrawn, servile or aggressive, or by denying the role. Others use it as a way of attracting attention or satisfying their masochistic impulses. Douglas (1995) describes the ancient roots and gives contemporary examples of scapegoating.

The dysfunctional roles are:

Lobbyist: uses the group setting to introduce suggestions aimed at achieving personal goals or focussing attention on personal hobby-horses; committed to self at the group's expense.

Playboy/Playgirl: creates a nuisance by horseplay, whispering, writing notes, ostentatiously doing things unrelated to the task.

Recognition seeker: calls attention to self by loud talking, extreme ideas, unusual behaviour; seeks sympathy by playing 'poor me', or seeks praise by boasting.

Blocker: interferes with progress by raising irrelevancies, going off at tangents, arguing too long on a point, being stubbornly resistant.

Pessimist: expresses thoughts and feelings of doom; discourages and disillusions others; harps on past failures; disapproves or is cynical of all attempts to succeed.

Aggressor: criticises, blames, deflates or disapproves of others in a hostile manner.

Rebel: attacks authority, breaks group norms for the hell of it, refuses to cooperate.

If a group is to be effective, it must develop an appropriate mix of formal and informal roles. One such mix is described in a classification of work team roles put forward by Belbin (1993). These are based on findings from extensive management research in the U.K. carried out originally by the Industrial Training Research Unit, Cambridge, and the Administrative Staff College, Henley. The findings indicated that management groups are characterised by nine fairly distinctive types of roles, certain combinations of which make for an effective team structure. The roles can be summarised as follows:

Coordinator: team leadership, coordinating style; a good chairperson; clarifies goals, promotes decision-making, delegates.

Shaper: team leadership, directive or controlling style; challenging, dynamic, thrives on pressure.

Implementer: a good 'company worker', buckles down to the task; practical and conservative, works within the rules and constraints.

Team worker: helps to promote team spirit, shows concern for others' needs and feelings; diplomatic, listens, calms the waters.

Plant: an innovator; advances new ideas; solves difficult problems; creative, imaginative and often unorthodox.

Resource investigator: explores opportunities and resources, makes contacts outside the team; often extrovert, usually enthusiastic.

Monitor-evaluator: cautious, strategic and discerning; sees all options; perceptive, judges accurately.

Specialist: single-minded, self-starter, dedicated; provides knowledge and skills that are in short supply.

Completer: keeps work up to schedule, conscientiously seeks out errors and omissions; gets work done to a high standard in good time.

Belbin rightly warns that each role in practice has a downside or 'allowable weakness' (p. 23) and sometimes an unacceptable weakness (p. 53). For example, in the case of Shapers, an allowable weakness would be their tendency to become irritable or to provoke other members, while an unacceptable weakness would be their inability or refusal to make amends with good humour or to apologise when they hurt another's feelings.

These research findings are mainly useful in two ways: as a basis for selecting the members of a work team prior to its formation., or in the diagnosis of interpersonal problems in an ailing group. In the latter instance, the group may be found to have an imbalance of roles, or to lack some important one. Belbin and his co-researchers originally concluded as a general guide that an ideal management team would have:

- *either* a coordinator *or* a shaper (the two styles tend to clash);
- one plant;
- one monitor-evaluator
- one or more implementers, team workers, resource investigators and completers.

It is of more practical value, however, to plan or analyse the role structure of a work team in the light of Belbin's most recent findings on the way the different roles interact with each other in ways that are either mutually productive or counter-productive (Belbin, 1993, pp. 59–69).

One type of role almost totally ignored except by Moreno (1964) is the concept of the *psychodramatic role*. Mother, father, childhood games and fairy stories all have a profound effect on the roles played or avoided in the adult's daily life. The behaviour we bring to the enactment of our organisational roles (as well as such social roles as parent, musician, nurse etc.) is also significantly influenced over many years by our internalised images of admired heroes and heroines or feared villains. A person develops his or her group roles as a response to reality, at the same time retaining the internalised fantasy and archetypal roles as developed throughout the childhood years. These are the roles that individuals desire to enact even when they are outside the work and social roles they are permitted in their normal daily life. Heroes, heroines and villains are the models that cause us to become a particular type of leader, joker or comforter, bringing to those roles vestiges of a Nelson Mandela, a Bill Cosby, or a Mother Teresa. Equally, one might emulate Hitler, Machiavelli, or the Wicked Witch!

Playing out the psychodramatic role involves a process that is largely unconscious. Bringing these behaviours to conscious awareness increases the possibility of enhancing the productive ones and reducing the effects of the destructive ones. Together, the complex of psychodramatic roles form the individual's internal role structure, and are far more extensive and driving than the public roles. As such, they have been greatly underestimated and under-researched as influences on motivation, behaviour and the performance of organisational roles.

For detailed reading on classical role theory, see Biddle and Thomas, 1979.

For detailed reading on organisational roles see Belbin, 1993; Hirschhorn, 1991, pp. 34–42;

For detailed reading on psychodramatic roles, see Clayton, 1993.

Norms

As a group begins to develop, members begin to have shared and predictable responses to particular issues or situations, and a strong 'group position' emerges. Certain behaviours come to be acceptable, others not; certain beliefs are valued and shared, others not. As this value system develops, members experience rewards for conformity, punishments for deviance. From this emerge the group norms: *'those attitudes, values and forms of behavior that the group as a whole requires or expects of its members'* (Fessler, 1976, p.91).

Rules that a group makes deliberately to regulate behaviours or procedures could be regarded as explicit norms, but in the true sense of the term, norms are implicit rather than explicit: that is, they only become known when tested. They are the ways of doing things that have come to be regarded as appropriate or proper behaviour, and are specific to each group.

Because norms refer to the expected behaviour rewarded or punished by the group, there is a strong 'ought' or 'should' quality to them. The potential rewards and punishments may be overt or covert, but members are at least subconsciously aware of their existence and may modify their behaviour significantly because of hope of approval or fear of censure by the group as a whole.

Some norms require more strict observance than others, with a corresponding variation in the degree of reward or punishment handed out. The more adherents there are to a group norm, the greater will be the pressure to conform to it. Conformity may be rewarded by acceptance, praise, approval, pay rises, promotion. Deviance or refusal to conform may be punished by rejection, criticism, hostility, ridicule, fines, ostracism or expulsion.

Norms, formed as they are during the course of group interaction as individuals learn to 'fit in', are also influenced by the culture of the society in which the group exists. Luthans (1985, p.375) said that group norms will be strongly enforced if they

- ensure group success or survival;

- reflect the preferences of the leader or other powerful members;

- simplify or make predictable what behaviours are expected of members;

- reinforce specific individual roles;

- help the group avoid embarassing interpersonal conflict.

As Alexander (1977) pointed out, norms can be classified as basically positive or negative; he gives the following examples:

Positive norms viewing self and group with pride; √
wanting to improve on past performance;
sharing information and working co-operatively;
leaders as helpers and developers of subordinates;
saving money to reduce costs;
maximising customer satisfaction;
supporting and encouraging innovation and change;
training and development seen as essential;
trust and openness of communication. √

Negative norms negative view of organisational goals;
'near enough is good enough';
'every man for himself';
secrecy;
leaders as policemen;
lack of concern for cost effectiveness;
customers as obstacles, to be avoided;
support the status quo;
discourage experimentation;
training and development a non-essential luxury;
closed and defensive interpersonal communication.

For detailed reading on norms, see Spencer, 1995; Napier and Gershenfeld, 1993, Chap. 3; Feldman, 1985b; Bierstedt, 1970, pp. 208–41.

Culture

The culture of an organisation is best expressed in the phrase 'this is the way we do things around here'. It arises from the long-term values, beliefs and customs shared and adhered to by its members. Culture includes, in addition to rules and norms, long-established conventions and standards of protocol and etiquette; rituals and ceremonies; mores, ethics and taboos. All these make up the total pattern of familiar and expected ways of thinking and doing that are part of culture at all levels: nation, organisation or group.

In work groups, similar cultures develop as the group itself develops its norms and working practices, and establishes its underlying value system. From the outset, the culture of a work group may be strongly influenced by the prevailing culture of the larger organisation or society of which it is a part. Each time a critical incident or theme emerges it will be dealt with in ways which then tend to become accepted as the 'ways we do things around here'. Other influences may stem from the group's own history of successful or unsuccessful patterns of work, communication, and leadership.

A strong internalised and widely-shared group culture can have positive or negative effects on a group's performance. Greenpeace, for example has a strong culture that is based on desirable human values and clearly supports its goals. Equally strong cultures prevailed in David Koresh's Branch Davidian sect in Waco, Texas, and in Jim Jones' Jonestown cult in Guyana: the negative aspects of these were obvious. In contrast, weak group cultures, those that are undeveloped, fragmented or polarised into a culture and a counter-culture can be either an impetus for change or a source of energy-draining friction or mediocrity.

As in the case of norms, the stronger or more desirable the culture the greater pressure there is on members to preserve it. Moving into a group with a distinct but unfamiliar culture can result in mild or severe 'culture shock'. Newcomers are subject to a socialisation process that helps (or forces) them to 'fit in' – some groups hold initiation rites for this purpose, others use less dramatic degrees of social influence such as incentives, rewards or punishments. Group culture, once established and shared by the members, is reinforced in a number of ways:

- symbolically by behaviour such as bestowing rewards or punishments;

- symbolically by artifacts such as uniforms, badges, furniture, group name or logo;

- linguistically by stories, myths, slogans or 'in' jargon;

- ritualistically by events such as ceremonies recognising achievement, group outings;

- attitudinally by stance towards authority figures; the opposite sex; people from different races or religions; ethics and social responsibility; the natural environment.

Changes in a group's culture frequently occur in response to significant changes in the group's environment, at transition points or crises in its life-cycle, or when it persistently fails to achieve performance standards. A change of leadership or the existing leader's adoption of a more transformational style (see Key Concept 7) will often precipitate the emergence of new cultural norms and values. Culture change is easier in a young group than in a long-established one, but many other variables must be taken into account in order to anticipate and manage resistance or instability.

A group culture can also be manifested over a relatively short time period as a cohesiveness arising from a collective *group emotion* (Smith and Crandell, 1984). Rice (1969) defined this as *sentience*: the feelings and meanings arising from the common emotional bonds among group members who share a particular reality in a particular situation. As an example of a sentient culture, Smith (pp. 816–7) cites the case of a particular baseball team comprising 18 players, male, female, black and white. In the year that led up to their winning a local championship, the team and its supporters coalesced to act as one unit and felt a 'wonderful sense of bondedness'. In the following year, the team lost all of their first six games, with the result that the sentient system was fractured. Female players who did not get to play at all in one match shared a feeling of vindictiveness, of being blamed for the team's losses. Another split was along racial lines when one of the white players noted that the black players were more frequently seen sitting close together. This had the effect of creating two sentient systems where previously only one, the team (undifferentiated into male/female or black/white) had existed.

As individuals seek to act out their psychodramatic roles, so do groups with a strong culture or sentient system sometimes seek to act out their fantasised *sociodramatic role*, coming to behave and see themselves as if they were the Knights of the Round Table, The Mafia or The Simpsons. Group culture can to some extent also be moulded by the sociodramatic role that outsiders bestow on the group, welcome or not. Groups with different cultures (for example cooperative, entrepreneurial, compassionate, combative) provide quite different experiences for their members, and as a corollary require quite different understandings and actions from leaders and followers alike.

For detailed reading on organisational culture, see Morgan, 1997, Chap. 5; Brown, 1995; Hampden-Turner, 1992; Harrison and Stokes,

1992; Schein, 1992, 1990; Bolman and Deal, 1991, Chaps 12–14; Allcorn 1989; Pondy et al., 1983.

Status

> *In spite of the fact that most of us are quick to declare how unimportant status is, most of us are greatly concerned with acquiring status symbols. Fortunately, or unfortunately, depending on your predilections, we live in a class-structured society. In spite of attempts to make our world more egalitarian, we have made little movement toward a classless society. As far back as scientists have been able to trace human groupings, we have had chiefs and Indians, noblemen and peasants, the haves and the have-nots. This continues to live with us to-day. Even the smallest group will develop roles, rights and rituals to differentiate its members. Status is an important factor in understanding behavior because it is a significant motivator and has major behavioral consequences when individuals perceive a disparity between what they perceive their status to be and what others perceive it to be.*

With these words, Stephen Robbins (1979, p. 184) introduced his view of status, more briefly defined as 'a socially defined position or rank given to groups or group members by others' (Robbins et al., 1994, p.389). Status is conferred by others, and is therefore a matter of perception based on personal and group values and, to a lesser extent, on personal idiosyncracies. It can be ascribed on the basis of *inherited attributes* (family background, age, sex, physical characteristics, religion or charisma) or on the basis of *achieved attributes* (education, income, skill, contributions, visibility, privileges earned, title, position held). A person who is a member of several groups may enjoy a different status in each, while his/her status in any one group may change over time, sometimes – as politicians often discover – quite rapidly.

Status is closely related to the role, office or position held in the group, and directly determines the hierarchical and 'pecking order' aspects of group structure. However, to regard status differences as a linear distribution from low to high is to over-simplify reality: groups tend to sort out the highest and the lowest early on in the life-cycle, but further status differentials are defined more slowly and with frequent fluctuations thereafter.

It is possible for two status hierarchies to co-exist in a group, one formal and based on organisational roles (position, office or title), the other informal and derived from the idiosyncratic perceptions of the group members, who may prefer to confer status as a result of valuing such personal characteristics as leadership style, friendliness, trustworthiness or charisma. Usually, the latter is the stronger and more significant of the two hierarchies. Conflicts occur whenever there is *status incongruence*: for example, when a person with prestige in the informal hierarchy is not rewarded with status in the formal hierarchy or vice versa; or when a person with low status enjoys privileges which the other group members perceive as appropriate only to people of high status. Interpersonal conflict or stress can result when an individual's own perception of his or her status is not at one with the perceptions held by others, particularly others whose opinions are important.

A member's status has extensive consequences for behaviour and communication by influencing the amount and kind of interactions, privileges, power and responsibility he or she has relative to others in the group. In brief, research findings are (i) that more communications are initiated and received by high status members than by low status members; (ii) that high status members usually conform to group norms more than low status members do, although the group is usually more ready to permit high status members to deviate from group norms; (iii) the higher the status, the higher the power, with a frequent tendency on the part of high status members to consolidate and legitimise their power and deter low status members from trying to usurp it; and (iv) high status members take the initiative or lead more than low status members do.

The *circularity* of all the aspects of status is emphasised by many writers: for example, as the possession of power increases status, so high status in turn increases personal power; persons performing roles at the bottom of the hierarchy, if classified as low status or if denied privileges, may be actively prevented from rising higher.

Power

All members of a group are in relationship with each other, and therefore exercise some degree of influence and are themselves open to being influenced. The degree of power that members possess varies greatly, as does the degree to which different ones may value or seek power. It is this pattern, and the ratio of high-power to lower-power members that is the power structure of the group.

The mainstream view usually defines organisational power as the ability to create the conditions we want by influencing others to change their thoughts, feelings or behaviour in some way. Oshry's view (1977, p.i) is that 'power is not position; power is the ability to recognise and realise the potential of *whatever* position we are in'. The Gestalt view is that power is latent (potential) *until the right conditions are presented for its activation.*

Authority is distinct from but closely related to power, and is the right to influence others, and in an organisational sense is legitimate power vested in a person either by virtue of his or her position or role in the organisation, or by tradition. The exercise of power without authority can lead to group members feeling dominated or powerless. At the personal level, power and authority are more closely related. Personal power refers to the possession of desired skills, knowledge, resources and character attributes; personal authority is the ability to self-authorise: to give oneself permission to supply or use any such attributes or resources in direct action. In groups, leaders and members need to have both power and the appropriate type and degree of authority to exercise it responsibly in the service of the task.

Authority and authority relations are central concerns in the Bion/Tavistock psychodynamic approach, particularly with regard to the relations between the leader and the group. Long (1992, pp. 71–4) gives, in a nutshell, an indication of the importance and the complexity of this aspect of group and organisational dynamics.

While power is a *potential*, influencing is a *process* of affecting the behaviour of others. The relevant action verbs connected with influence include persuade, encourage, inspire, reward, direct, control, manipulate, distract, convert, mould, bribe, deceive, hinder, threaten, punish. Control is an extreme form of influence in which one person or group influences another's behaviour and enforces limits to that behaviour. Compliance (or conformity) refers to the yielding of one person or group to another's influence, a 'going along with' the other's wishes or pressures.

In their now classic study, French and Raven (1959) described five types of power involved in the ways an agent 'A' influences a target 'T':

Reward power: A has the ability to reward T, T needs or values the reward (e.g. the power of a manager to promote a subordinate).

Coercive power: A has the ability to punish T, T wishes to avert punishment (e.g. the power of an employer to sack a worker).

Referent power: A is admired by T, who wishes to be like A (e.g. the power of a pop star to set a fashion).

Expert power: A is perceived by T to have specialised or superior knowledge or skills (e.g. the power of a doctor to persuade a person to undergo surgery).

Legitimate power: A has social permission (originating in society's norms) to influence T, who believes that A has the right to do so (e.g. the power of a policeman to halt traffic).

The above types of power are not mutually exclusive, and a person may possess several concurrently. Of all the five types, coercive power is the least likely to lead to group effectiveness, and the most likely to produce fear, alienation, frustration, or desire for revenge. Expert and referent power are most positively correlated with effective performance. Morgan

(1997, p. 170–99) adds other sources of power that provide members with the means of furthering their interests, not necessarily at the expense of others. These include:

* formal authority;
* control of scarce resources;
* control of decision processes;
* control of boundaries;
* control of technology;
* control of informal networks and alliances;
* the ability to cope with uncertainty.

Once the power structure has become differentiated, the high-power members entrench themselves by attempting to legitimise their power. They may do this by reinforcing norms and procedures that make it difficult or threatening for low-power members to reduce the power differences between them. They also may establish severe penalties for low-power members who attempt to 'rock the boat', rewarding those who fit in or refrain from being rebellious.

Powerful group members are treated with deference, attract a disproportionately large share of interpersonal communications, and have their wishes complied with more often than do other members. In turn, powerful members are more attracted to the group, have more control over it, and derive greater satisfaction from their position in it.

Group effectiveness is diminished when power is not distributed fairly evenly. Co-operation takes place through the exercise of mutual influence; unequal power hinders the building of the trust and open communication levels so essential for dealing with group conflicts and for working in the collaborative mode.

A consideration of power would be incomplete without mentioning personal power and personal authority. Individuals are deeply affected by early childhood experiences of parental authorisation or de-authorisation to act in and on the world. These later combine with situational factors to affect the degree of self-authorisation a person brings to his or her work-group role. The individual who has developed only a weak sense of self will be largely im-potent to act, while those who have developed a strong sense of self will be their authentic 'unbound selves free to truly be themselves, to live the best way they can, and to take full responsibility for who and what they are and do' (Gould, 1989, p. 3).

For detailed reading on power and politics in organisations, see Ivancevich and Matteson, 1997, Chapter 10; Morgan, 1997, Chapter 6; Vecchio et al., 1996, Chapter 10; Johnson and Johnson, 1994, Chap. 9; Robbins, 1994, Chapter 13; Pfeffer, 1992; Mintzberg 1983; Oshry, 1977.

For detailed reading on authority, see: Sennett, 1993; Raz, 1990; Watt, 1982; Milgram, 1974.

For detailed reading on personal power and authority, see Zander, 1994, Chaps. 8 and 9; Gould, 1993, 1989; Wing, 1986; Rogers, 1977.

Sociometry

An important aspect of the structure of a group is the pattern of interpersonal relationships that develop based on feelings of attraction, rejection and indifference between members. Pairs, cliques, clusters, isolates, rejectees and 'stars' emerge from this pattern of likes and dislikes among members and are features of all established human groups. Sociometry is a way of measuring relationship patterns, and was originally developed in the 1920s by Jacob L. Moreno. Moreno, a doctor, philosopher and mathematician, was the founder of the psychodrama and group psychotherapy movements, having rejected the psychoanalytic imperative that psychotherapy be a one-to-one relationship in a consulting room.

Moreno used the word 'tele' to refer to the attractive force between individuals that occurs as soon as people are in each other's presence, close or distant. We might nowadays call it 'chemistry' or 'vibes': the feelings transmitted from one individual to another, reciprocated or not. The source of positive or negative tele may be sexual or merely social, but anyone who has ever been in a group will recognise that it exists whenever they feel like getting to know another member better or, conversely, like avoiding them. Indifference is the absence of any noticeable tele between two people.

In the workplace of the 90s, the patterns of attraction and rejection are further complicated by the greater diversity of the workforce. This brings with it more complex issues involving, for example, racial stereotyping, the new status of women, working with the disabled, tolerating alternative sexual preferences, understanding different religious beliefs.

Tele strongly influences both the structure and effectiveness of the work group through the quality of the working relationships developed by the members. Sociometry incorporates techniques for measuring current or proposed relationships in a group and then portraying them in the form of a *sociogram* (Moreno, 1956; Hale, 1981). Figure 4.3 illustrates a hypothetical but typical sociogram depicting the relationships between members of an established group of ten.

Conducting a full sociometric analysis is tedious for large groups, and may be threatening unless trust levels are well-developed, as it requires members to reveal their preferences for each other. Such analyses have at times enjoyed wide use in social work and family therapy for the mapping of past and present systems in which clients have been or are embedded. It is a useful exercise for groups that wish to deepen the quality and increase

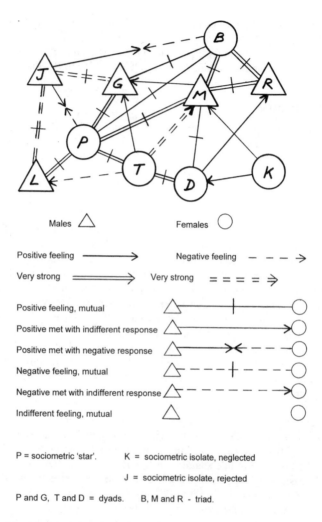

Figure 4.3 A small-group sociogram.

the potential of their socioemotional connections, particularly if this is pursued as part of a team-building program. Simpler techniques than a full sociometric analysis will often suffice for everyday work groups, and a sociogram can easily be constructed from personal observation without recourse to collecting data from the members.

Perhaps the most significant contribution of sociometry to the study of group behaviour is the way it assists to identify the sources of strengths and weaknesses, for example, the positive and negative potentials of certain alliances and processes between group members around the core work of the group. 'Stars' reflect what is valued in the group. Persistent isolates and rejectees can cause distraction and disruption – if they disrupt progress significantly, they need to be integrated into the group, perhaps by linking them to key members such as stars or leaders, or by using isolation as a criterion in an exploratory sociogram. Wherever possible, members and leaders alike should seek to harness positive tele relationships to serve the task, and avoid couplings or groupings that are characterised by negative tele relationships unless these can be easily improved.

Below the surface level of work roles, the sociometric structure of the group is subject to sometimes quite dramatic fluctuations as individuals experience mood swings and shifts of allegiances. The processes that drive these changes are more often than not at the unconscious level, and consequently are difficult to predict. The energy exchanges that constitute Moreno's tele may be of either short or long duration. It is also important to recognise that couplings which work very well on one type of task might be much less productive on a different task, on different days, or in different environments.

For detailed reading on sociometry, see Hale, 1981; Moreno and Jennings, 1960; Moreno, 1956; Northway, 1952.

Subgroups

One important aspect of the structure of a group that is usually self-evident, and will certainly be revealed in even a casual sociogram, is the existence of subgroups (cliques, coalitions, clusters, alliances). They are neither necessarily good nor bad and arise as a normal part of organisation and development, or as an inevitable result of a group increasing in size. According to Fisher (1980), subgroups typically arise because of some conflict within the larger group, and often command greater loyalty from their members than does the main group. They may also arise out of common interests held by a few members or when a number of admirers gather around a sociometric 'star' or a high status member. Other functions which subgroups may serve are managerial (leadership, liaison) or production (work tasks, support services). Once established, a subgroup may be fostered because it offers its members support, fellowship and activities that the larger group might deny them.

Subgroups can be a potent force if their energy is mobilised towards achieving benefits for the whole group. Equally, they can be potentially destructive if they become nuclei for obstructive or frustrated minorities. Northen (1969) pointed out that in evaluating these subsystems, the basic concern is how they relate to the group as a whole, whether there is harmony or conflict between different ones, and whether or not they are functional for the work being undertaken by the group at a given time. When subgroup boundaries become strengthened or threaten to become closed, or when competition and discord between subgroups increase, then it is time to stem the fragmentation of the whole group by dealing with the issues around which these two processes are occurring. Heap (1977, p.210) suggested the following interventions to re-stabilise the group structure at such a time:

- keep alive the identity and cohesion of the group-as-a-whole by reflective observation;

- stimulate interaction across subgroup boundaries;

- focus on 'superordinate' goals (goals which are important to all members and which require their cooperation);

- recall satisfactions derived from earlier cooperative whole-group tasks.

One subgroup in particular, which Kotter (1978, p.20) called 'the dominant coalition', is the one that – legitimately or otherwise – oversees the group as a whole and controls its basic functioning. In an organisation this would perhaps be the Board of Directors; in a club the President, Vice-President and Secretary; in a committee the Chairperson and his or her closest lieutenants. By definition, the dominant coalition occupies the top power position in the group, and with that goes the ability to exert maximum influence, for better or worse. Hopefully, that coalition will be in good shape, for as McDonald (1972) said: *'If the power centre at the top is in chaos, what hope is there for the rest of the organisation?'*.

Cohesion

Group cohesion is variously defined as:

- the degree to which the group is united, or 'hangs together';

- the sum of all the forces which bind the members to each other;

- the forces acting on the members to remain in the group rather than leave it.

Cohesion results from the process of interaction in the group: it builds gradually as the group matures, with fluctuations due to single incidents or situations that might have a more sudden (but usually only temporary) effect.

As cohesion increases, members become more committed to group goals, and accept roles and norms; absenteeism and lateness decline; participation increases and more resources become available; members tend to create group symbols such as a group name or logo, a constitution or manifesto, nicknames for members; induction rituals for newcomers etc; members communicate more effectively, with better listening and greater acceptance and valuing of each other; the group persists longer in working on difficult or frustrating tasks.

While cohesion and productivity (output) are not necessarily positively correlated, high cohesion is likely to result in improved productivity provided that members accept and value the group goals. High cohesion also leads to greater social influence: greater pressure on members to conform to the group norms and standards. This may have positive outcomes (for example: when a group encourages open expression of differences and even hostile feelings in an effort to confront and work through conflict), or negative outcomes (for example: when excessive conformity results in the group falling victim to 'groupthink'). Highly cohesive groups, if fortunate, function effectively with an 'esprit-de-corps' that provides members with a sense of security by reducing anxiety levels and raising morale.

Cohesion is more likely to occur if:

- group members like each other;
- group members enjoy or are satisfied with the group experience, and trust levels are high;
- group members agree on the group goals;
- the group is homogeneous in terms of common values, interests and backgrounds of its members;
- the group is small: larger groups have less frequent interaction between members, and a greater tendency to split into subgroups that may compete with each other or cause friction;
- the group membership is stable and not often disturbed or rearranged, i.e. has a low turnover;
- the group is isolated from other groups;
- the leadership is effective and well balanced between task and maintenance functions;
- the task requires physical proximity of members rather than separation from each other;
- the group experiences successful completion of tasks or achievement of goals;
- the group exists in a facilitating (i.e. comfortable, convenient, well-equipped) environment.

Cohesion will be less likely to occur if:

- membership of the group is not voluntary;
- goals or tasks are imposed from outside;
- no progress is made on the task;
- tasks are approached in a competitive win/lose manner;
- conflicts do not get resolved;
- a few people dominate;
- the group is negatively evaluated.

Group leaders can foster cohesion by taking steps to establish or enhance the conditions listed above. However, the group may slide into dependency on any leader or member who tries to force cohesion. Temporary or reactive cohesion can occur if a group is faced with an external threat or danger, e.g. appointment of a new leader, an attempt to destabilise or disband the group, conflict or competition with other groups, etc.

For detailed reading on cohesion, see Hogg, 1992; Kellerman, 1981 pp. 225–329; Shaw, 1981 pp. 213–26.

Key Concept

5

PROCESS

Process and Group Dynamics

When I am having a conversation on the telephone and discussing the weather, that is *what* I am doing. The process is about the *how* of the event: how the initial rapid exchanges of information give way to slower pauses as we begin to change the subject; I begin to speak more hesitantly about our recent conflict; then my voice hardens, the other person begins to get angry, we both raise our voices, and finally I slam the phone down. *Group process* is how the group is behaving from moment to moment, the sequence of activities, interactions, and movements of the members as they go about their work and relate to each other. It is nicely defined by Steiner (1972, p. 176) as *'a series of behaviours, one following after another, each to some degree determined by those which have gone before and each in turn, influencing those that will come later'*. Process is dynamic, continuous and ever-changing. It must not be confused with progress: it cannot be 'interrupted' or 'spoilt', and doesn't 'stop' or 'go backwards'. Understanding it is essential for effective group membership, particularly for leadership and team-building.

Most of the above processes may also be referred to as *group dynamics*, a term coined by Kurt Lewin in 1939 and still in use in a universal rather than a specific sense. It is more useful however to reserve the term for the specific purpose of referring to the moment-to-moment shifting patterns of *energy* in the group as the members move and interact. The changes in mood, noise and vitality, the ebb and flow of activity and inactivity: all these are the dynamics of the group as it goes about its task. As an orchestra plays loud or soft, fast or slow, with patterns of light, shade, harmony and discord, so does the group manifest similar dynamic changes. These energy shifts are fuelled by underlying forces which include motivation (a *driving force*) and anxiety (a *restraining force*) and all are part of, affect and in turn are affected by the on-going sequences of behaviours we call process.

Lewin's Field Theory (Lewin, 1951; Deutsch, 1954) assisted the study of group process by viewing it as the result of behaviour of the individual members in the context of their total here-and-now situation, which is called the individual's 'field' or 'life-space'. Lewin saw the 'field' as composed of driving forces that strongly support action and change, and restraining forces which act as obstacles to prevent action and change. Individuals communicating and relating to each other behave as systems seeking to maintain a state of equilibrium in the face of these opposing influences. Some years later, Whitaker and Lieberman (1964) developed a theory of group process with its roots in Lewin's work, and applied it specifically to the field of group psychotherapy. They referred to the two opposing forces as the 'disturbing motive' and the 'reactive motive' which together create focal conflicts for which individuals and the group continually seek resolutions. Group process and group dynamics are largely the outcome of these 'driven-to-act *versus* fear-of-consequences' dilemmas.

Process Observation

To understand and practise process observation, a 'process checklist' will be found helpful. Directly observable process variables include arriving, talking, arguing, withdrawal, silence; sharing and assembling information, giving feedback, asking questions, recording; modifying the physical environment; disintegrating, re-organising, disbanding, departing. Processes which can be deduced from an analysis of *content* (what people are talking about, or the materials and objects being used) include goal setting and clarification; information processing and evaluation; role differentiation, power struggles and scapegoating; norm development; planning and problem-solving; reviewing and team-building. A process checklist is given below:

Arrival   Are members chatting, milling around, getting seated?
Are some members forming cliques or subgroups?
Are members close or far apart?
Are some members being shunned or shut out?

Organisation   How is the group getting started?
What roles and procedures are being established?
What is the interest level?
Is the group being railroaded or dominated by a few?
What is the tempo: slow, hurried?
What is the climate: warm, chaotic, hostile?

Task	Is attention focussed or scattered? Are the members competing or cooperating? Are goals being set or clarified? Are resources being assessed? What decision-making methods are being used? What problem-solving techniques are being used? Is the group staying on track? bogged down? going round in circles? Are alternatives being assessed? Are records being kept? Is information being collected? shared? processed? evaluated?
Maintenance	Are any members dropping out, becoming tired or disillusioned? Is anyone being ridiculed, punished, ignored, scape-goated or ratpacked? Are members supporting and valuing each other? Are dissenters or minorities being listened to? are less vocal members being invited in? Is the group moving towards crisis, returning to stability?
Leadership	How is the leader behaving? Is a power struggle under way? Are indigenous leaders emerging? Is leadership being distributed? Is progress being made?
Team-building	Is group process and progress being reviewed? Are questions being asked or statements being made about the group's effectiveness?
Environment	Is a change to the physical setting being made? Are materials and equipment being assembled or used? Is the seating being rearranged? Is the group moving to a different location? Are there interruptions originating outside the group?
Departure	Is attention being withdrawn? Are members beginning to pack up? Are some members attempting to keep the session going? Is a ritual or ceremony taking place? Are members leaving?

One way of measuring the flow of interactional events in group discussions was devised by social interaction theorist R.F.Bales (1950, 1952).

His Interaction Process Analysis (IPA) classified process events as follows:

Social-emotional or maintenance realm, positive acts:

- Shows solidarity, raises other's status, gives help, rewards.
- Shows tension release, jokes, laughs, shows satisfaction.
- Agrees, shows passive acceptance, understands, concurs, complies.

Social-emotional realm, negative acts:

- Disagrees, shows passive rejection, formality, withholds help.
- Shows tension, asks for help, withdraws out of field.
- Shows antagonism, deflates others, defends or asserts self.

Task realm, asking questions:

- Asks for orientation, information, repetition, confirmation.
- Asks for opinions, evaluation, analysis, expression of feeling.
- Asks for suggestions, direction, possible ways of action.

Task realm, giving answers and information:

- Gives suggestions, direction, implies autonomy for other.
- Gives opinion, evaluation, analysis, expresses feelings, wishes.
- Gives orientation, information, repeats, clarifies, confirms.

Bales' research findings were that the interactions in the four categories above display a fairly stable content of 25% positive and 11% negative contributions in the social-emotional (maintenance) realm, and 7% questions and 57% attempted answers in the task realm. This was one of the earliest attempts to analyse process in discussion groups.

For detailed reading on different approaches to group process, see: Schein 1987; Colman and Geller, 1985; Main, 1985; Luft, 1984; Balgopal and Vassil, 1983; Burton, 1982; Banet, 1976; Colman and Bexton, 1975; Turquet, 1974; Whitaker and Lieberman, 1964; Bion, 1961; Lewin, 1951.

Motivation

Mullins (1996, p. 480) defines motivation as '*some driving force within individuals by which they attempt to achieve some goal in order to fulfil some need or expectation*'. There are many ways to look at motivation, a word derived from the Latin 'movere', to move. The concept is built on the observation that an individual with an unsatisfied need will engage in self-serving (but not necessarily selfish) behaviour with the aim of satisfying that need. Feeling thirsty, buying a drink and drinking it is an example that obviously fits the simple process model shown in Figure 5.1.

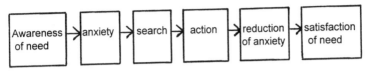

Figure 5.1 The need satisfaction process.

In the belief that the motivating force originates with need, Maslow (1954) put forward a theoretical 'hierarchy of needs' in a classification system which has become widely popular (Figure 5.2).

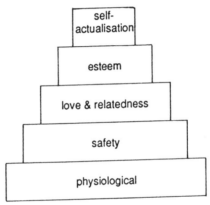

Figure 5.2 Maslow's hierachy of needs.

The basic need, physiological, is for food, air, water, shelter and other bodily needs. When this need is at least partly satisfied, its importance as a motivator decreases, and the next higher one begins to emerge: the safety need. This includes security, stability, and freedom from pain, illness and threat. Again, as this need becomes substantially satisfied, the need for love and relationship comes into prominence, and so on up the hierarchy. Esteem includes self-esteem as well as status and recognition or respect from significant others. The highest need is for self-actualisation: fulfilment and realisation of one's potential.

Critics of Maslow's theory, arguing that there is little research evidence to support the idea that the fulfilment of one need automatically activates the next higher one, have produced other classifications. Alderfer (1969) separated the core needs into three clusters – existence, relatedness, and growth – that he saw as interdependent rather than sequential sources of motivated behaviour. McClelland (1961) classified needs in terms obviously significant to work-group settings:

- the individual need for *achievement*: to excel;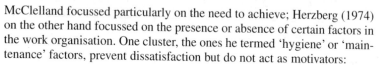
- the interpersonal need for *power*: to influence others;
- the interpersonal need for *affiliation*: to be close.

McClelland focussed particularly on the need to achieve; Herzberg (1974) on the other hand focussed on the presence or absence of certain factors in the work organisation. One cluster, the ones he termed 'hygiene' or 'maintenance' factors, prevent dissatisfaction but do not act as motivators:

- company policy and administration
- quality of supervision
- working conditions
- job security
- fringe benefits
- salary

A second cluster, which he termed 'motivators', relates to the higher-order needs of the individual:

- responsibility
- recognition
- meaningful work
- achievement
- advancement
- personal development

In small work groups, the intensity and direction of what Mullins calls the 'driving force' manifests in each member's choice of role, style of behaviour, and level of commitment to the task. Past experience, current mental sets and future projection combine with here-and-now situational elements in ways which are complex and difficult to identify. Certainly, motivation is not a phenomenon that triggers isolated acts, rather it is a continuous orientation that affects the on-going interaction between the individual and the group (Nuttin, 1984 p.75). An individual will at any moment be internally influenced by his or her idiosyncratic perception, psychodramatic role hunger, emotional state and hidden agendas. At the same time, he or she will be contending with the task and the relationship dimensions of the group. Attempts to understand motivation must therefore be set in this total context, the 'field' or 'life-space' of the individual and of the group itself.

For detailed reading on motivation, see Adair, 1990; Maslow, 1987; Klein, 1982; Vroom and Deci, 1979; Herzberg, 1974; McClelland, 1961.

Hidden Agendas

Group process works on two levels: the level of the *open* or *surface agenda* (the advertised purpose of the group, and its real task) and the level of the *hidden agenda* (the undisclosed needs and motives of individuals or subgroups). Hidden agendas often siphon off energy that could be available for work on the task, and an ability to recognise and deal with them will help a group to perform more effectively.

Members of work groups are often inhibited from disclosing even their most basic personal needs for security, belonging, acceptance, recognition, self-expression and creativity, all of which are legitimate reasons why people seek to join groups in the first place. Other, less innocent needs (such as the desire for power or prestige, the need to control others, the desire for revenge etc.) are unlikely to be aired at all, yet they are often present and can result in manipulative behaviour that seriously impedes the group's progress. Lack of progress on a group task during any part of the life-cycle may mean that hidden agendas are being worked on covertly. A subsequent sudden spurt of progress on the open agenda may mean that a hidden agenda has just been worked through and cleared out of the way.

A hidden agenda will often surface when the group runs into a crisis, or when its continued thwarting reaches an intolerable level. The final solution for some individuals is to sabotage the group or leave it. Although hidden agendas are covert, they are very much the concern of the group: it is unfortunate that, for a variety of reasons, they cannot just be laid 'on the table'. For that to happen the trust level in the group must be high, and it is only in the later phases of the group's life-cycle that hidden agendas are usually aired or reduced. Burying them or pretending they are not related to the group is ineffective, although it must be recognised that not all of them can be successfully resolved, and times will occur when potentially dangerous ones are best left 'under the table'.

Hidden agendas operate in the following areas:

- between members
- between a member and the group
- between a member and the leader
- between the leader and the group
- between groups or subgroups

The signs of hidden agendas are:

- emotions overtaking logical thinking;
- coalitions and cliques forming;
- personal attacks, scapegoating, complaining, grumbling;
- interruptions and over-talking;
- ambivalence of opinion or commitment;
- scattered, fragmented work procedures;
- withdrawal into silence;
- backing away from decisions at the last minute.

What to do about them:

- minimise the likelihood of hidden agendas becoming obstacles by creating opportunities for airing opinions, doubts and complaints about work and relationship concerns;
- learn how to recognise the inevitable signs and carefully bring them to the notice of the group and the member(s) concerned – this must be done in a way that is appropriate to the existing trust level in the group;
- avoid reprimands, criticism, punishment and ridicule – recognise agendas as a legitimate part of group life, to be dealt with just as open agendas have to be dealt with;
- use problem-solving techniques to define and resolve them, inviting information and feedback from all members concerned;
- recognise those that are potentially too dangerous to an individual or to the group as a whole, and leave them 'under the table'.

Defence Mechanisms

Defence mechanisms may be considered special cases of hidden agendas: they are unconscious and aimed at defending the person or the group from anxiety, guilt or shame or painful memories. Being hidden yet ever-present, they are difficult to detect and even more difficult to deal with, since any attempt to do so usually increases anxiety and reinforces them. When activated, defence mechanisms profoundly affect interpersonal, group and intergroup processes (see also the Bion/Tavistock approach in Key Concept 3). At the individual level they create barriers to interpersonal communication; at the group level, they interfere with the task.

The common goal in all the defence mechanisms described below is the elimination of anxiety, or at least its reduction to manageable proportions, but the common outcome at best is temporary relief, at worst a prolonged reduction of the group's available energy for the primary task.

Repression: is the complete and involuntary exclusion from memory of painful or embarrassing present and past experiences. These are kept out of awareness by being pushed down into the unconscious and 'forgotten' to the point that they are virtually inaccessible. In a group, for example, there may be an instance of highly unethical behaviour in its history that can no longer be recalled: it has been 'forgotten' completely by all members – a form of 'group amnesia'. Repression of thoughts and feelings is an underlying component of most of the other defence mechanisms.

Denial: is a refusal to acknowledge that a disturbing external threat actually exists. Common examples in groups are ignoring or refuting persistent unfavourable feedback about performance, or denying that some external person or group is angry with them. Denial differs from repression in that while the latter is a covert unconscious process, the former is acted out overtly.

Rationalisation: is usually brought into play when it is desirable to find socially and rationally acceptable reasons (i.e. excuses) for failure or disappointment, or for behaviour of a shameful or unethical nature. A well-known rationalisation for the latter, and one that hides the unconscious desire to be considered good rather than guilty, is 'Well, we couldn't have avoided doing that, it was clearly in the company's interest'.

Regression: is the process of reverting to more primitive, childlike behaviour in the face of insecurity, confusion, guilt or shame. The shift from Bion's Work Group mode into one of the Basic Assumption modes (see Key Concept 3 above) is a typical example of regression.

Introjection: is 'taking on board' some attributes, behaviour patterns or projections of another person or group. Examples might be the absorption of early parental injunctions to behave in certain ways in certain situations; the adoption of values espoused by admired figures in the family, in society or from history, literature, myths and legends; the emulating of respected or idealised heroes or heroines.

Projection: protects people and groups from acknowledging that they have undesirable traits or behaviours, or are incompetent in some way. It is the process of attributing their own unwanted or denied negative feelings to another person or group, the aim being to preserve the projector's current positive self-image. Groups may seek a scapegoat to carry their unacceptable 'bad' aspects instead of owning and integrating them as inevitable manifestations of their own 'shadow' side. Through scapegoating, blaming or 'bad-mouthing' others (particularly minority groups) the projector is able to feel blameless. (The more complex process of projective identification has been discussed in detail in Key Concept 3 under the Bion/Tavistock approach).

Reaction formation: occurs when a group engages in a task that has them acting out of a particular value framework that actually conceals a propensity for the very opposite. For example, a protest group lobbying for weapons control may be concealing from itself and others a fear of their own predilection for violence. Such a group may also employ denial or rationalisation to prove their 'purity' when accused of aggressiveness in the tactics they use in waging their campaign.

Intellectualisation: is the process of distancing oneself from emotionally disturbing events or fantasies by responding to them in intellectual or abstract terms. Example: 'I'm feeling very guilty, so I know there is some unexpressed resentment to be explored'. Protection from the reality of accidents, illness or death is a necessity for many groups such as nurses, rescue teams or the military, particularly if they are to defend themselves in order to cope with daily or prolonged scenes of great distress.

Displacement: is a substitute activity where blocked or forbidden behaviour is redirected into safer or more socially acceptable channels, thereby reducing anxiety or evading the possibility of censure. The instinctual sexual energy of members of a work group may be channelled into horseplay or 'touchy-feely' training exercises. A supervisor's anger at a senior manager's rebuke may be displaced onto his secretary.

Fantasy: is the process of creating an entirely make-believe situation to replace the real one. Being neurotically, perhaps even psychotically, disassociated from reality would be an extreme case of a defence mechanism, yet it is far from being an unknown phenomenon in work groups. In the face of prolonged threat or unresolved conflict, individuals may retire into their psychodramatic role, a group into its sociodramatic role. Problems occur when they do not recognise that they have substituted fantasy for reality, or cannot move between the two and know the difference.

Defence mechanisms are not always negative or manipulative – they are after all the organism's protective/adaptive response to situations of stress or conflict, and play an essential part in maintaining the ability to stay in control. They can serve an important purpose while the person or group is maturing or learning better ways to deal with the difficulties of reality in the workplace. It is only when they are distorted or deeply entrenched ways of relating that they become dysfunctional processes.

For detailed reading on defence mechanisms, see: Kleinmuntz (1974); Mahl (1971); Freud (1946).

PART 3

WORK

When work is a pleasure, life is a joy
Maxim Gorky

Key Concept

6

COMMUNICATING

Communication is not a matter of being right,
but of starting a flow of energy between two
people that can result in mutual understanding.
John Sanford

The Communication Process

For a group to come into existence, organise itself, and develop into an effective team requires above all else good communication between members. There is more to this than just talking or exchanging information: cooperative action depends for its success on the accurate transfer of *meaning* between individuals or between groups. The aim is to achieve an understanding between the sender and the receiver whereby the meaning received is the same as the meaning intended. When this happens, we have what Jones (1972) called a '*shared common-meaning experience*': that moment of understanding that occurs when each 'meets' the other and attributes the same meaning to the data or symbols being exchanged. It is an intriguing definition of human communication.

Organisations use the communication process in a number of ways and for a variety of purposes. One-way communication may be used to inform, instruct, control or persuade; two-way communication is usually preferred for interactive functions such as task coordination, problem-solving, conflict resolution, decision-making and team building. In the classical hierarchical organisation, further distinctions may be made between vertical and horizontal flows (top-down, bottom-up, crosswise) and between formal and informal channels and procedures. Koontz et al., 1980) offer the following list of functions served by communication:

- to establish and disseminate goals of an enterprise;

- to develop plans for their achievement;

- to organise human and other resources in the most effective and efficient way;

- to select, develop, and appraise members of the organisation;
- to lead, direct, motivate, and create a climate in which people want to contribute;
- to control performance.

In small groups the main concerns are with face-to-face interaction and the factors that assist or hinder effective interpersonal and intergroup communication. Figure 6.1 depicts a simple model of the process.

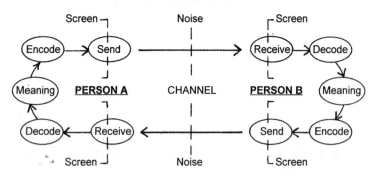

Figure 6.1   The communication process.

Person A starts the interaction by encoding: transforming a thought into symbols (written or spoken words, sounds, visuals etc.) for transmission as a signal through a channel or medium. The act of sending the encoded message assumes a recipient (Person B), who in turn decodes the message and transforms it into thought and meaning. B's response to A follows a similar sequence, and so the process continues. During this flow back and forth, there will be two main sources of message distortion: screens and noise.

A screen is the totality of the individual's personality, experience, emotional and physical state, attitudes, beliefs, values, biases and assumptions. Any message must pass through A's as well as B's screen, and in doing so each may distort, confuse or add to the content unintentionally. When B is responding to A, it is to what B actually heard or saw rather than to what A intended B to hear or see.

Noise refers to any interference with the message in the space between the sender and the recipient, i.e. in the channel. Channels include the air space between the parties, telephone lines, mail and courier services and so forth. Each of these may cause further distortion by generating background noises, discomfort, obstructions, static, fading, tampering etc. Noise may also affect the screens of each party by playing on their emotional and/or physical state.

Apart from screens and noise, a particular instance arises when two communicators have to contend with the problem of different sensory preferences. People take in and give out information through three basic sensory channels: visual (seeing), auditory (hearing) and kinaesthetic (feeling). A clinical therapeutic approach to interpersonal communication known as Neurolinguistic Programming (NLP) has provided strong evidence that individuals tend to have a preference for one of these channels over the others when talking or listening (Bandler and Grinder, 1975; Laborde, 1983; Lankton, 1980). Misunderstanding can occur if the sender's mode does not match that of the receiver, for example, when a strongly visual person is talking to a strongly kinaesthetic person. 'I don't *see* what you mean…' and 'I *feel* you're not really with me…' contain verbal clues to differing preferences.

NLP proposes ways that one or both parties may improve their understanding of each other by matching their words and imagery more closely. It is of little use replying to 'I don't see what you mean' with 'Didn't you hear what I said?' The single most important tenet of the NLP approach is that *the success of communication must be measured with reference to the framework of the recipient rather than that of the sender.*

Levels of Communication

We can use the model in Figure 6.1 to examine three different *levels* of communication, and a number of different *modes*. The first level is *communication as sending* (one-way). At this level, only half the process takes place (from 'encode message' to 'meaning') and the receiver remains passive. Office memos, orders, advice and pronouncements from superiors can all be sent quickly, but it may take a long time to discover that the message was not properly understood or acted upon. Where immediate feedback is impossible or discouraged, there is no way to determine whether what B received was what A intended. This type of communication is dependent on the sender's competence in expression and on the hopeful assumption of a high degree of rapport between the parties.

The second level is *communication as exchange* (two-way). At this level, A and B are in dialogue for as long as it takes to establish a mutual understanding. The full process continues as each party sends a message then listens to the other's response and responds in turn. Through reflecting back what is heard (feedback) and through the sharing of emotional as well as intellectual reactions to each other's messages, a state of consensus of understanding may eventually be reached.

The third level is *communication as union,* a deeper experience of mutual understanding than would normally be expected in everyday work situations. It implies a moment of inspiration shared by two people as their communication reaches a level of meaningfulness that unites them, albeit for an instant, in a moment that may have almost a mystical quality. Even in work groups, such an event may sometimes be witnessed when two members resolve a difficult interpersonal conflict with an obviously deeply-felt sense of relief and acceptance of each other. This is truly communion, a meeting of two people who are at that moment whole in themselves and in their encounter with each other. It is the 'I-Thou' level of human contact as proposed by Buber (1958) and discussed by Batros (1996). The moment of communion is usually followed by silence, any further interchanges being unnecessary or, at most, nonverbal.

Nonverbal Communication

There are two basic modes or types of signals used in the interpersonal communication process: verbal and nonverbal. In communicating verbally we use the spoken or written word, and in that simple fact lies the source of much of the difficulty that occurs between people attempting to understand each other. A word is only a label or symbol for a thing, not the thing itself. Because individuals experience the world in ways that are never identical, the meanings we attribute to words and the emotions we attach to them may be markedly different. In addition, words are often inadequate in themselves as tools for describing complexity fully and clearly, particularly the complexity of interpersonal behaviour. Differences in life experience, age, ethnic origins, values and the myriad other factors listed later all contribute to problems in verbal communication.

The nonverbal mode refers to the ways that we transmit messages other than by the written or spoken word. They are largely involuntary, and include body language, vocalism, and symbolism. They contribute very significantly to the communication process between two individuals, but often on a subconscious or covert level. Mehrabian (1981, p.76) claimed that we derive only 7% of the meaning of a message from the sender's words, but 38% from the tone and inflection of the voice, and 55% from the body language. Body language includes posture, gestures, eye contact, movement, touch and personal distance. Vocalism refers to non-word sounds such as grunts, 'ums' and 'ahs', and the tone, volume, pace and emphasis of the voice. Symbolism includes the clothes, hairstyle, and adornments that we choose, and even our furniture, cars and living spaces, all of which give out signals of their own which may mould the message further. Our use of political language and metaphors, the way we arrange our office or work space, and enjoyed personal rituals all give out powerful nonverbal messages (Pfeffer, 1992, pp. 279–98).

The constant stream of signals from voice, body and possessions are a real and significant part of our communication – if our verbal and our nonverbal signals do not complement each other (i.e. are not *congruent*), the receiver will likely find the nonverbal component more valid when trying to construct meaning. A large proportion of the process of two-way communication is given over to achieving congruence as well as consensus of understanding. In addition, sending and receiving often takes place simultaneously: a person can be speaking and at the same time processing the other's nonverbal responses to what is being said.

Communication and Context

The flow of communication depends in part on the group structure and culture, in particular the number and direction of channels available, the differences of power, role and status, and the procedural rules and norms that become established. These variables can ease or constrict the flow of messages, and may also affect the message content and the frequency of transmissions.

It was noted earlier that communication networks reveal patterns that vary from completely centralised at one extreme to all-channel at the other. The different patterns have direct influences on morale, leadership, cohesion, problem-solving and group development (Fisher, 1980, pp. 158–65; Shaw 1981, pp. 150–61). Interactions through the various channels are regulated by rules (of task, procedure, etiquette, protocol or social custom) and relationships (e.g. boss–subordinate hostility, peer rivalry). Members of a group with a charismatic or feared leader may behave differently in the way they communicate with each other depending on whether the leader is present or absent.

Differences will also be observed in groups that exist in, say, a collaborative as opposed to a combative culture, or consist of members with a respectful/supportive *versus* a dehumanising/threatening attitude to each other and to people in general. A supportive non-threatening climate lets people express their opinions, be straightforward, and not be defensive or feel they will be criticised for being honest (McCroskey et al., 1986 p. 260).

The seating pattern in small-group meetings is another factor that has significance in terms of ease or difficulty of communication. Much of this stems from issues of power/status/leadership that may be reflected in the seating arrangements. Some typical configurations are depicted in Appendix A.

Sources of Distortion

The many conditions which may hinder, block or distort a communication transaction can be attributed either to the people involved (the sender, the receiver or both) or to the circumstances of the situation at the moment when the attempt is made. Koontz et al. (1980), Napier and Gershenfeld (1985) and Pfeiffer (1973) provide many examples of sources of interference and distortion. These have been added to and re-categorised as follows:

Work-space conditions:

- excessive noise, heat, cold; inadequate lighting or ventilation;
- badly arranged or uncomfortable furniture;
- poor aesthetic quality;
- overcrowding;
- intrusions and distractions (e.g. interrupters, telephone, TV).

Psychological:

- negative past experiences leading to fearful expectations (e.g. cynicism, unwillingness to be honest);
- false beliefs, unclarified assumptions and stereotyping;
- information overload (an accumulation of inputs resulting in faulty or partial processing);
- emotional overload (e.g. accumulated hostility, sadness, suspicion);
- low self-concept;
- lack of interest in subject matter; pre-occupation and mind-wandering;
- hidden agendas;
- emotional blocks (use of defence mechanisms such as repression, projection, or denial to cope with increased anxiety or threatened self-esteem – refer back to Key Concepts 3 and 5 for a discussion of these).

Physiological:

- speech or hearing defects;
- poor health;
- bodily distractions (pain, hunger, thirst).

Language/cultural:

- semantics (multiple, ambiguous, or disputed meanings to words and phrases);
- diction (e.g. too fast, too soft, mispronunciation);
- incongruence (contradictory verbal and nonverbal content);
- inarticulateness (poor command of vocabulary or expression due to age, education, or use of an unfamiliar language);
- jargon, slang, dialect, accent or brogue.

Interpersonal:

- charisma or perceived trustworthiness (i.e. credibility, reliability) of sender;

- power, status and role relationships between sender and recipient;

- proxemics (inappropriate interpersonal distance, intrusion into personal space).

Any part of the communication process – encoding, sending, signal transmission, receiving or decoding – can be affected by the presence of even one of the hindering conditions listed above. Since most transactions take place with several present, it is important not to compound the problem with ineffective behaviour.

Ineffective Communication Behaviour

Group members must develop the ability to communicate clearly and openly with each other in a process based on sharing. If they are to share their reactions, opinions, doubts, fears, interests, strengths and weaknesses, the climate must be safe and encouraging. Controlling, hiding or defensive behaviours and attitudes are not conducive to the creation of trust and safety and will further impede communication. (The literature on Gestalt Therapy by Perls, 1969, 1973, and Passons, 1975, is particularly helpful for understanding the linguistic bases underlying ineffective interpersonal dialogue). The following list includes the most common habits that contribute to ineffective communication behaviours:

Judging: evaluative, critical or moral judgements put the recipient on guard, and usually reduce willingness to share and be honest. Criticism is sometimes unavoidable, but wherever possible, descriptive statements are preferable to evaluative ones.

Shoulding: this is a 'trip' laid on the other party by means of 'shoulds' and 'oughts'. It accentuates guilt and puts the person further away from what he or she is actually experiencing: the image of what they *should* be doing obscures the experience of what they *are* doing.

Putting-down: 'put-downs' and statements that patronise, ridicule or shame the other party are likely to be immediately countered by aggression at one extreme or withdrawal at the other.

Blaming: refusing to accept responsibility for oneself usually evokes an equally angry response and almost guarantees an escalation of hostility. In addition, it doesn't repair damage or resolve conflict.

Explaining: seeking causes and reasons, interpreting, or intellectualising is talking about experience rather than experiencing. The result is that contact with the other person is diminished.

Interrupting: if the receiver cuts off the sender, the complete message cannot be absorbed. Interrupters are unwilling to listen, being more concerned with dominating or impressing the other party than with achieving understanding or communion.

Generalising: using 'people ...', 'we ...,' 'you ...', or 'one ...' instead of 'I' impersonalises the conversation and avoids responsibility for the view expressed. 'I' statements make the experience and understanding of each other more immediate.

Alwaysing: the word 'always' is a sure sign that the exchange is going to be 'a wild one', as Sanford (1982, p.7) puts it. He continues *'when we use this word, it brings up such a sweeping generalization that discussion is almost impossible'.*

Butting: Gestalt therapists have long advised clients to substitute the unifying 'and' for the divisive 'but'. Consider the change in meaning when 'I love you darling, but I don't agree with your opinion' is changed to 'I love you darling, and I don't agree with your opinion'. The word 'but' is usually taken as if it negates the statement that precedes it, when in fact it may not.

Using cliches: tired and worn-out phrases result in communication that shares little of value or significance, e.g. *'Better late than never ...', 'Can't see the wood for the trees ...', 'It's an open and shut case ...'.*

Asking pseudoquestions   (Pfeiffer and Jones, 1974): questions that conceal an attempt to manipulate, influence or control rather than to elicit information or opinion fall into a number of categories illustrated by the following examples:

- 'set-up' questions that control by manoevring the other into a vulnerable position (ready for 'the kill') or by attempting to narrow the possible responses, e.g.
'Would you agree that ...?'
'Am I correct in saying that you ...?'

- 'kill' questions or 'gotcha' questions that are meant to trap the other person rather than obtain an answer, e.g.
'Didn't you say that ...?'
'Weren't you the one who ...?'

- questions that hide a command or a reprimand, e.g.
'When are you going to ...?'
'Have you done anything about ...?'

- questions that screen the questioner's preference, e.g.
'Would you like to eat Chinese food tonight?'

- questions that hide the questioner's beliefs or opinions, e.g.
'Don't you think that ...?'
'Wouldn't you rather ...?'

- questions that hide the questioner's criticism, e.g.
  'Wouldn't it be better to ...?'

Shifting: changing the focus away from the self and introducing 'red herrings' are ways of diverting the discussion to avoid being confronted with anything uncomfortable or threatening.

Reacting defensively: people who are insecure will tend to hear questions as accusations and turn their replies into justifications or counter-accusations. Defensive behaviour is also a common response to being judged, de-valued, criticised, reprimanded or controlled – in short, to almost any of the behaviours listed above! To respond defensively invites reciprocal, defensive behaviour and an escalation of miscommunication (Gibb, 1984).

Suppressing feelings: anger, fear, sadness, and even excitement or joy are often hidden or denied for fear of ridicule, rejection or reprisals, with the result that the communicators as well as their communication become impoverished. Anger, if continually suppressed, may finally erupt in a great emotional avalanche. Joy, if continually suppressed, will turn into deadness and loss of spontaneity. Sadness, if continually suppressed, will result in depression and withdrawal.

A helpful framework for analysing the causes of ineffective communication is the widely-popularised TA (Transactional Analysis). Originally developed by Eric Berne (1961, 1964, 1972) for use in individual and family therapy, it has also been applied to training in leadership and interpersonal communication in groups and organisations (for example, Albano, 1974; Rendero, 1974). Transactions take place between people at an unconscious level as each acts out of a hypothesised *ego state* similar in structure to Freud's superego, ego and id (see Figure 3.1 in Key Concept 3). Berne labels these the Parent, Adult and Child, and describes interpersonal process as transactions taking place between different combinations of these with varying degrees of communication effectiveness (see Figure 6.2).

The Parent may be a critical parent (concerned with rules and regulations, proper behaviour, matters of morals and conscience), or a nurturing parent (encouraging, supporting, protecting). The Parent provides the value system and the 'shoulds' and should nots'. The Adult behaves responsibly: the rational, data-processing, reality-testing and decision-making part of the person. Adults are in touch with their inner thoughts and feelings *and* with events that are happening around them *and* are able to connect the two processes. The Child may be a natural child (creative, fun-loving, curious), a manipulative child (seductive, selfish, evasive), or a maladapted child (belligerent, blaming, complaining). The Child is the 'feeling' or 'acting out' part, particularly vulnerable to strong emotional reactions linked to earlier childhood experiences.

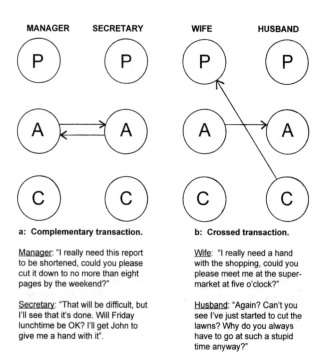

a: **Complementary transaction.**

Manager: "I really need this report to be shortened, could you please cut it down to no more than eight pages by the weekend?"

Secretary: "That will be difficult, but I'll see that it's done. Will Friday lunchtime be OK? I'll get John to give me a hand with it".

b: **Crossed transaction.**

Wife: "I really need a hand with the shopping, could you please meet me at the super-market at five o'clock?"

Husband: "Again? Can't you see I've just started to cut the lawns? Why do you always have to go at such a stupid time anyway?"

Figure 6.2 Transactional Analysis.

Theoretically, people can act out of all of these states to some degree, and can move between them quite rapidly at times in response to the other party. The TA framework could equally well be applied to encounters between groups as a way of analysing critical incidents in intergroup processes. There are clear resemblances here to Bion's Work Group mode (the group-as-a-whole in an Adult state) and Basic Assumption mode (the group-as-a-whole in a Child state).

Effective Communication Behaviour

To be effective, communicators must first of all strive to become aware of the conditions and behaviours that may be hindering their communication, and then actively seek to minimise them or compensate for them. To be truly successful, however, requires more than just reducing the effects of screens and noise. There are some specific skills that need to be mastered if the process is to start effectively and then proceed to build trust and achieve clarity and understanding. These skills are grouped under five headings: starting, owning, active listening, creating safety and taking risks.

Starting: Sanford (1982, p.7) says *'starting effective communication requires giving some thought to the opening remark, since the way the dialogue starts often determines the way it will go'*. If the opening toss is offensive, i.e. includes accusations, put-downs, threats or attempts to manipulate the recipient, the return toss is likely to be defensive, and listening will be impaired. Effective initiators are very much in the 'here-and-now': centred, confident, prepared and focussed, considerate of and tuned in to the recipient.

Owning: effective communicators use many of the techniques that grew out of the tradition of Gestalt therapy. They use 'I' statements (*'I don't understand what you mean'* rather than *'You're confused'* or *'No-one knows what you mean'*). They 'own' and accept responsibility for their opinions, feelings and actions (*'I'm scared of conflict'* rather than *'People can't handle conflict'*). They communicate with more integrity by changing 'I can't' to 'I won't', 'I need' to 'I want', 'I have to' to 'I want to', and 'I know' to 'I imagine'. Overall, they express themselves accurately and simply; their verbal and nonverbal signals are not contradictory; and they use language and style appropriate to the recipient's frame of reference. After their message is delivered, they become active listeners.

Active listening: this skill is not easy to acquire but it is of paramount importance. Something much more than just hearing words is needed. The listener must be still and attentive: both the facts and the feelings that underlie the content of a message must be grasped. *Feedback* is an essential component, both reflecting back (paraphrasing what the sender said and checking for accuracy) and giving back (sharing thoughts and emotional reactions to what was said). Active listeners are genuine in their desire to hear and understand and are alert to nonverbal cues. They suspend judgement and criticism, refrain from interrupting, and respect the sender's viewpoint and value system. They resist distractions, and confront the sender if he or she is inaudible, ambiguous, or incongruent. They also confront and deal with any dislike or hostility between them.

All proponents of active listening (e.g. Rogers and Farson, 1984 pp. 255–67; Sanford, 1982 pp. 17–30; Egan, 1970 pp. 248–60) agree that *empathy* is another essential component. Where sympathy is feeling *for* someone, empathy is feeling *with*. If listeners absorb and reflect back the whole message, (facts, feelings and meaning), express their reactions, and accept the sender's feelings and values as legitimate, then an empathic sharing has occurred.

Creating safety: clear and open communication can only flourish in a safe environment where group members can share their thoughts, express their negative as well as their positive feelings, and receive support and encouragement when they risk being honest. No-one will take risks in a threatening situation: controlling or judgemental behaviour will increase

defensiveness and reduce trust levels. Trust and openness need a climate of safety in which to grow steadily; they cannot be produced instantly. Active listening plays a major part in the creation of a safe environment, but two specific behaviours are also vital: *being supportive* and *coping with negative feelings.*

Showing support must be a genuine act, not counterfeit or ritualised: it may be better to admit to being at a loss for words than to engage in cliches such as *'I know how you feel'.* Genuine support can be shown in two ways: by giving encouragement or recognition. It is encouraging for others if you are the first to trust, to be honest, or to disclose something of your self. If done appropriately, these behaviours will be seen as invitations to behave in an equally open and involved way towards you. It is good for others to be recognised as likeable, worthy, important. Responding warmly, keeping eye contact, giving compliments and acknowledging the value of another's idea or viewpoint are effective demonstrations of support.

Negative feelings need to be expressed rather than suppressed, so that internal pressure does not build up. Responsibility for them needs to be owned rather than dumped on someone else. The group needs to develop norms that permit members to share and work through their uncomfortable emotions.

Anger is probably the hardest emotion to deal with. Some people handle their own anger by denial or bottling up, others by projection or violence. It is more constructive, but often far harder, to admit to it, own it, and then investigate the fear that lies behind it. Coping with someone else's anger may also be done directly by withdrawal or counter-attack, or indirectly by attempting to invalidate, deflect, or ridicule the other's hostility. It is better to stand your ground, actively listen, and try to identify the source and motivation (anger may be a show of strength, a defence, a punishment, an expression of individuality or an attempt at closeness).

Taking risks: paradoxically, it can be seen that creating safety requires taking risks. Self-expression and involvement with others will always entail some element of risk, but it is in the more 'advanced' behaviours of *self-disclosure* and *confrontation* that the highest risks are taken in the pursuit of effective communication.

Self-disclosure is a powerful way to build trust if done authentically. Chartier (1974, p.127) says *'a person's ability to engage in self-revelation is a symptom of a healthy personality'.* Nevertheless, it is advisable to guard against over-exposure: too much too soon can be as damaging as none at all. Unrestricted honesty or emotional expression can be alienating or, at worst, destructive. Whether or not to reveal one's thoughts or feelings is a question of appropriateness, of assessing the other person's readiness to be receptive. Unwillingness to disclose at all may stem from guilt, shame, shyness, collusion (a tacit agreement between the parties to pretend or hide), or group norms that make it unwise or unsafe to do so. It is best done at a level at which you feel comfortable, or preferably a little beyond that so as to deepen the dialogue a little. Pfeiffer and Jones recommend that openness and honesty generally should be a matter of strategy plus acceptable risk, which means '*determining how much open data flow the system can stand and then giving it about a ten percent boost – enough to stretch it but not to shatter it*' (Pfeiffer and Jones, 1972 p. 198).

Confrontation is not the same as attack. If you learn to confront in a declarative rather than an abusive or interrogative manner, communication will improve. The desire to find a common ground must be genuine, and hopefully mutual. *Responsible* confrontation may be an invitation to self-examination, a challenge, or calling a bluff, but it is not an act of aggression. The instinctive response is, nevertheless, to be defensive or retaliate. To shelve this response is also taking a risk and will certainly be difficult, but it will be rewarding. Confrontation is an exercise in which all the effective behaviours described above need to be brought into play as the issue is worked through (Egan, 1970 pp. 287–335; Kurtz and Jones, 1973 pp. 135–38). Giving and receiving feedback is the core interaction for confrontation. Feedback will be most useful when:

- it is offered with concern and attention
- it is specific rather than general or vague
- it is direct rather than oblique or half-hearted
- it is descriptive rather than evaluative or interpretative
- it is immediate rather than delayed
- it is declarative rather than hostile or punitive.

Communication is the core activity which enables the group to develop its structure and do its work: that is, it is the key to successful organisation. It is also the key to successful leadership, for without effective communication neither leaders nor members of a group can take those specific actions that will move a group towards its goals.

For detailed reading on communication in groups and organisations, see Johnson and Johnson, 1994, Chap. 4; Robbins, 1994 Chap. 11; Fisher, 1980 Chaps 3 and 4; Farace et al, 1977; Johnson, 1977.

For detailed reading on interpersonal communication, see DeVito, 1995; Johnson, 1986; Gibb, 1984; Argyle, 1983; Boas, 1982; Sanford, 1982 Chaps 4 and 5; Tajfel and Fraser, 1978 Chap. 5; Rendero, 1974; Satir, 1972; Egan, 1970.

For detailed reading on nonverbal communication, see Pease, 1985; Malandro and Barker, 1983; Mehrabian, 1981; Argyle, 1975.

Key Concept

7

LEADING

Leaders are the agents of renewal. Like contemporary
alchemists, their role is to bring forth gold from the vast array
of talents, knowledge and values hidden in the people of
an organisation.
P. McKinnon

But of a good leader, who talks little, when his job is done,
his aim fulfilled, they will all say 'We did this ourselves'.
Lao Tzu

Leadership is the art of influencing people so that the group is moved one
step closer to its goal. A group leader may be appointed or elected (the
'designated' leader) or may emerge from the ranks as the person who most
frequently or persistently performs acts of leadership (the 'indigenous'
leader). Leading is an art that can be practised by any group member, not
just by the official leader, although this has not always been a widely
accepted view.

Leadership Theories

The dimensions of effective leadership have been the subject of intensive
research and debate for more than fifty years, yet no single satisfactory
theory has so far emerged. Prior to the 1930s, the *trait* theories predomi-
nated, in which it was held either that individuals are born with certain
characteristics that make their emergence as leaders almost inevitable (the
so-called 'great man' theory), or that such traits could be acquired through
training. These theories largely failed to prove any cause-and-effect relationship between traits and effectiveness, but the popularity of listing
'desirable attributes' has a persistent history. The examples below show
one early and one more recent such list:

Tead (1935):	**Stogdill (1974):**
Physical and nervous energy	Adaptable to situations
Sense of purpose and direction	Alert to social environment
Enthusiasm	Ambitious and achievement-oriented
Friendliness and affection	Assertive
Integrity	Co-operative
Technical mastery	Decisive
Decisiveness	Dependable
Intelligence	Dominant
Teaching Skill	Energetic
Faith	Persistent
	Self-confident
	Tolerant of stress
	Willing to assume responsibility

Pioneering studies by Lewin, Lippitt and White (1939) at the University of Iowa introduced one of the first classifications of leadership *styles*:

Autocratic: very directive, stresses discipline, allows little or no participation, makes all decisions, usually conservative, may be strict, patronising or benevolent. Group members may be happy with this style, or they may rebel, become dependent, or harbour resentful feelings.

Democratic: encourages group discussion and participation in decision-making, assists and encourages group members, and has confidence in members' abilities, respects their needs, treats them as peers. Group members may be happy with this style, or they may attempt to load responsibility back onto the leader.

Laissez-faire: provides little or no control or supervision, allows complete freedom to the group, gives direction or advice only if requested. Group members may be happy with this style, or they may lose interest and commitment, compete with each other, split into factions, or disintegrate.

Subsequent research efforts led to the conclusion that the 'one best style' approach was limited. Different situations were seen to call for different styles, and the research focus broadened to include the whole group and the changing conditions in which it exists at any moment. First, Tannenbaum and Schmidt (1958) proposed a *continuum* of styles from boss-centred to subordinate-centred, reflecting a progressively increasing range of freedom to group members to influence decisions. Later, the *situational* or *contingency* theories (e.g. Fiedler, 1967, 1978; Hersey and Blanchard, 1977; Vroom and Yetton, 1973) focussed on the way a leader's effectiveness is moderated by the circumstances of the moment, such as the group composition and mood, the leader's attributes, the task, the setting and organisational environment, and so on. Situational leadership theories clearly imply that any particular leader may be right for one group

and wrong for another, or effective in one situation and ineffective in another, even with the same group.

Eventually, the realisation that constantly shifting situations demand an impossibly high degree of versatility and flexibility on the part of the leader led to the *distributed-functions* theory (Johnson and Johnson, 1994, pp. 187–9; Barry, 1991; Katz and Kahn, 1978; Cartwright and Zander, 1968). This theory states that the leadership function may be and indeed should be fulfilled by different members performing a variety of relevant behaviours. More explicitly, it advocates that any member may take a leading role if they have the information, style or skills appropriate to the situation.

For group members to initiate a leading act, they must (a) be aware that a particular function is needed, and (b) feel that they have the ability to perform it and that it is safe for them to do so (Cartwright and Zander, 1968, p.310). The task and maintenance roles described earlier are all examples of leading behaviours, as much as any of the classical and more general managerial roles (coordination, planning, liaison, negotiation etc) customarily expected only of a formal leader.

Distributed leadership does not come about by edict, but by evolution. The deliberate creation of a climate of trust and a willing (but not necessarily total) delegation of power and control on the leader's part are necessary conditions for this to occur. Distributed leadership is central to the concept of self-managing teams, an integral part of the sociotechnical approach used in the Tavistock Institute's action research programs since the 1950s. In the contemporary corporate world, many organisations are espousing self-managed teams for a wide variety of work groups, with varying degrees of success (see also Key Concept 13).

A recently emerging theory, *transformational leadership*, refers to leaders who have sufficient personal power or charisma to inspire their followers to achieve fundamental internal change both in the organisation and in themselves (Tichy and Devanna, 1990; Ackerman, 1984). This is achieved primarily by transmitting a sense of mission, stimulating and rewarding learning and innovation, and vigorously persisting in seeing their vision carried through into action and achievement (Egan, 1988). In short, transformational leaders bring about radical change in the organisational culture, mainly by intervening in three areas identified by Stace and Dunphy (1996, p. 133) as: structural interventions (restructuring, changing layout and technology, replacement of leaders); process interventions (human resource policies, relations with external groups); and symbolic interventions (new mission statements, public and visual acts and artifacts).

Transformational leaders strongly support their change strategies by modelling: behaving with integrity, self-directedness and self-critical evaluation; being unequivocally committed to the organisation, its members, and the primary task. Through this type of exemplary behaviour they are able to arouse in their followers extraordinary levels of enthusiasm, loy-alty, and performance. It is not surprising that the role of the leader as edu-cator (Dyer, 1995, pp. 51–6) is gaining emphasis following the rise of the concept of 'the learning organisation' (see Key Concept 12).

The Leader's Role

The formal leader must coordinate, unite and direct the members until such time as the group becomes more self-directing and autonomous. The leader must create opportunities along the way for leading initiatives on the part of the followers to occur and be validated, so that the completion of the task is felt to be a truly collaborative effort. In this endeavour, a leader imposed on the group from outside will most likely experience greater difficulty than will a leader who emerges either spontaneously or by election from within the group and enjoys the members' mandate to lead.

In a maturing group committed to developing into a team, the *functions* required of the leader by the group will vary according to which stage of its life-cycle the group is in. This aspect of the leader's role is clearly shown in Figure 7.1, the last column of which shows the leader's changing role in detail (see also Corey and Corey, 1987).

The leader has two other roles of a more on-going nature: the execu-tive role and the boundary role. The former includes responsibilities such as convening meetings and starting and finishing on time; arranging venues and facilities; providing necessary documents and materials; arranging for implementation of decisions reached, etc. The boundary role requires the leader to take responsibility for the relationship between the group and its environment, for example other groups, the parent organisa-tion, consumers or the community at large. In this role, the leader, if caught between conflicting demands and expectations, can often experi-ence high stress.

When a leader or other member intervenes, i.e. enters into the ongoing group process for the purpose of assisting the group to pursue its goals, it is essentially an act of communication: a verbal message accompanied by nonverbal signals which hopefully reinforce rather than contradict the ver-bal content. The intervention may take almost any form: instruction, observation, question, suggestion, interpretation, criticism; offers of infor-mation, ideas or resources; confrontation; self-disclosure; acts and expres-sions of emotion that interrupt, surprise, encourage, distract, provoke or inspire.

The manner in which the group leader intervenes profoundly affects the interpersonal and developmental processes occurring in the group (Heron, 1975). With the overall responsibility of ensuring that the group survives and performs optimally, the leader's value system is also of

Stage of Group Development	Work Issues Facing Group	Social-Emotional Issues Facing Group	Patterns of Group Behaviour	Leadership Functions Needed
Forming	Identifying group's task and obtaining agreement about it. 'What are we here for?'	Establishing contact between members. Awareness of and uncertainty about leader. 'What will this group be like?' 'What is appropriate behaviour in this group?'	Dependence on leader. Politeness. Uncertainty about what to do or how to do it. A search for a sense of direction and a 'strong' leader.	Clarification of task. Promoting interaction. Enough guidance to let members feel safe, enough freedom to let them start to take initiative.
Storming	Need to have a more detailed understanding of task, and of how it can be achieved. 'Can we achieve this task?'	Testing of leader and other members in power struggles. Personal commitment of members to the group and their ambivalence about this commitment.	Either rebellion (especially against leader or any dominant members) or a sense of apathy, drifting hopelessness.	A sense of security: 'holding' the group through a difficult period. Showing that the leader is strong and/or competent, but not inflexible.
Norming	More detailed procedures set up for achieving task. Allocation - overtly or covertly - of roles.	Development of closer relationships. Growth of trust.	New sense of enthusiasm. Trying out new ideas, new ways of working; members beginning to take more responsibility for the group.	Modelling of appropriate behaviour by leader, along with 'shaping' of member responses and validation of helpful behaviour. Clarification of boundaries and rules.
Performing	Activity to achieve the task. Concern for quality and time availability.	Maintenance of adequate degree of cohesion in the group.	Sense of group 'getting on with the job', with only occasional pauses or detours to resolve problems in functioning.	Monitoring progress: keeping a balance between task and social-emotional activity in the group. Encouraging the indigenous leadership of the group.
Terminating	Evaluation of task: 'Did we do what we set out to do?' and 'Could we have used more effective methods to get the same or better results?'	Coping with impending end of group and associated feelings. Handling the difficulties of disbanding.	Regression to earlier behaviour and problems. Reminiscing about the group's past. Planning of ending 'ceremony' and/or reunions.	Helping group to face up to task and social-emotional issues involved in ending. Help members make individual plans for future as appropriate.

Figure 7.1   Leadership functions (adapted from Crawley, 1978, 1979).

decisive significance. His or her world view, intellectual honesty, authenticity, ethics, temperament, and concern for the best interests of the group members are of vital importance. There is undoubtedly a mystique of leadership deeply rooted in mythology and history (see for example Mindell, 1993; Sun Tzu, 1988; Heider, 1985) with which followers tend to endow their leaders. However, in the more mundane life of a typical work group, leadership comes down to a dependence largely on the dynamic interaction between three sets of variables: the leader, the led, and the situation.

In striving to provide the appropriate function and make effective interventions, leaders bring to their behaviour an *orientation* that has its roots deep in their personal system of values and beliefs. At this deeper level the origins of the leader's psychodramatic role will be located, while at the surface level of the group interactions, the organisational (managerial) role is more in evidence. How leaders value the world, the organisation and their fellow beings, and how they believe all of these *ought to be*, will have a profound influence on the way they enact their roles and formulate their interventions. Numerous theorists have conceptualised leadership orientations in distinctively different terms, yet most of their schemas are compatible and promote similar prescriptions as the basis of 'good' leadership. Three such schemas, all of which apply equally well to large organisations and small groups, are described next.

The Leader's Orientation

Douglas McGregor (1960) suggested that understanding leadership must start with the basic question of how leaders see themselves in relation to others, and that this in turn requires thought on the perception of human nature. He identified two sets of assumptions – Theory X and Theory Y – that he considered would influence the way leaders enact their role:

Theory X assumptions
1. Most human beings have an inherent dislike of work and will avoid it if they can.
2. Because of this human characteristic of dislike of work, most people must be coerced, controlled, directed, and threatened with punishment to get them to make adequate effort towards achieving the organisation's objectives.
3. Most human beings prefer to be directed, wish to avoid responsibility, have relatively little ambition, and want security above all.

Theory Y assumptions
1. The expenditure of physical effort and mental effort in work is as natural as play or rest.
2. External control and the threat of punishment are not the only means for bringing about effort towards organisational objectives. People will exercise self-direction and self-control in the service of organisational objectives to which they are committed.
3. Commitment to objectives is a function of the rewards associated with their achievement, particularly at the self-actualisation level.
4. Most human beings learn, under proper conditions, not only to accept but also to seek responsibility.

5. Imagination, ingenuity, and creativity in the solution of organisational problems is widely, not narrowly, distributed among people.
6. In our modern industrial society, the potential of the average human being is only partially utilised.

These two theories are obviously fundamentally different, and represent two extremes. Most leaders tend to have a leaning towards one or the other of these. Theory X is rigid, pessimistic and static; leaders who tend this way would differ substantially from those who lean more towards the flexible, optimistic and dynamic Theory Y. Theory X and Theory Y leaders correspond closely to Lewin's autocrat and democrat respectively.

Rensis Likert (1961, 1967) proposed four basic systems or styles of organisational leadership (Figure 7.2).

System 1 (exploitive-authoritative)	System 2 (benevolent-authoritative)	System 3 (consultative)	System 4 (participative)
Control and decision-making located at the top	Some delegation of control and decision making	Considerable delegation of control and decision-making	Control and decision-making widely dispersed
Members motivated by fear, coercion and punishments	Members motivated by a system of rewards and penalties	Members motivated by rewards and the opportunity to participate	Members motivated by rewards and genuine involvement
Leader has no confidence or trust in group members	Leader has condescending confidence and trust	Leader has substantial but not complete confidence and trust	Leader has complete confidence and trust in members in all matters
Members do not feel at all free to discuss things about the job with the leader	Members do not feel very free to discuss things about the job	Members feel rather free to discuss things about the job	Members feel completely free to discuss things about the job
Leader seldom gets ideas and opinions of members in solving problems	Leader sometimes gets ideas and opinions of members	Leader usually gets ideas and opinions and usually tries to make constructive use of them	Leader always asks for ideas and opinions and always tries to make constructive use of them

Figure 7.2   Systems 1, 2, 3 and 4 (adapted from Likert, 1961, 1967).

The leader who operates under a System 1 approach is very authoritarian, and actively exploits subordinates. The System 2 leader is also authoritarian, but softer and more paternalistic: the 'benevolent dictator'. The System 3 leader consults, asking for and receiving inputs from subordinates. The System 4 leader involves all members in decision-making, giving only direction and limited inputs, and aiming for consensus on all important decisions. The four systems can be seen to have Theory X-type assumptions at one extreme (Lewin's 'autocrat'), and Theory Y-type assumptions at the other (Lewin's 'democrat').

A different but compatible model formulated by Blake and Mouton (1964, 1978) focusses on and represents the task and maintenance dimensions of leadership, i.e. concern for production (goal-achievement, task completion) *versus* concern for people (relationships, needs, feelings, self-esteem). Other theorists have called these two dimensions production-oriented *v*. employee oriented; task-centred *v*. subordinate-centred; initiating structure *v*. consideration. They are the two axes on which Blake and Mouton's Managerial Grid (Figure 7.3) is set out, showing five basic orientations. The 1.1 manager shows a minimum of concern on both axes, the 9.9 manager a maximum. The 5.5 position is 'middle of the road'. Harmony and friendliness take precedence in the 1.9 style, output in the 9.1 style.

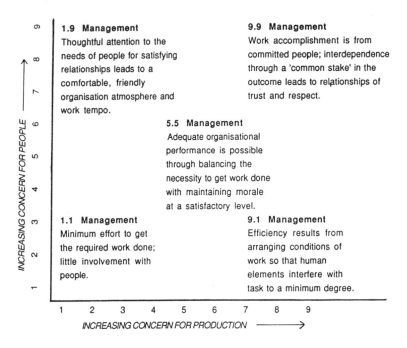

Figure 7.3   The Managerial Grid (Blake and Mouton, 1964, 1978).

The foregoing theorists all have a human relations emphasis, and are predominantly male. Although they have conceptualised leadership style and orientation with supposedly value-neutral terminology, they do not disguise the value they place on the Theory Y/System 4/9.9 orientation as the ones most likely to yield optimum results. However, this could be seen as inconsistent with the contingency theory view that holds there is no 'one best way'. The resolution of this may be found in the idea of a leader who is openly committed to a truly democratic approach, while being capable of intervening in whichever style is called for to match the situation and meet the legitimate needs of the group at that moment.

The Leader and the Led

Designated leaders have power: they are either backed by the authority that appointed or elected them, or they at least are endowed with expert or referent power. As soon as anyone is placed in the group as some kind of leader, they not only influence the members but are reciprocally influenced by the members. Multiple transactions take place between leader and followers in which each gives and receives rewards which, if the transaction is to be beneficial to both parties, must be perceived as equitable (Hollander, 1978). In practice a leader might be followed, abused, admired, rejected or loved. Members might successively view their leader first as someone who promises some kind of help or promotion; then as a surrogate father, mother, brother, sister; next as a human being with weaknesses; and finally as a human being with strengths. No matter how skilful a leader may be, his or her actions are likely to be met with mixed reactions – approval and compliance from some, disapproval or rebellion from others. This is largely due to the make-up of the average heterogeneous work-group: some dependent personalities, some counter-dependent, and some interdependent, all of them with different motivations and aspirations. The leader who can satisfy the needs of all three types with a single intervention is lucky.

When leaders are perceived as failing or refusing to perform in the way the group needs or wants them to, the members' anxiety levels increase rapidly. Even if the leader follows all the 'rules' of effective communication, he or she may be ignored or deposed, or become a target for the group's anger or disdain. When this happens, the members cease to behave as a work group in the sense that Bion (1961) uses the term, and cling to one or another of the Basic Assumption modes. When the group is fully in one of these modes, the leader will only be followed if he or she fulfills the group's Basic Assumption needs. Rather than colluding with the Basic Assumption behaviours, the leader has to help confront the members' behaviour and assist them to identify and deal with the underlying source of their anxiety. Until this is done, the group cannot return to working effectively on its task and becomes a closed system which can do no work (de Board, 1978, p.138): either the leader cannot function or the group can't, each 'side' being caught up in attempts to mobilise behaviours that will 'win'. These behaviours are defences against anxiety, and prevent the members from engaging in the realities of the task. (For a full discussion of the psychodynamics of followership, see Rioch, 1975b).

When leaders fail to match up to the personality image which has been constructed by the group members out of their projections and fantasies, similar processes may occur. The fantasised image has to be peeled away to reveal the leader as just another human being, care being taken that the reality so revealed is not too abrupt a let-down. This can only be done easily if the leader's behaviour has been authentic from the outset, and a fair degree of trust has been built between the leader and the led.

Followership as a concept has received much less attention in the literature than leadership, yet the art of good following is crucial to the success of any task group. The first requirement is acceptance of the role, that is, supporting, complementing and when necessary responsibly challenging the designated leader without the intention to compete or depose him/her. Followers, like leaders, also need to be able and ready to take up appropriate task or maintenance roles when needed and without competing with each other in doing so. At times, followers might need to step into the designated leader's shoes and act in that role for a time, then graciously step back again into their follower role.

Not all followers are effective, as pointed out by Kelley (1988). He classified ineffective followers as:

Sheep	passive, uncritical, lacking in initiative, merely followers of instructions;
Alienated followers	acquiescent, disgruntled, often cynical;
'Yes' people	dependent on leader, sometimes aggressively deferential or servile;
Survivors	live by the slogan 'better safe than sorry', adept at surviving change.

In contrast to these, Kelley speaks of self-confident followers who 'see colleagues as allies and leaders as equals' (p. 144), and courageous followers who 'can keep a leader honest – and out of trouble' (p. 146). Finally, in claiming that 'good leaders know how to follow', he seems to be echoing the words of Lord Melbourne, a former British Prime Minister. '*I am their leader*' he said of his constituents in a period of crisis, '*I must follow them*'.

The Ideal Leader

In addition to personality traits, interpersonal style, orientation, and leader-follower relationships as significant variables affecting leadership effectiveness, versatility must also be considered. Leaders need *repertoires* of models and roles (e.g. cognitive models for understanding group development, behavioural models for intervention and communication) and they need *mobility* to shift easily among them in order to respond appropriately to the changing dynamics of the group. Taking all of the above into account, plus the enduring features embodied in leadership theories of the past fifty years or so, it is possible to construct a profile of the 'perfect group leader':

He or she has:

- a sense of purpose and direction;
- integrity, humour, sensitivity, caring and faith;
- technical competence;
- energy and attention;
- ability to stimulate emotion and provide cognitive meaning;
- commitment to self-evaluation and evaluation of the group functioning.

He or she will:

- model direct, open and accurate communication;
- show respect for self and others;
- engage in appropriate risk-taking and self-disclosure;
- give support and build trust in the group;
- take easily to the basic task and maintenance roles and make interventions based on these appropriate to the group's needs of the moment;
- encourage the distribution of leadership behaviour among all group members.

He or she understands the consequences of each style and type of intervention well enough to use the one that is best for :

- the structure and history of the group;
- the amount of time and other resources available;
- the nature of the task being worked on;
- the kind of climate the group wishes to establish;
- the type of setting in which the group is working.

For detailed reading on leadership (group level), see: Johnson and Johnson, 1994, Chap. 5; Yukl, 1994; Barry, 1991; Hirschhorn, 1991;

Corey and Corey, 1987; Wilson and Hanna, 1986, Chap. 7; Adair, 1984, 1983; Turquet, 1974.

For detailed reading on leadership (corporate level), see: Stace and Dunphy, 1996; Gardner, 1995; Ghoshal and Bartlett, 1995; Hames, 1994; Limerick and Cunnington, 1993; Krantz and Gilmore, 1990; Rosener, 1990; Jacobson, 1985; Peters and Austin, 1985; Stead, 1985; Argyris, 1983.

For detailed reading on leadership (philosophical level), see: Mindell, 1993; Sun Tzu, 1988; Heider, 1985.

Key Concept

8

PLANNING

The major areas of concern for work groups – planning, problem-solving and decision-making – are seldom plain sailing. Unclear goals, intractable disputes, lack of progress in reaching a decision are familiar experiences. Cries of 'wasting time', 'going round in circles' and 'grinding to a halt' are well-known accompaniments to the endeavours of the best-intentioned groups, and clearly indicate the need for attention to process as well as content. More often than not, members either do not have appropriate process models, or do not have an adequate repertoire of problem-solving skills (groups that have neither probably terminate early!). This Key Concept and the next three examine a number of interrelated activities common to all work groups: goal-setting, action planning, problem-solving, decision-making, and managing conflict and diversity.

Goal-Setting

A goal is *an image of a future state of affairs towards which action is oriented*. All groups have goals: to win a race, invent a new product, build a better city. The group's ability to define its goals and achieve them successfully is a measure of its effectiveness. A group goal is more than a summation of the goals of all the group members. It is a goal that is desired by enough members to motivate them to work collaboratively towards its achievement. The motivation of members to work towards achieving the goal of their group is increased by participation in setting them: goals imposed from outside may not arouse much authentic motivation or commitment.

Most groups have a number of goals, ranging from the long-term to the immediate. Group members are affected by both, but usually it is the immediate goals that directly influence behaviour. Commitment to working to achieve a goal depends on the following:

- how attractive or desirable it seems in terms of the anticipated rewards for achieving it;
- how likely it seems that it can be achieved;
- whether it was imposed from outside or group-defined;
- how challenging it is;
- whether members will be able to tell that it has been achieved.

In setting goals, it is important to distinguish between the definition of the goal itself, the tasks that must be carried out to achieve it, and the interaction processes that the members will have to engage in. For example, the goal may be to produce a report on an investigation; the tasks may include carrying out interviews, analysing data; the processes may include a division of labour, sharing information, constructively resolving conflicts. The goals themselves can also be regarded as (i) guides for action, and (ii) the driving force without which members would take no action at all, becoming apathetic, disenchanted, or frustrated. As members commit themselves to work towards their group goals an inner tension is aroused that makes them restless and dissatisfied until the goal is reached or some other sort of closure is achieved concerning it (Johnson and Johnson, 1994, p.71).

Initial goal-setting should start with a clear understanding about the purpose for which the group has been formed. This is the **primary task**, a term coined by the Tavistock Institute's A. K. Rice and defined by him as 'the task the group must perform if it is to survive' (Rice, 1958). For example, a residents' action group may have been formed with a primary task 'to improve the local environment'. This is a *fuzzy* goal and says nothing about what the group will actually do. The next step is to refine the goal to be more *operational*, i.e. directly indicating the sort of actions to be taken. Such a statement might be 'to pressure the local council to act to reduce pollution'. In this form the goal is still not fully operational; in the next step the group might then decide 'to hold a public protest meeting in the Town Hall on March 2nd'. From this sort of clear and operational goal stem the tasks (book the venue, print leaflets, invite speakers, etc). These general-to-specific levels of goals and subgoals are commonly referred to as a *goal hierarchy*. Should the group define several goals (e.g. hold a public meeting, get an activist elected to Council, write an article for the local paper), these would constitute a *goal set*.

Finally, goals must be capable of modification without sacrificing clarity or specificity. This requirement also relates to the conflict-resolving skills in the group: goals inevitably raise conflicts, and modifying the goals is one way (not always a good way) of resolving such conflicts. Of special significance are the conflicts that arise between a private (individual) goal and the group goal. The importance of these intrapersonal conflicts as a source of hidden agendas is often underestimated.

For detailed reading on goals, see Johnson and Johnson, 1994 Chap. 3; Shaw, 1981 Chap. 10.

Action Planning

As outlined above, if goals are sufficiently operationalised downwards through the goal hierarchy, they in fact virtually transform into tasks. The terms goal and task are often either confused or used as if synonymous, and it is helpful if tasks are defined simply as all those things that must be done if the group is to succeed in achieving its goal. Planning, used here in a specific sense, is defined as *setting out a course of action to achieve a goal*. Usually, a course of action can be seen as a collection or sequence of specific tasks.

Tasks vary enormously, and there are many ways of classifying them. One of the most comprehensive systems is that of Steiner (1972), who divided them basically into two main categories: divisible and unitary. The former are tasks that can be broken down into separate assignments each of which can be carried out by a different individual or subgroup. Group members may decide for themselves who will be matched with which assignment, or rules may be in force, for example demarcation, which predetermine who will do what. Productivity is affected by the appropriateness of this matching of person to task. An example of a divisible task is the planning of a public exhibition, which might be divided into venue preparation, building the display boards, inviting a celebrity to open it, arranging publicity, and so on. Unitary tasks on the other hand require the collaborative effort of all the group members, and cannot be subdivided. An example of a unitary task facing the planners of the exhibition might be making the final decision on the venue.

Tasks also vary in their degree of difficulty, attractiveness, familiarity, and suitability (how suited it is to the group's structure and accessible skills and resources). Some are highly structured or routinised, others relatively unstructured or unpredictable. To all of these dimensions, Shaw (1981, p. 364) adds *solution multiplicity*: the degree to which there is more than one possible solution. This dimension ranges from tasks with only one right solution which is easily seen to be correct, to those with many acceptable solutions, many ways of reaching them, and no easy way of verifying which are good or bad.

How a task is initially described and the manner in which it is allocated will have an effect on the members' attitudes to working on it. The type and number of tasks to be performed, the time and resources available, and the anticipated rewards for success will all influence the way

dispute over topics

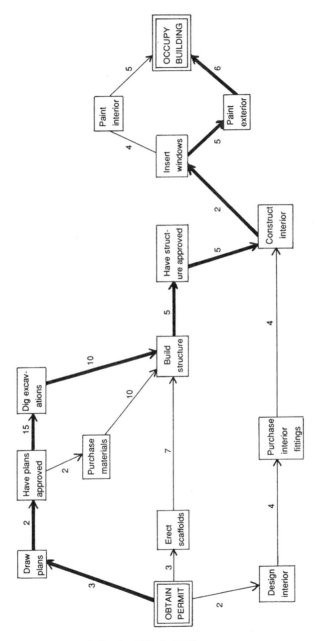

Figure 8.1 A critical path flowchart (Wyatt, 1989).

the group organises itself and approaches any difficulties that may be encountered.

For each goal agreed upon by the group, action planning can be assisted by the *critical path technique.* Working backwards from that moment when the goal has to be achieved, the members first determine what tasks need to be completed and roughly in what sequence. Responsibilities and resources for these are then allocated, and an estimate is made of the length of time each task will take to complete. The tasks and times are now assembled on a preliminary time-line. If the job is to be divided up among a number of subgroups who will work concurrently, the diagram will have several paths and loops. Some of these will feed each other, and they will all eventually converge on the final stage. In this way, the time-line takes the form of a flowchart (Figure 8.1).

The critical path is the one through the diagram that takes the longest time to complete, and it is this path therefore that determines how long the whole project will take. The chart helps to find ways to reduce the length of the critical path and to allocate resources and personnel most economically. People allocated to tasks on less critical paths might be re-assigned to more critical tasks to make the work-flow more balanced. In Figure 8.1, for instance, since the critical or longest path up to the 'build structure' node is the one involving digging the excavations (30 days), some of the scaffolders could be put to digging. The path the scaffolders are on is much shorter (10 days), and they would otherwise have to wait around until the workers on the critical path catch up to them at 'build structure'. The whole process can be kept under review and appropriately modified, and all members work to a clear and common schedule.

Problem Solving

Every creation is preceded by the right kind of chaos.
William Thompson

As tasks get under way, it is almost inevitable that problems of one kind or another will confront the group. These may be internal (whatever impedes the group's own functioning, such as absenteeism, unresolved conflict, dominance by a few members), or external (whatever directly impinges on the task, such as inappropriate technology, insufficient information, inadequate funding). In some instances, the group task itself may be to solve a given problem, as in the case of a research team commissioned to find a safe way to dispose of radioactive waste.

A problem of any kind is traditionally looked upon as a barrier across the path to a goal (Figure 8.2), but if a creative approach is to be adopted, then it is advisable to cultivate a broader perspective and approach it also as a challenge and opportunity for learning and growth. This is in line with Adams' Gestalt view (Adams, 1993, pp. 16, 17, 23) expressed earlier in Key Concept 3. It is not unreasonable to go even further and suggest that persistent substitution of the word 'challenge' for the word 'problem' will result in a significant attitude change which in turn will engender enthusiasm for acquiring *challenge-meeting* (rather than problem-solving) skills.

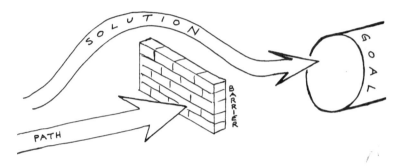

Figure 8.2   Elements in a problem/challenge situation.

Probably the most common problem is interpersonal conflict, and this will be given special attention in Key Concept 10, together with an examination of the 'problem-solving approach' to conflict resolution. Problems which are more product- than process-related are usually approached via the traditional linear problem-solving process with its five main stages:

Stage 1: Recognising and agreeing that there is a problem.
Stage 2: Defining and refining the problem statement.
Stage 3: Diverging – generating options and possible solutions.
Stage 4: Converging – evaluating the preferred or most viable options.
Stage 5: Deciding – choosing and agreeing on the final solution.

Two things need to be said about the linear model above apart from the fact that it is simplistic. First, it omits the important initial step of setting out and exploring the field or system in which the problem (as yet unrefined) is embedded; and second, it obscures the fact that divergent and convergent thinking are also used in stages other than 3 and 4.

The way a group approaches a problem will be influenced by the group culture. Some will approach the metaphorical brick wall in Figure 8.2 with a view to circumnavigating it, others will try to blast their way through or will dismantle it piece by piece. Others still may just sit tight and wait for it to crumble. Both the approach and the techniques used will also be influenced by the levels of cohesion, trust and commitment enjoyed by the members. The most creative work is done when the group

is free of negative norms and the majority of members are capable of acting in accordance with the following rules:

1. **Suspension of disbelief and pessimism:**   An attitude which is prejudiced against or cynical of any idea offered by another will not foster group creativity. The following sort of comments should be regarded as detrimental :

    (a) That would cost too much
    (b) The boss would never accept that
    (c) It's too radical
    (d) We tried that before and it didn't work
    (e) It's against company policy
    (f) That's much too airy-fairy
    (g) It's too early to look at that now
    (h) It's too late to look at that now
        etc.

2. **Balanced criticism:**   Since authentic negative criticism is valuable, negative comment should not be ruled out altogether. The tendency to dwell on 'what's wrong' can be countered by adopting a policy of giving at least an equal number of 'what's right' comments about any suggestion put forward. The right of a member to make a negative criticism might, for example, have to be earned by first offering two or three comments in favour of the suggestion.

3. **Associative thinking:**   The creative thinker encourages word associations and trains of thought to develop, looks for associations between apparently divergent suggestions, thinks laterally, and modifies and transforms ideas and possible solutions. Thinking aloud and indulging in apparently crazy or even outrageous ideas are actively encouraged.

4. **Tolerance of ambiguity:**   It is essential to be able to profit from contradictory, ambiguous, unclear, or incomplete notions rather than discard or retreat from them. Often, contradiction is the origin of new ideas and spurts of progress.

5. **Tackling specific rather than general problems:**   A manager trying to deal with the problem of absenteeism is trying to solve a general problem. Specifically trying to find out why Smith has been absent from all the divisional committee meetings since July may be easier, and may also throw useful light on the general problem.

6. **Delaying solution-mindedness:**   There is a natural tendency to rush towards solutions, particularly when a task group has to meet a deadline. Many groups approach every new problem by trying to use only those solutions which worked in the past. The creative group gives attention to all the elements of the situation: the path so far that has led up to the

impasse, the alternative ones not chosen, the nature and parameters of the barrier itself, the various ways that might be taken around, over, under or through it, and the nature of the goal being aimed for.

7. **Detachment:**   From time to time it is important to 'sleep on it', or at least take time out of the problem-solving session to do something totally different and unrelated. At these times, standing back from the problem allows for the incubation of ideas, which may be followed on occasions by the 'eureka' experience, that all-important moment of insight.

The degree to which a group succeeds in solving a problem will also be determined by the available repertoire of skills in utilising creative techniques. Thumbnail sketches of a range of popular methods are given in Appendix C.

For detailed reading on problem-solving, see Pfeiffer, 1994, Vol. 9; Adams, 1987; de Bono, 1968; Le Grew et al., 1980; Maier, 1970.

Key Concept

9

DECISION MAKING

It has been my experience to put aside a decision for future pondering. Then one day, fencing a piece of time to face the problem, I have found it already completed, solved, and the verdict taken.
John Steinbeck

Making a decision is generally defined as choosing one of a number of alternative solutions or courses of action. Meaning literally a 'cutting away', it is a *process* whereby proposals are put forward and debated, and then progressively evaluated until a preferred one is selected. Whether the decision involves and is supported by all or only some of the group members is a matter of the decision *method*: consensus, majority vote, decision by authority, and so on. The *type* of decision refers to the degree to which its implementation will result in significant or substantial change for the group itself or for its environment. 'Vital' decisions are ones which either implicate the basic values and needs of the group members, or involve commitments of considerable permanence or duration with substantial investments of time, resources or emotional energy. 'Routine' decisions are everyday, repetitive decisions of a less important nature.

The *quality* of a decision refers to its degree of effectiveness, and is measured by a comparison of actual outcomes with anticipated or intended outcomes. Decisions can also be evaluated in the light of the way the group's time and resources were utilised, how many members are committed to implementing it fully, and whether the group's problem-solving ability was enhanced. Intuition, too, plays a part: one can 'sense' a good decision by being aware of one's feelings of satisfaction, relief, or excitement, and of a bad decision by one's feelings of anxiety or a sense of prematurity or incompleteness: what might be called the 'hunch' factor. A knowledge of the indicators of *groupthink,* described below, can alert members to the dangers of a defective process that might lead to a poor-quality decision.

Group decisions are made in a *climate*: some are made coolly and rationally as a result of routine problem-solving, while others are made amidst struggles of emotion, ethics or conscience that embroil the members of a group in sometimes severe levels of pre-and post-decisional conflict. The more vital the interests of the group members, the more likely it is that there will be significant degrees of stress and difficulty. Stress can result from a member's wish to escape from the need to make a difficult choice between alternatives, anxiety about the nature of the commitment that would follow the decision, or apprehension about its anticipated outcomes.

Regardless of whether the climate is calm or stressful, difficulties can arise in the process if the group is lacking in problem-solving skills adequate for the task, or lacks effective mechanisms for dealing with stress and conflict. Conditions which can further reduce decision-making effectiveness include insufficient or false information; group size too small or too large; lack of group maturity; egocentrism and dominance of a few members and non-participation by others; fear of the consequences of making the decision; collusion to avoid disagreement or argument; excessive homogeneity; power differences with low levels of trust; and pressure of time. A diagnostic aid for determining the causes of prolonged indecision is included in Appendix D.

Decision-Making Methods

Method 1   Consensus
The most effective but also the most time-consuming and demanding of members' skills. Everyone gives their assent in what amounts to a unanimous decision, but there is not necessarily an absence of dissent or doubt. All members can show that they understand the decision, all have had a chance to express how they feel about it, and those who still have reservations nevertheless say publicly and willingly that they will support the decision and commit themselves to its implementation. In a vote, all hands must be raised to signify assent – if there are any 'no' votes it would be a case of majority rule, not consensus; if there are any abstentions, the decision would have to be agreed or passed 'nem. con.' (*nemine contradicente* = no-one against) which again is not consensus. Innovative, creative and high-quality decisions result from the effective practice of consensus-seeking. False consensus, such as groupthink, (see page 114) is the opposite extreme, and dangerous. Assumed consensus, resulting from a failure to obtain an indication of assent and commitment from each member can be equally dangerous. The frustrations and conflicts inherent in true consensus-seeking can lead not only to better decisions but, if effectively managed, to enhanced group skills and relationships. Consensus is unlikely to be achieved if there is an emergency in progress nor in immature groups, and is probably unnecessary for most routine and minor decisions.

Method 2   Majority Vote

The most commonly-used method in western society, and effective when time is short or the decision is not vital. Its main disadvantage is the tendency to divide the group into winners and losers. The latter may form a potentially disruptive force in the implementation stage unless any feelings of resentment or apathy are confronted and effectively responded to.

Method 3   Minority Vote

A working group, sub-committee, or task force is often appointed to make the decision on behalf of the group. When the members constitute less than 50 percent of the total group, the legitimate minority can save time, help to deal with backlogs or contribute special knowledge or resources. A disadvantage of this method is that it does not necessarily ensure commitment of the whole group to implementing the decision.

Method 4   Decision by Leader after Group Discussion

The group proposes ideas and holds discussions, but the designated leader makes the final decision. The greater the leader's listening skills, the greater will be the benefits of the discussion, but the members may end up feeling powerless or show low commitment; conflicts do not necessarily get aired or resolved.

Method 5   Decision by Leader Alone

The designated leader makes a decision without consulting the group members at all. In emergencies, or for minor and routine decisions it can be a useful method, but there are widespread disadvantages: group interaction and learning is lost, no commitment is built, conflicts are not worked through, and there is no insurance against later resentment or outright sabotage.

Method 6   Decision by Expert

The procedure is to select the expert, have him or her consider the issues with or without group discussion, and then make the decision on behalf of the group. Similar in its disadvantages to methods 4 and 5, this has the added difficulty of agreeing on who the expert is, or differentiating between the 'most powerful and 'most expert' member.

Method 7   Averaging or Ranking

Each member is asked for his or her opinion and the results are averaged. Even though discussion is allowed and may be fruitful, there is the disadvantage that the least knowledgeable members may annul the opinions of the most knowledgeable. Commitment to the final decision may be so varied or weak that implementation will be hampered. If rank ordering or rating is used, the group decision is the proposal with the highest aggregate score.

Group members should view the above list as a repertoire from which they may select the one most appropriate for the history and characteristics of their particular group, the task being worked on, and the resources and time available. Also on the theme of matching the method to the situation, and relating that to the amount of member involvement that is desirable, Vroom and Yetton (1973) proposed a leadership-participation model in the form of a *decision tree*. By a process of elimination through a branching set of yes/no questions, a leader can be assisted in judging the amount of participation on the part of the group members that would be appropriate under different sets of conditions. This normative model is somewhat rigid, and provides a contrast to the free-flowing descriptive model which follows.

The Decision-Making Process

When the method involves all group members in the pre-decision discussion and debate, there are generally clearly-defined phases through which the group passes. Out of these, the decision itself emerges, although the precise moment when this occurs is not apt to be pinpointed. Early theorists (Dewey, 1933; Bales and Strodtbeck, 1951; Simon, 1960) put forward strictly linear models of this process, while later thinkers such as Scheidel and Crowell (1964) and Fisher (1980) argued convincingly for 'spirals'. A spiral process can be summarised as follows: one person 'moves' the discussion to a 'higher' level, and others respond with agreement, disagreement, extension or revision. When the talk solidifies into consensus about that idea, the group 'anchors' that position and introduces a new idea. The spiral process involves both 'reach-testing' forward from an anchored point of agreement and 'back-tracking' when new ideas meet opposition, until a decision acceptable to all members emerges. Fisher combined linear and spiral thinking in his useful conceptualisation of the pre-decision process as one of 'decision emergence', whereby the group progresses through four distinct phases or levels, as follows.

1. **Orientation:** tentative searching for ideas and directions; opinions and attitudes towards proposals are expressed ambiguously at first, later more confidently as members become less socially inhibited.

2. **Conflict:** members now appear to have made up their minds, and disputes arise as they align themselves with or against the proposals. Members are now more tenacious, providing data to substantiate their views, and engaging in full-fledged debate and argument. Polarisation into 'for' and 'against' coalitions is typical.

3. **Emergence:** as overt conflict decreases, comments unfavourable to the emerging proposals diminish. There is a return to ambiguity, coupled with favourable opinion, as those who earlier voiced dissent now begin their change to assent *via* ambiguity. The emerging

decision becomes increasingly more evident as polarisation and dissent dissipate and consensus approaches.

4. **Reinforcement:**   conflict and ambiguity have all but vanished as members reinforce each others' favourable opinions and seek consensus and commitment to the preferred outcome. Eventually the announcement of the final decision is urged, signalling the end of the pre-decision phase.

The process that Fisher describes is gradual and cumulative, with occasional backtracking as the group moves towards its decision. Periods of 'skittering' are common: a random and sometimes chaotic series of disconnected suggestions and counter-suggestions, interruptions and distractions. (The word skittering originates from the eighteenth century verb meaning 'to move rapidly and lightly' – it captures the mood of such phases well). Members begin to feel they are wasting time, going round in circles, not getting anywhere. This time of 'muddling through' sometimes conceals a struggle for control (of the group, of the task), sometimes conceals anxiety (about being able to work as a team or cope with the task). So long as this phenomenon does not become too protracted, it can be appreciated as a necessary and potentially creative time, leading up to a turning point towards a more ordered phase of the discussion.

It is a characteristic of group decision-making that decisions are announced or made public in some way: by a declaration or 'statement of intent', a show of hands in a vote, or the signing of a document or contract for example. This 'symbolic display' signifies the end of the pre-decision stage, and the start of the implementation stage, and is a time to assess the group members' feelings about the quality of the decision and their level of commitment to its implementation. Higgin and Bridger (1965) suggested a simple questionnaire that could be used with a rating scale and be administered (written or verbally) for this purpose in the form of three simple questions:

1.   How satisfied are you with the decision just made by the group ?
2.   How willing are you to carry out the decision ?
3.   How satisfied are you with the way the group worked on the task ?

Groupthink

Under certain conditions, groups can prevent effective decisions from being made by the process Irving Janis calls groupthink (Janis 1971, 1982). He defines it as a *'deterioration of mental efficiency, reality testing and moral judgement'* that he says is associated with cohesive but dysfunctional groups, in which norms are present that put concurrence-seeking and morale higher than critical thinking or responsible conflict management. Such groups bring powerful social pressures to bear whenever a dissident voice begins to raise objections to what appears to be an emerging consensus. A typical norm of this type is that members remain loyal to the group by supporting the policies to which the group is committed even when there are warning signs that these might have unintended results. In the 80s, Janis's theory of groupthink, and particularly its presumed positive correlation with group cohesion, was revisited and questioned by a number of researchers (see Hogg, 1992, pp. 135–41 for a summary of their findings).

Groupthink has been responsible for some catastrophic decisions, the most famous and oft-quoted one being President Kennedy's invasion of Cuba in 1961 at the Bay of Pigs. Within three days, the whole brigade of 1,400 Cuban exiles, who had been aided by the CIA and the US Navy and Air Force, had been killed or taken prisoner. Kennedy, Rusk, McNamara and the other top-ranking policy makers had exhibited all of Janis's eight criteria of groupthink, summarised below:

1. Most or all of the group members share an illusion of being invulnerable that gives them a false sense of reassurance, and makes them take extraordinary risks and ignore warning signals.
2. The group collectively constructs rationalisations in order to discount warnings and negative feedback.
3. Members have an unquestioning belief in the inherent morality of the group.
4. Members hold stereotyped views of those who oppose them, labelling them as evil, weak or stupid. Genuine attempts at negotiation are thus sabotaged in advance.
5. The group applies direct pressure to any dissident voices that question the group's illusions, decisions, rights, etc.
6. A great deal of self-censorship takes place as members with doubts minimise them or set them aside and go with the consensus.
7. Members share an illusion of unanimity as the vocal members simply assume that the silent members are in agreement.
8. Members sometimes appoint themselves as 'mindguards' to protect the group (and particularly the leader) from adverse information and criticism.

The same US government group that was responsible for the Bay of Pigs disaster was faced with an even more dangerous situation only eighteen months later: the Cuban missile crisis. This time however, they negotiated a successful resolution of the crisis with the Soviet Union, in the process demonstrating considerable foresight and skill. As with most groups, their susceptibility to groupthink was variable.

Groupthink can equally well apply in small, everyday work groups. A knowledge of the above indicators can alert members to the dangers of a defective process that might lead to a poor-quality decision. As a counter concept to groupthink, Neck and Manz (1994) have coined the interesting term *teamthink* which they define as 'constructive synergistic team thinking' (p. 929). Their paper develops and extends Janis's own recommendations for safeguarding against groupthink:

- each member of the group should take on the role of 'critical evaluator', and at least one member the role of 'devil's advocate';

- group leaders should adopt an impartial stance at the start of a task, to encourage a norm of open enquiry;

- the group should guard against becoming insular: outside groups should be asked to work on the same problem or provide feedback and advice;

- outside experts should be co-opted or invited in;

- when the group is involved with other groups, special attention should be paid to warning signals and other information coming from the latter;

- after reaching a preliminary consensus, a 'second chance' session should be held at which all members air any residual doubts they may have.

With so many potential impediments, it is small wonder that most decisions are made by what Simon (1957) called 'satisficing' (looking for the solution which is just satisfactory or 'good enough') rather than by maximising (getting the best possible result). Even if maximising is an unrealistic goal in all but the most ideal conditions, higher levels of effectiveness will nevertheless be reached if even a few members are conversant with the following:

- the advantages and disadvantages of the common decision-making *methods* used by work groups;

- at least one good descriptive model of the *process* of group decision-making;

- a normative (prescriptive) model of effective group decision-making *behaviours*.

Effective Decision-Making Behaviours

Having reviewed the methods and process of group decision-making, some prescriptions in the form of a checklist of desirable behaviours and techniques can next be attempted. What follows is a synthesis of work by Hall (1971) on consensus-seeking; by Janis and Mann (1977) on 'vigilant information processing' and the 'decision balance-sheet'; by Janis (1971,

1982) on groupthink; by Yukl (1994) on leadership functions in decision-making groups; and by Neck and Manz (1994) on 'teamthink'.

Effective consensus-seeking includes the following prescribed behaviours

1. Avoid arguing blindly for your own position: present it as clearly and logically as possible, but be sensitive to the reactions of the group each time you do so.
2. Avoid 'win-lose' stalemates and competitive thinking, at the same time withstanding pressures to yield that have no objective or logically sound foundation.
3. Avoid changing your mind merely to achieve agreement and harmony.
4. Avoid conflict-reducing devices such as majority rule, averaging, bargaining and trading, coin-tossing, etc.
5. View differences of opinion as natural and helpful rather than a hindrance.
6. View early agreement as suspect, and ensure that people have arrived at the same conclusion for the same reasons, or at least for compatible reasons.
7. Be positive: assume that your group is capable of excelling at all the foregoing prescriptive behaviours.

The effective decision-maker

1. Thoroughly canvasses a wide range of alternative courses of action.
2. Surveys the full range of objectives to be fulfilled and the values implicated by the possible choices.
3. Carefully weighs what is known about the costs and risks of negative consequences, as well as positive ones, that could result from each alternative. The 'balance sheet' lists the following:
   (a) the tangible gains and losses for the group;
   (b) the tangible gains and losses for significant others;
   (c) group self-approval or disapproval (will we feel proud or ashamed of this choice?);
   (d) approval or disapproval of the group by others.
4. Intensively searches for new information relevant to further evaluation of the alternative by (i) inviting outside experts to group meetings and asking them to challenge the members' views, (ii) calling for at least one member to play 'devil's advocate'.
5. Correctly assimilates and takes account of any new information or expert judgement even when it does not support the choice initially preferred.
6. Re-examines the positive and negative consequences before making a final choice, perhaps making use of subgroups which meet separately to hammer out differences and express all residual doubts before re-forming to test the degree of consensus and commitment.

7. Makes detailed provisions for implementing the decision, with special attention to contingency plans that might be required if various known or anticipated risks were to materialise.

The effective leader of a decision-making group

1. Assigns the role of 'critical evaluator' to each member, encouraging the group to give high priority to open airing of objections and doubts.
2. Adopts an impartial stance instead of stating preferences and expectations at the beginning.
3. Encourages members to discuss the group's deliberations with outsiders (within the limits of security or confidentiality) and report back on their responses.
4. Listens attentively and observes nonverbal cues so as to be aware of members' needs, feelings, interactions and conflicts.
5. Models and promotes positive 'task and maintenance' behaviours: initiating, clarifying, process analysing, standard setting, summarising, gatekeeping and supporting.
6. Prevents the group making hasty decisions as a result of 'concurrence-seeking', a desire to agree regardless of consequences such as groupthink: the very antithesis of true consensus-seeking.

In conclusion, it is possible to construct a general model of the norms in 'the perfect decision-making group':

> Communication is two-way, and the open and accurate expression of both ideas and feelings are emphasised. Participation and leadership are distributed among members.

> Controversy and conflict are seen as positive opportunities for involvement and individual and group learning, leading to better quality decisions.

> Creativity, interpersonal effectiveness and self-realisation are encouraged. Members evaluate the effectiveness of the group and are committed to improving its functioning.

> Cohesion and consensus are sought through high levels of inclusion, acceptance, affection, trust and support, with respect for the dissenting voice. 'Unanimity without groupthink' is the motto.

For detailed reading on decision-making, see Johnson and Johnson, 1994 Chap. 6; Neck and Manz, 1994; Yukl, 1994, Chap. 14; Fisher, 1980; Johnson, 1977 Chap. 6.

10

MANAGING CONFLICT

When angry, count four; when very angry, swear.
Mark Twain

The Nature of Conflict

Conflict (literally 'a striking together') is inevitable in work groups, and must be effectively handled if it is not to be a barrier to progress, a cause of the destruction of the group, or a source of physical or psychological damage to an individual. If members of the group are committed to the task and involved actively in working to achieve its goals as well as their own, differences of opinion, beliefs and values are almost bound to be aired and will give rise to debate and argument as a matter of course. The emotional investment that each party to a conflict puts into the satisfaction of their needs, the achievement of their goals, and the protection of their belief and value systems may also be such that a debate or argument will rapidly develop into a more substantial conflict of interest, then into direct opposition, and – eventually – stalemate or possible violence. Moments of impasse call for particular skills and strategies if the group is to benefit from the opportunity each such incident offers for learning and positive change.

Conflict can occur at the personal level (internal conflict), between people (interpersonal conflict), or between groups (intergroup or international conflict). Most people in our society regard conflict in a negative light, due undoubtedly to the uncomfortable or stressful emotions that generally accompany the emergence of any confrontation between two or more parties. Such situations, if experienced as threatening, give rise to anxiety , fear or panic, depending on the degree of the perceived threat, and then to a reaction which typically produces one of three types of behaviour: attack, immobilisation, or flight. It is easy to conjure up images of these in the animal kingdom: charging buffalo, petrified deer, fleeing rabbits, for example. In groups, these behaviours show up when members engage in open and hostile verbal battle, are stunned into silence, or 'drop out' in some way, perhaps by becoming apathetic, busying themselves with other matters, or leaving the room. The responses to conflict are idiosyncratic and rarely predictable. Individuals usually first revert to their favoured or characteristic behaviour in the face of opposition (in extreme situations, a full regression to characteristic childhood behaviour may be observed) before attempting to deal rationally with the issue. Groups that become heavily conflicted may therefore manifest either hostile or apathetic behaviour – the troubleshooting chart in Appendix D helps to show some of the causes of these patterns.

Effective conflict handling requires that the energies which have either erupted or are still simmering below the surface are creatively channelled towards a resolution that will bring fresh insights, as well as improving the relationships between group members and enhancing the skills of the group as a whole. Ineffective handling results in a deterioration of the relationship between the opposing parties as hostility escalates into violence, or apathy degenerates into stagnation, either of which is capable ultimately of destroying the group or, at best, causing it to disband voluntarily. The sense of failure and frustration that follows these outcomes is neither pleasant nor healthy for the individuals who endure it.

Conflict is best handled by managing it, that is adopting appropriate strategies to bring about a desired end, whether that be resolution, abatement or suppression. This calls for purposeful action: *dealing* with the situation rather than merely *responding*. Basically, there are two types of strategy for managing conflict: *Win-Lose,* and *Win-Win.* Both usually involve negotiation, but the intentions in each type differ. In a Win-Lose approach, the aim is to find a solution more favourable to oneself, regardless of the effect on the other. In a Win-Win approach, also called the Problem-Solving approach, the aim is to arrive at a solution that is the most satisfying possible to *both* parties. Such an outcome would be true conflict *resolution*: both parties would win, and would be enhanced by and committed to the result.

Before exploring these strategies in more detail, it is important to consider the need for, and value of, a change in attitude towards conflict, away from the negative one predominant in our culture towards a more balanced one capable of being put to positive use. Although the attitudinal change may take time, the preferred attitude itself is easily described. It is, simply, that *conflict is positive, necessary, and manageable, but also has a negative potential for destructiveness that must be approached with understanding and respect.*

Conflict as a positive and necessary phenomenon is nicely argued by Drucker (1977, p.379): '*The understanding that underlies the right decision grows out of the clash and conflict of opinions and out of the serious consideration of competing alternatives* / In addition, group cohesion can be improved as a result of conflict with other groups as members band together to reaffirm and maintain the group's identity and boundaries in the face of interference or opposition from the surrounding social or organisational environment. In the course of a conflict, new situations can arise that require the establishment of new rules and norms or the modification of existing ones, and these processes can increase group learning and effectiveness.

Conflict as manageable is a proposition supported and illustrated by the Thomas-Kilmann model, an adaptation of which is shown in Figure 10.1. Most of us will be only too familiar with the negative potential, or at least with the ugliness, pain or fear associated with the realisation of that potential. At the time of writing these words, countless wars are being fought around the globe, while national governments are adding enormously to the distress of all peoples in their consistent inability to relinquish their win-lose approach to arms reduction and other international peace and social justice initiatives.

Conflict Management Strategies

Figure 10.1 shows five basic methods of managing conflict: coercion, accommodation, avoidance, compromise and collaboration. The axes of the model refer to the attitudes taken by either party in a conflict situation towards the other. These attitudes give rise to the five strategies described below.

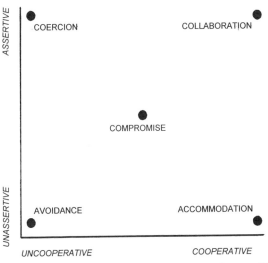

Figure 10.1   A conflict management model (Thomas and Kilmann, 1974).

Coercion: is assertive and uncooperative – a power-oriented 'win-lose' mode characterised by competition, stand-over tactics, brute force etc. Individuals use whatever power seems appropriate to win their goals even at the other person's expense.

Uses:

- when quick, decisive action is vital, e.g. emergencies;
- on important issues where unpopular decisions have to be implemented, e.g. cost-cutting, discipline etc.;
- as protection against those who take advantage of non-competitive behaviour.

Disadvantages:

- conflict may not be resolved and may re-surface later with increased vigour and complexity;
- the loser may become more angry , rebellious, or devious;
- the chances of a subsequent negotiated resolution may be lessened or destroyed;
- the conflict may erupt into open violence.

Accommodation: is unassertive and cooperative – the opposite of coercion. Individuals neglect their own needs to satisfy those of the other, by capitulation, selfless generosity, charity, obedience, self-sacrifice, etc.

Uses:

- when preserving harmony outweighs other goals;
- when continued competition would damage your cause;
- when you realise you are wrong, to learn from others;
- to allow others to learn by making their own mistakes;
- when it is useful to build up credit for later use!

Disadvantages:

- feelings of self-worth may be diminished;
- winners may come to regard their tactics as condoned or justified;
- winners may press further their domination of the accommodator until the conflict re-surfaces in heightened form.

Avoidance: is both unassertive and uncooperative – the individual does not address the conflict, maybe by withdrawing totally or by denying that there is a conflict. Other terms may include sidestepping, looking the other way, de-fusing, and postponing.

Uses:

- when an issue is trivial or relatively unimportant;
- when your power is low – impossible opposition, no chance at all to win;
- when the potential damage of confronting the issue would be greater than the benefits of resolving it;
- to allow people to cool off or recover their balance, to reduce tension;
- when gathering more information is judged to be necessary;
- when a mediator is attacked by one or both of the parties in conflict.

Disadvantages:

- low satisfaction, tends to leave fears and doubts about meeting the same type of situation again;
- perpetuates low valuing of traits such as courage, persistence, self-respect;
- may increase the opponent's frustration and power tactics.

Compromise: is intermediate in assertiveness and cooperativeness. It is an attempt at problem-solving, but only seeks to find a mutually accept-able solution which partially satisfies both parties' goals. It might mean splitting the difference, exchanging concessions, or finding a quick mid-dle-ground position. Usually, neither party is satisfied for long; at best, it is a temporary solution, and not a *resolution.*

Uses:

- when two opponents with equal power are strongly committed to mutually exclusive goals;
- to achieve temporary settlements in complex matters;
- to achieve expedient solutions under time pressure or other duress;
- when the goals are only moderately important.

Disadvantages:

- the conflict is likely to re-emerge later in the same form, or in disguise;
- leaves both sides with residual feelings of dissatisfaction;
- may leave both sides with low commitment to implementing the solution.

Collaboration: is both assertive *and* cooperative, and literally means 'co-labour', or work together. It means delving into an issue and the concerns and goals of the persons or parties involved, with a view to finding a creative solution that will meet *both* parties' needs to the highest extent possible, with neither emerging as a loser. Successful negotiating behaviours will be needed – active listening, self-disclosure, mutual trust, responsible confrontation, clear communication. A repertoire of creative problem-solving skills is also a priority.

Uses:

- to find an integrative solution when both parties' concerns are too important to be compromised;

- to transcend the 'either-or' polarity and find a truly creative solution;

- to work through hard feelings which have been interfering with the group's progress;

- to maximise commitment by incorporating other's concerns into a consensual decision;

- when it is important to learn from others or to understand the views of others.

Disadvantages:

- can consume large amounts of time and energy;

- can require expensive additional resources (experts, consultants, materials etc).

The five strategies are best treated as a repertoire: the effective conflict manager understands the consequences of each strategy well enough to adopt the one that is appropriate to the moment, while giving priority to cooperative and assertive collaboration whenever possible. Whether a party chooses to work cooperatively and assertively towards resolution, or employs one of the other strategies will depend on a number of variables:

- Present-time situational factors and constraints: structure, purpose and goals of the group; the time available, the nature and urgency of the task; the importance of the values underlying the issue; the relative strength, resources and skills of the opposing parties.

- Past experience: individuals enter the arena with memories, emotions, scars and insights from earlier similar situations, all of which result in a pre-disposition for a particular way of behaving.

- The stage in the process in which the parties find themselves: particular strategies may have a different appeal in the early stages or after some time has elapsed, or a switch to a different strategy might be made as a last resort, or as a surprise tactic.

Negotiation and Mediation

At this point, more needs to be said about collaboration as the strategy most likely to result in conflict *resolution* as distinct from conflict abatement or suppression. Collaboration holds the same position in the conflict management repertoire as consensus does in the decision-making repertoire: it is the ideal, the process deemed to be the most likely to lead to a satisfactory outcome and to enhance the group's learning and effectiveness. The conflicting parties may work together unassisted, or they may seek the assistance of a facilitator or mediator. In either case, there is a process to be followed, as outlined below:

Step 1   Preparation

A diagnosis must be made to ascertain whether the issue concerns facts (an information issue), or anticipations (a prediction issue), or values (an ideological issue). Value conflicts are the hardest to resolve; it is important to look for the tangible effects, the precise nature of the impasse, block, or difficult decision to be made. It is helpful to clarify whether the issue concerns content (ideas, problem areas) or behaviour (actions, attitudes). It is also helpful at this stage to spend some time identifying and exploring the *trigger*: the key word or act that precipitated the discussion into an argument or fight. If a review of the process immediately prior to and just subsequent to the outbreak of hostile feelings can pinpoint the trigger, there will be an opportunity for one party or the other to focus on the crucial word or action, perhaps bringing in one of the appropriate problem-solving techniques such as tableaux, graphics, analogy or role-play (see Appendix C). A vital part of each party's preparation is to get clear about what they really want to achieve, how far they are prepared to meet the other's needs, how they would best like to conduct themselves, and when and where the issue will be broached.

Step 2   Confrontation

Initiating a *responsible* confrontation means presenting and arguing your case to the other party as a request or proposal expressed as an 'I' statement, including not only the facts but the *thoughts and feelings* which underlie your case. Initiating must be done effectively: it is not a good idea to immediately attack or demean the opposing party – an angry or defensive reaction will be guaranteed. Kurtz and Jones (1973) conclude that it helps if (i) the confronter has a good relationship with the confrontee; (ii) the confronter distinguishes between thoughts, feelings, actions, and facts; (iii) concrete behaviour is addressed rather than emotions; (iv) the confrontee is open and willing to explore himself or herself and the issue; (v) the confrontee responds flexibly to the situation and the confronter's style, rather than in a stereotyped inflexible way; and (vi) both parties are willing to accept some temporary disorganisation.

Step 3   Listening

Each party must be capable of *active listening*: really hearing what the other is saying, reflecting back to the speaker a paraphrase of what they have said to check for accuracy. Active listening also involves shelving preconceptions, giving the other party plenty of time to put over their point of view, avoiding being defensive or critical, etc.

Step 4   Collaboration

This step involves the parties in jointly agreeing on a re-definition of the problem or issue, the generation of options and solutions, and the choice of a mutually satisfying solution. Each party must take on the role of *negotiator*. The task is easier if the conflict is *symmetrical*, i.e. the parties are approximately equal in terms of power or status, and much harder if the conflict is *asymmetrical*, with one party in a position of dominance or control. There will be serious problems if either of the collaborators is a coercer, avoider, or compromiser in disguise! The less symmetrical the conflict is, or the greater the difficulty being experienced in the collaboration, the greater the need for a third party or mediator. The roles of negotiator and mediator are substantially different, as the guidelines below make clear. The full range of creative problem-solving skills (see Appendix C) available among the members of the group may need to be mobilised.

The negotiator role

1. Define the conflict as a mutual problem, and pursue goals held in common.
2. Operate from a position of strength (prescribing, proposing and asking, rather than begging, pleading or coaxing); stay respectful, firm and centred, avoid personal attacks, vacillation and lies or misrepresentation.
3. Assess one's own needs accurately, and disclose them.
4. Avoid harassment, harm, or embarrassment of the other party, expressing anger only to get rid of hostile feelings that may interfere with future cooperation.
5. Work to increase empathy and understanding of other's position, feelings, and frame of reference.
6. Try to equalise power, and maintain commitment to a problem-solving orientation.
7. Reduce the other's defensiveness by avoiding threats and communicating flexibility of position.
8. Promote clarity and mutual interdependence; project trustworthiness and predictability.
9. Explore both the similarities and the differences in positions.
10. Seek help from third parties when appropriate.

The mediator role

1. Focus on process rather than content.
2. Get the parties to define their basic wants and goals, and to state the lengths to which they are prepared to go to achieve those ends.
3. Help determine the relationship, for each party, between ends and means – how far are they reasonably prepared to make concessions without resorting to compromise.
4. Include an exploration of internal conflict, that is, conflicts which exist within an individual or group and which are more than likely significantly contributing to the open conflict.
5. Avoid putting forward proposals or giving advice.
6. Avoid conflict between the mediator and the mediated.

In conclusion, it is possible to construct a general model of the norms in 'the perfect conflict-handling group':

Members do not try to eliminate, deny or avoid conflict, but view it as healthy , offering opportunities for involvement, growth, change, new insights and creativity.	

Members strive to create a climate of trust and support in which parties in conflict may safely work towards a a resolution.	Members value the 'problem-solving' approach rather than the 'win-lose' approach, looking for the creative solution most satisfying to *both* parties, with neither being the loser.

Members are committed to evaluating and understanding the processes and outcomes of their conflict management performance and to improving their effectiveness in this area.	

For detailed reading on conflict management, see Moore, 1996; Johnson and Johnson, 1994, Chaps 7 and 8; Pfeiffer, 1994; Condliffe, 1991; Cornelius and Faire, 1989; Wilson and Hanna, 1986, Chap. 10.

For detailed reading on intergroup conflict, see Zander, 1994, Chaps. 11 and 12; Fisher et al., 1991; Susskind and Cruikshank, 1987; Feldman, 1985a; Blake and Mouton, 1984; Smith, 1982.

Key Concept

11

MANAGING DIVERSITY

Contact is the appreciation of differences.
Fritz Perls

Acknowledging Diversity

Managing diversity has emerged as a major area of professional and scholarly attention over the past decade, yet it is what leaders and managers of groups have always had to do. Group membership has always been characterised by diversity both in terms of members' backgrounds and their here-and-now behaviour in group sessions. In the contemporary workforce, Affirmative Action and Equal Opportunity legislation, while enjoying only limited success around the world, has not only increased the degree of diversity in organisations, but has also highlighted the need to deal equitably with the many issues that this increase has raised. The workforce in general has become more vocal about the legitimacy of difference, and in many instances displays a growing consciousness of and pride in uniqueness. This has been accompanied by an increasing intolerance of intolerance!

Some personal characteristics of group members that are elements of group structure are discussed in Key Concept 4. In other parts of the book it has been shown how personal differences also contribute in complex ways to interpersonal, group and intergroup psychodynamic processes. The management of diversity, in the contemporary sense of the term, addresses both the here-and-now differences in behaviour of group members at work, and the inherent differences that underlie and drive those behaviours, particularly those that hinder or block progress on the task. Diversity in all types of groups creates opportunities for discovering other ways of doing things, other ways of being. Diversity is a decided advantage in problem-solving and decision-making groups where a multiplicity of viewpoints and prior experiences contributes richness to the process

and content and helps to avoid groupthink. Diversity is most disadvanta-
geous in groups that require members to think or behave in similar or nar-
rowly-defined ways or to act out of a uniform value system.

There are three areas to be explored: first, the nature of diversity in
terms of the dimensions of difference most commonly found in work
groups; second, the behaviour of those who are different and those who
respond to difference; and third, the strategies available to directed or
self-managed groups for improving their chances of managing diversity
effectively.

Diversity exists first of all within the individual: each will bring to the
group a range of attitudes, feelings, fears, hopes, preferences and values,
personal agendas, role hunger, and past experience. Add to this demographic statistics such as ethnic or cultural mind-sets, or physical statistics
such as energy level or disability, and there are the beginnings of a complex *intrapsychic* management task on the part of each member even
before any interaction occurs. Figure 11.1 portrays a group as if the members have crossed the boundary and taken up their role in the group, trail-
ing behind them a comet-like tail which represents the totality of who and
what they are at that moment.

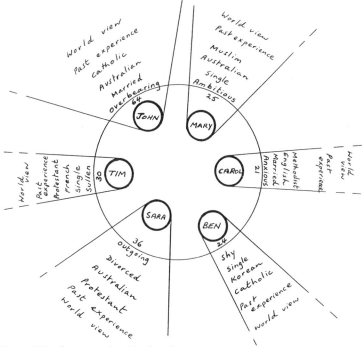

Figure 11.1   Group membership diversity.

Directly behind the public face of each of the members are their personality and personal characteristics, a little further back are their goals and agendas, and behind that their life circumstances and past experiences. Such a diagram could be used to map the group's unique diversity as a tool for anticipating and positively managing it as a resource rather than a weakness. Once each member comes to take up their role with others for the task at hand, there will be new and significantly more complex intragroup dynamics to be handled. Whether there is a group leader or whether the group is self-managing, sooner or later there will be critical incidents that stem more or less directly from differences in attitudes, abilities, values, and styles of relating and working together on a task. The dimensions of difference that might have a significant impact on work and require management would include at least the following:

- **Professional** level of expertise, level of commitment, locus of control, career stage.

- **Demographic** gender, age, ethnicity, nationality, language.

- **Social** education level, marital status, parents' marital status, religious beliefs.

- **Psychodynamic** psychological presence, attitude to authority, vulnerability to stress, personality type (e.g. introvert/extrovert), preferred learning style, sociability, degree of self-awareness, sexual orientation.

- **Physiological** energy level, state of health, disabilities or impairments.

- **World view** values, tendency to prejudice (stereotyping, racial intolerance), tendency to bias (ethnocentrism), stance on ethics and social responsibility.

Responding to Diversity

Much of the attention in the literature on organisational diversity seems to have been paid to the dimensions of difference that are concerned with the influence of members' ethnic or national backgrounds, that is, *cultural diversity* in the broadest sense of the term (for example, Thiederman, 1993; Kogod, 1992; Adler, 1986). Thiederman (1993, p. 257) noted that group members who are fearful because of their cultural difference tend to act in one or a number of the following ways:

Hesitance to take initiative;
Reluctance to complain or make negative comments;
Failure to admit lack of comprehension;
Reluctance to seek or accept promotion;
Reluctance to praise self.

Thiederman offers the following possible interpretations for these behaviours: fear of or respect for authority; fear of job loss; fear of reprimands, ridicule or loss of face; desire for harmony in the group; desire not to be set apart from the group; desire for anonymity. At the same time, managers and other members typically respond in predictable ways such as those described by Kogod (1992) and Adler (1986):

Parochially   denial, or 'cultural blindness': concerned only with the member's professional skills; not recognising differences since 'our way is the only way'.

Ethnocentrically   acknowledging the existence of diversity, but viewing it as the cause of problems, since 'our way is the best way'.

Synergistically   working with the differences to explore and combine the advantages of each.

It is the synergistic approach that leads to the most appropriate ways to manage diversity. A number of writers have proposed guidelines for this, varying from organisation-wide change programs (Thomas, 1990) to targetted training programs (Johnson and Johnson, 1994). The latter provides the following recommendations for action directed towards valuing and managing diversity in groups (pp. 448–53):

- recognise that diversity is ever-present and unavoidable;

- maximise diversity of personal characteristics and abilities to maximise productivity and success;

- face and resolve barriers to the utilisation of diversity such as racism, sexism, exclusive or derogatory language, etc;

- structure constructive procedures for managing conflict and clarifying miscommunications among members;

- create a context where diversity is seen as a resource and a strength rather than a problem or hindrance;

- focus on the higher level of group identity and the importance of being a group member to unite diverse personal identities;

- encourage members to develop an appreciation for their ethnic, religious, cultural and personal backgrounds;

- promote a pluralistic set of values concerning equality, freedom, the rights of the individual and the responsibilities of group membership.

In conclusion, Carnevale and Kogod's comment that 'diversity creates opportunities for learning' (1996, p. 11) could stand as an apt slogan for the management of diversity. It also provides a fitting introduction to Part 4.

For detailed reading on managing diversity, see Carnevale and Kogod, 1996; Chemers et al., 1995; Daft, 1994, Chap. 13; Gentile, 1994; Johnson and Johnson, 1994, Chap. 10; Gordon, 1993; Thiederman, 1993; Jackson, 1992; Kogod, 1992; Thomas, 1990.

PART 4

LEARNING

A fellow-learner is the best
teacher you can have

Key Concept

12

GROUP EFFECTIVENESS

It is not enough to aim, you must hit.
Italian proverb

Effectiveness and Learning

Over the past decade, questions of effective performance and learning in small groups have been somewhat overshadowed by the burgeoning interest in 'The Learning Organisation'. The concept was firmly put on corporate agendas worldwide with the publication of Peter Senge's 'The Fifth Discipline' (Senge, 1990). Since then, the field has grown steadily (French and Bazalgette, 1996; Kilmann, 1996; Field and Ford, 1995; Wardman, 1994; Kim 1993; Schein, 1993; Garrett, 1992; Huber, 1991; Sweiringa and Wierdsma, 1991). In this Key Concept and the next the focus is on effectiveness and learning in small groups, but it must be remembered that attitudes towards and opportunities for learning in the parent organisation is always a significant context.

Models of group development and maturation presented in Key Concept 1 all implied movement towards higher levels of effectiveness, usually as a desirable goal. Definitions and measures of group effectiveness are not simple matters however – they can be based on any one or a number of criteria: efficiency; goal-achievement; output; contributions to the parent organisation or to society; organisational growth, endurance or survival; control over the environment.

Efficiency is defined as the ratio between energy input and energy output, the difference between the two being the amount of energy absorbed by the system's processes in order to do the required work. Effectiveness, in a frame of reference that values only achievements or productivity, would be measured only by the quality of its products – reports, decisions, solutions, plans, artifacts etc. – with little or no regard for the group's inner workings or the satisfaction of the personal needs of its members. In a frame of reference that puts relationships before task achievements, the criteria would be related more to personal growth and group cohesion. Ideally, both productivity and social-emotional aspects are taken into account and balanced when assessing effectiveness.

Models of Effectiveness

A group can be evaluated for effectiveness in terms of how well it measures up to a profile of 'an ideal group'. Some of the attributes of such a group, as seen through the eyes of a number of prominent theorists, are given below.

Chris Argyris (1970) briefly described the effective group as having three main abilities:

- the ability to gather relevant data;
- the ability to make sound, free and informed choices or decisions;
- the ability to implement those decisions with commitment.

Jay Hall (1971) suggested four concerns that underlie and distinguish the effective group:

- commitment level and how it is achieved;
- conflict and the manner in which it is handled;
- creativity and whether it emerges;
- consensus as a decision rule incorporating all the former.

Johnson and Johnson (1994), Dunphy (1981), Likert (1984) and McGregor (1960) are among the many other writers who have suggested longer checklists which describe the ideal work group. Many of their views are synthesised in the profile which follows.

Working atmosphere: all the activities take place in a supportive atmosphere, where suggestions, ideas, information and criticisms are offered and received in a helpful and respectful way. Members are involved, interested, and committed to their work, and have a high degree of confidence and trust in each other. Individual differences are accepted and individual needs acknowledged.

Roles: individuals are permitted to behave in accordance with their personal needs as well as with regard to the range of group needs. The skills required for the task will basically be available within the group; external help will be welcomed or sought as appropriate. Roles are clearly defined and of the right 'mix' to achieve a balance between productivity and relationship-building (task and maintenance functions). The group is of a size appropriate to its purpose.

Goals: group goals are cooperatively rather than competitively structured; if externally imposed, the goals are only accepted if clarified and formulated in such a way that members can commit themselves to achieving them. Self-determined goals are clear, well-understood, achievable, worthwhile, 'stretching', and capable of providing the best possible match with the members' personal goals. Goals are consistently achieved.

Commitment: group members are committed to the task and to each other. All do their best to achieve the group goals and to build satisfying relationships within the team and with other significant groups when appropriate. Individuals are encouraged to take responsibility for leadership and decision-making initiatives. Self-development, creativity, innovation and team-building are all valued highly. Cohesion is promoted, but not at the expense of the worth of the individual.

Communication: there is high motivation to give and receive information which is relevant, uncensored and of value to the group's purpose. Interpersonal communication is two-way, open and accurate. All members participate in discussion, which remains focussed and pertinent to the task in hand. Members are free to express feelings as well as thoughts, and are not ridiculed or punished for sharing their doubts and fears or putting forward creative or unorthodox ideas. Criticism is frequent.

Leadership: the designated leader is competent, and is aware of and sensitive to the needs of individuals and to the characteristics of group behaviour. The leader does not dominate, nor do the group members defer unduly to him/her. Power struggles are resolved on the basis of how best to achieve the task rather than on who should control the group. Different members are in a position at different times to take leading initiatives, and the designated leader accepts and encourages this diffusion of responsibility. Leaders and members help each other to perform their roles better, and time is allocated to team-building activities. The leader adheres strongly to principles that create a supportive and cooperative atmosphere: information sharing, trust, respect, and equality of opportunity.

Conflict management: the group is comfortable with disagreement and committed to seeking resolutions through open negotiation. Conflict is viewed in the light of the group's task or mission. It is seen as healthy and affording opportunities to strengthen the group by increasing trust, cohesion, and decision-making effectiveness.

Decision-making: the group has a repertoire of decision-making procedures from which the one most appropriate to the situation can be selected. For all important decisions, consensus-seeking is the rule, with all members sharing in that process. The full expression of members' opposition to as well as support for the proposals under discussion is encouraged. The final decision is made not by coercion or by appeals to the emotions, but by fully exploring the different contributions, weighing them, and endeavouring to find a solution that contains the best of all of them. The full range of creative problem-solving techniques is employed for all difficulties encountered in the process.

Evaluation: the group is self-conscious about its operations, and frequently examines its procedures and progress. Criticism is frank and honest, without evidence of personal attack, and is made with the intention of improving personal and group performance. Steps are taken to learn from experience by altering behaviours and procedures in the light of review and feedback.

Few work groups can match the above model of excellence in all elements. If the model is regarded as one extreme of a continuum of effectiveness, then the opposite extreme also needs to be considered. Kahn and Boulding (1964, p.135) provided this in a nutshell in their description of what they called 'chronically defeated groups':

> Such a group tends to divide into subgroups and to develop both cliques and social isolates. There is also mutual disparagement among the cliques. Rumor, especially gloomy rumor, is usually abundant. The group itself becomes unattractive to its members. Some members leave, and those who leave are usually considered the 'good' ones, leaving those who remain to become even more insecure. The group develops a 'servant' self-image; it stops initiating ideas, squashes would-be innovators, and does only what it is sure will be wanted by superiors. An increasing bureaucratization takes place, partly to prevent potentially dangerous ideas from getting out to the line and bringing more trouble to the group. The group perceives itself as a weak competitor of groups with related functions. Other groups are no longer seen as entities to be co-operated with, but as more powerful groups with which this group must compete but against which it cannot win. In short, as the group comes to feel less and less valued, its capacity to respond adequately deteriorates.

Somewhere between the two extremes described above lie those more commonly-found work groups, the 'organised anarchies' described by Cohen, March and Olsen (1972, p.1) in their rather disparagingly-labelled 'garbage-can model'. These types of groups are seen as being plagued by problematic preferences, unclear technology, and fluid participation. Any such group appears to have three general properties:

- it discovers preferences through action more than it acts on the basis of preferences;

- its own processes are not understood by its members;
- the audiences and decision makers for any particular kind of choice change capriciously.

Groups that come to recognise themselves as falling somewhere unacceptably low on the effectiveness continuum, and who seriously want to become more competent, must engage in team-building. A prior necessity for that, though, is a basic understanding of how groups learn (or fail to learn) from experience.

For detailed reading on group effectiveness, see Johnson and Johnson, 1994; Argyris, 1983; Kotter, 1978; Argyris and Schon 1974; Hall, 1971.

Experiential Learning

> If I hear, I forget
> If I see, I remember
> If I do, I understand
> *Confucius*

Three conceptual models which help to understand the way groups can learn from experience are outlined below. Unlike the descriptive models presented earlier, these are frankly normative in that they advocate behaviours or procedures that will encourage members to evaluate the progress of the group, to sound alarms when developmental needs are not being met, and ultimately to modify the group's existing normative system.

The Kolb model

The origins of experiential learning go back to the pioneering work with learning groups in human relations training and group dynamics carried out by Kurt Lewin and his associates in the 1930s and 40s (Lewin 1944, 1947). The *experiential learning cycle* (Figure 12.1) was formulated by David Kolb from the findings of Lewin and his co-workers, and extended into a major theory of learning and development (Kolb and Fry, 1975; Kolb, 1984). In the cycle, here-and-now experience (CE) is followed by reflection and observations (RO), which are then assimilated into general abstract concepts or theories (AC). From these, new implications for action can be derived in what Kolb called the active experimentation phase. Tyson and Low (1987) prefer to call this the active programming phase (AP), as it is at this time that an active learner will be preparing to move towards a new round of the cycle by anticipating or planning the next experience (CE).

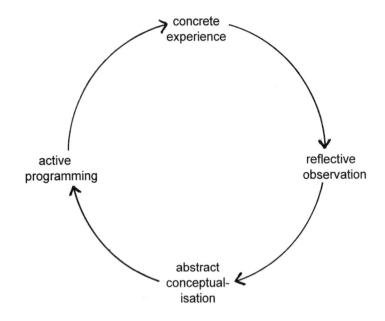

Figure 12.1   The experiential learning cycle.

Although essentially a model of how individuals learn, it can also be applied to groups as they confront and deal with (or fail to deal with) the succession of concerns, themes and problems that arise in group life. As Lewin claimed, *it is necessary to complete the cycle for effective learning to occur.* Thus, a number of needs arise: first, the group members must take time out to reflect on all their processes: data handling, interpersonal relations, leadership, conflict management, problem-solving, use of resources, and so forth. How the members handle personal anxiety and intragroup conflict is of paramount importance here. Second, it is evident that leaders and members of groups committed to learning from experience must accumulate a repertoire of conceptual models of group behaviour, models which they are continually willing to modify in the light of reflection and observation. Third, the conclusions reached in the conceptualising phase must be available to the group for use in the free choice of new behaviours in future experiences.

Periods of ineffectiveness or difficulty may in reality be periods when the members are struggling to learn the next step. The group will only 'move on' to a new level of competence if the cycle is effectively completed so as to result in new awareness, knowledge, and ability. This permits each successive cycle to reflect a higher order of performance as the group meets and overcomes each obstacle or challenge (Figure 12.2).

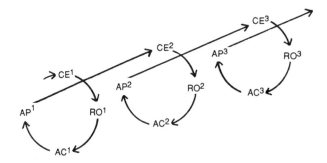

Figure 12.2 Development and growth through experiential learning.

The 'pinch' model
Sherwood and Glidewell (1973) described a dynamic learning process which necessitates continued negotiation and up-dating of mutual expectations as old learning needs are met and new needs emerge. Known as the 'pinch' model, it is also cyclical and includes four phases (Figure 12.3).

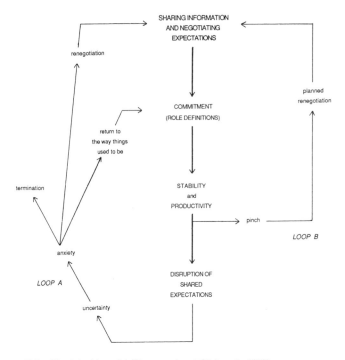

Figure 12.3 The 'pinch' model (Sherwood and Glidewell, 1973).

Phase 1 – sharing information and negotiating expectations – leads to mutual commitment to defined roles (Phase 2), which results in stability and productivity (Phase 3). The individualised nature of groupwork inevitably leads to conflict and disruption (Phase 4) which can have a number of outcomes as members decide how to respond to the anxiety and uncertainty this phase entails (Loop A). If, however, during Phase 3 members are allowed to announce signs that they think herald an imminent disruption, then such signs (or 'pinches') provide new data for preventive re-negotiation of expectations through an alternative Loop B. Whereas Loop A is unplanned and reactive, Loop B is planned and proactive. Learning to opt for the latter strategy will depend initially on the group's ability to detect pinches, and then on their willingness to take the time needed for a commitment to learning via Loop B. Examples of pinches are:

- meetings don't start on time;
- absenteeism increases;
- participants tune out of a discussion or are reluctant to speak up;
- there is a last-minute retreat from a decision;
- dissident voices or divergent thinkers start to be suppressed or punished;
- progress on the task slows down;
- interruptions, impatience and attacks start to increase;
- cliques form, with private discussions to one side;
- complaints are made that the task is impossible.

While the model should not be read as advocating avoidance of healthy controversy and conflict, it can be utilised to make changes and minor adjustments without having to go through costly disruptions and repetitive crises that drain the group's energy. 'Pinches' may also be signs that hidden agendas are coming into play – these may need to be investigated as part of the planned renegotiation loop.

Argyris and Schon's Model I and Model II
The development of a group towards maturity and higher levels of effectiveness is always a matter of *learning*. Argyris and Schon (1974, 1978) describe organisational learning as taking place when members detect and correct errors in their functioning. In *single-loop learning*, the corrections are made within existing group norms, whereas it is preferable to engage in *double-loop learning*, which requires that the norms themselves are subjected to inquiry and restructuring.

Most work groups resemble what Chris Argyris (1983) called a Model I group (Figure 12.4). By way of contrast, he and co-worker Donald Schon proposed their idealised Model II (Figure 12.5) in the form of prerequisite conditions for maximising effectiveness.

Groups composed of individuals programmed according to Model I tend to create defensive norms, reduce the production of valid information,

1 Governing variables for action	2 Action strategies for actor and toward environment	3 Consequences on behavioral world	4 Consequences on learning	5 Effectiveness
Achieve the purposes as I perceive them	Design and manage environment so that actor is in control over factors relevant to me	Actor seen as defensive	Self-sealing	Decreased effectiveness
Maximise winning and minimise losing	Own and control task	Defensive interpersonal and group relationships	Single-loop learning	
Minimise eliciting negative feelings	Unilaterally protect self	Defensive norms	Little testing of theories publicly	
Be rational and minimise emotionality	Unilaterally protect others from being hurt	Low freedom of choice, internal commitment, and risk taking		

Figure 12.4   Argyris and Schon's Model I (Argyris, 1983).

and reduce free choice. There is little public testing of ideas; members do not seek feedback that genuinely confronts their actions; learning tends to be within the confines of what is acceptable, i.e. *single-loop* learning. The group dynamics include quasiresolution of conflict, intergroup rivalry, conformity, avoidance of uncertainty, parochial interests, and miscommunication.

1 Governing variables for action	2 Action strategies for actor and toward environment	3 Consequences on behavioral world	4 Consequences on learning	5 Effectiveness
Valid information	Design situations or encounters in which participants can be origins and experience high personal causation	Actor experienced as minimally defensive	Disconfirmable processes	
Free and informed choice	Task is controlled jointly	Minimally defensive interpersonal relations and group dynamics	Double-loop learning	Increased effectiveness
Internal commitment to the choice and constant monitoring of the implementation	Protection of self is a joint enterprise and oriented toward growth	Learning-oriented norms	Frequent public testing of theories	
	Bilateral protection of others	High freedom of choice, internal commitment, and risk taking		

Figure 12.5   Argyris and Schon's Model II (Argyris, 1983).

In contrast, Model II (Figure 12.5) leads to consequences that are the reverse: valid information, free and informed choices, and internal commitment. Groups composed of individuals programmed according to Model II engage in *double-loop* learning: members invite each other to confront their views and to alter them in order to produce a position that is based on the most valid information possible, to which the people involved can become internally committed.

The challenge for group leaders and members alike, is to discover ways to extricate themselves from the Model I trap and increase effectiveness by moving towards Model II. The path is neither self-evident nor simple – even though group members may want to move towards Model II, they tend to use Model I behaviours in the process, thus unwittingly erecting their own barriers along the way. It is Argyris and Schon's emphasis of this particular point that lends weight to the contention that learning must itself be understood if team-building is to be successful.

Turning points

Groups will often experience a circularity of process that sees them repeatedly bogging down over the same issues or going round in circles to arrive time and time again at the same sticking-point. In the Kolb model, this could be interpreted as a short-circuiting of the cycle, perhaps a failure to reflect or conceptualise and so do things differently next time round. In the other two models discussed above it might be seen as 'getting hooked on Loop A' or 'trapped in Model I'.

Most people with experience of work groups other than chronically defeated ones would probably agree that the fortunes of the group tend to rise and fall in a pattern in which there are definable turning points. Such moments are usually unplanned and palpably felt: the group suddenly shifts out of a pattern of ineffectiveness and gets going again, to the members' obvious relief. Sometimes there seem to be specific moments when a single act or incident will see a stuck group suddenly surge forward in a bout of productive work. At other times the transition is more gradual, a series of events that seem to build on each other until the failing group has noticeably emerged from a trough and changed back into a succeeding group. At the trough, one would expect to find instances of attempts to adopt 'right' (as opposed to 'wrong') behaviour as set out in models of communication, leadership, decision-making or conflict management such as those discussed earlier.

Alternatively, as in the case of a decision-making group comprised of indecisive people, so frustrated by prolonged skittering that one member finally bursts his banks and passionately makes a personal decision, a moment of emotional honesty might catapult a group into a new more productive phase. The unconscious working through of some hidden agenda has already been mentioned as a possible cause of the surge forward. Whether the phenomenon is a turning *phase* or a turning *point*, it has something to say to the group members if they are open to learning. An analysis of that moment should lead to a naming of the behaviours that contributed to the pre-turning point bogged-down phase and the post-turning point on-the-move phase. Learning can be said to have occurred if, next time a similar pattern of stuckness is recognised, its duration is significantly cut short by consciously mobilising the behaviour or intervention needed to create the turning point.

For detailed reading on experiential learning, see Boud, Cohen and Walker, 1993; Boud, Keogh and Walker, 1985; Kolb, 1984; Brown, 1980; Argyris and Schon, 1978; Rogers, 1969.

Key Concept

13

TEAM-BUILDING

Taking planned action to bring about increased effectiveness is known as 'OD' (organisation development), or 'team-building' if applied to small groups. It is a conscious attempt first to examine and evaluate problems the group may have in its functioning, then to select and adopt educational strategies for appropriate changes. Changes may include: introducing and practising improved interpersonal behaviours; modifying the beliefs, attitudes and values of individuals; altering particular elements of the group structure; upgrading or streamlining task or meeting procedures; acquiring additional or better resources, facilities and support services; changing the leadership and conflict management styles; learning additional creative problem-solving techniques; integrating regular process review and feedback sessions into the working life of the group.

Diagnosis and Commitment

Team-building interventions are needed whenever a group is consistently experiencing the following difficulties:

- lack of progress towards its goal;
- inappropriate leadership;
- failure to make sound decisions;
- interpersonal hostility;
- individual stress, low motivation;
- role confusion or alienation;
- high turnover, absenteeism.

Team-building can also be beneficial for competent groups wishing to develop an even more open problem-solving approach, or for groups facing new demands and challenges requiring special commitments and creativity, as in the case of self-managing teams. Care must be taken in all cases not to force change of this sort, nor to impose it on an unwilling team. Should this happen, equilibrium is shattered and resistance occurs.

There are three main phases in a team building strategy: first, an open self-examination of the group and the way it functions; second, the selection of and commitment to appropriate training devices; third, the ongoing evaluation of changes in functioning that result from the training efforts.

When the group examines its own functioning, it will be looking for its strengths and weaknesses: identifying which behaviours and procedures are conducive to effective collaboration, and which are obstructive. This may be done by group discussion following observations from members well-versed in process observation, possibly supplemented by the use of questionnaires of the type included in Appendix B. In this way, a group begins to 'process' its own functioning. By focussing on the strengths of the members rather than on their weaknesses, by holding processing sessions regularly, and by making a clear commitment to increase those behaviours considered most effective, the group will have started on a path that will be likely to lead to benefits of the type described by Francis and Young (1979, p. 15):

- **Management of complexity:** the breadth of resources available to the team enables complex situations to be creatively managed.

- **Rapid response:** well-developed teams are capable of responding quickly and energetically.

- **High motivation:** the team feeds the individual's need to have personal significance, and team processes encourage activity and achievement.

- **Collective strength:** individuals often feel that it is hard to influence organisations and make any impact outside their immediate area. The team changes this as members extend their viewpoint to see that they, together, can achieve much.

A 'do-it-yourself' team development kit has been published by Rubin, Plovnick and Fry (1978) and is suitable for use by any small work group. Eunson (1994), Francis and Young (1992) and Woodcock (1989) provide similar programmes. More ambitious training programmes can be undertaken with the assistance of a facilitator with expertise in on-going consultation with groups over a substantial period of time. Worthwhile OD and team building programmes consume time and energy, and should not be undertaken lightly. They will be unlikely to succeed if imposed from above without the commitment of the group as a whole. The full exposition of how such programmes can be designed and implemented is beyond the scope of this work, but the detailed reading references below will furnish a useful overview. Ultimately, any substantial OD programme must be custom-designed by collaboration between a client group and a consultant, rather than drawn from books or manuals.

For detailed reading on team-building, see Dyer, 1995; Johnson and Johnson, 1994, Chap. 13; Pfeiffer, 1994; Stott and Walker, 1994; Katzenbach and Smith, 1993; Francis and Young, 1992; Woodcock, 1989; Blake et al., 1987; Kormanski and Mozenter, 1987; Hastings et al., 1986; Eitington, 1984; Woodcock and Francis, 1981.

Self-Managing Teams

For work groups in organisations that have opted to operate on a basis of a network of self-managed teams, the question of embarking on a team-building program is not left to the whim of the work group members but is deliberately planned and implemented as a corporate strategy. This requires a major commitment of time and resources to a phased team-building program aimed at progressively empowering the teams, distributing the leadership functions, and multiskilling. 'The road to self-managing teams is difficult and conflict-filled as well as exhilarating and liberating' (Tjosvold & Tjosvold, 1995, p. 203). Most such teams are semi-autonomous rather than entirely autonomous, and are held accountable to a supervisor, senior manager, or stakeholder group of some kind. As the team will tend to take on the roles traditionally performed by a supervisor or team leader (Taylor, 1993, p.16), a major question to be addressed is the role of the person to whom the team is accountable.

Dyer (1995, pp. 20 and 31) indicates clearly that supervisors and former leaders to whom the team is now accountable must make decisions about their attendance and inputs at team sessions, the most appropriate way to enact their boundary role, and the extent to which they offer training and facilitation in groupwork skills. They may be faced with having to redefine their traditional role quite dramatically, and not all will find that easy or welcome.

Together with accountability goes an increased level of responsibility on the part of the team for their internal management of all tasks and processes, including pacing the work, managing interpersonal conflict, responding effectively to mistakes and setbacks, and the induction and training of new members.

Self-managed teamwork typically produces a variety of performance outcomes, from increased productivity and a sense of pride in the product, to higher stress levels and a reduction in the opportunities for initiative and innovation. Tjosvold and Tjosvold (1995, p.210) identify a number of conditions that are necessary for the facilitation of effective self-managed teamwork. The most important of these are:

- leaders and employees discuss how their team's task complements and furthers the organisation's goals;

- leaders back up the talk about the importance of the self-managing teams by assigning people and financial resources;

- employees discuss their previous accomplishments, experiences and credentials, and disclose their personal strengths;

- employees take on self-education projects such as attending courses, reading, reflecting, and discussing.

For detailed reading on self-managing teams, see: Tjosvold and Tjosvold, 1995, Chap. 12; Wilson, 1995; Neck and Manz, 1994; Fisher, 1993; Barry, 1991; Wellins and George, 1991.

PART 5

CASE STUDIES

1

THE JOINT MANAGEMENT COMMITTEE

*As part of a major re-structuring in a large industrial
organisation a team approach was instituted for policy planning
at the middle management level. As a result of this, eight
divisional managers found themselves brought together as a team
and charged with the responsibility for establishing new
guidelines for liaison and cooperation between their respective
divisions. The following case study looks at three training
meetings held over a period of two weeks by the newly-formed
management team. Group developmental stages and themes were
identifiable in each meeting as well as over the two month period
as a whole. After describing the meetings, an analysis is given in
order to illustrate how these concepts relate to this group's
specific experience.*

On the 3rd October, a memorandum is received by each member of the
newly-created Joint Management Committee (all of whom know each
other at least slightly) to the effect that the next three consecutive Monday
mornings will be spent in workshops focussing on their aims and objectives. The first workshop is to be held in the Board Room starting at 9 a.m.
on October 10th. The memorandum is signed by the committee Chairman,
Geoff Spender, and advises that the session will be run by Jim Trainer, a
senior staff development officer.

First meeting
Geoff and Jim are already in the Board Room at 9 a.m. on the first
Monday morning when the first of the divisional managers, Jane and
Mandy, arrive. They are closely followed by Peter and Kent. While the
others are busy arranging the chairs in an informal setting away from the

large tables, Peter informs Geoff that two of the other three members of the committee would not be able to arrive until about 9.30. He explains that Jean and David had both phoned in to say that they were delayed by the transport strike. Following a query by Geoff, it appears that no-one knows where the last member (Craig) has got to, but while they are discussing this, Craig himself arrives and apologises profusely for his late arrival (2 minutes!). For some minutes after that, everyone is quiet. Peter, Kent and Mandy form one group sitting quietly near the tables, Geoff has taken Craig aside, while Jane and Jim sit by themselves reading some papers.

At about ten minutes past nine, Jim gets up and asks for everyone's attention. After getting them to bring their chairs into a circle, he explains that he has mapped out a framework programme for the morning, and expresses the hope that it will be flexible enough to accommodate both their professional and personal concerns related to the subject of aims and objectives of the Joint Committee. He points to a whiteboard just behind him, on which he has drawn up the outline programme. No-one responds when he asks if there are any questions, but after a moment or two Jane looks at her watch and asks 'How long are we going to wait for the others?' Jim replies that he thought it would be best to start the first session on time at 9.15, and catch Jean and David up when they arrive, since there is no way to tell how long they might be delayed. He immediately goes on: 'As you can see, it's almost 9.15 now, so I'd like to get started. This first session is scheduled to last for an hour. Since all of you on this Joint Committee are expected to get your respective divisions effectively coordinated, a good place to start is with the question of how you will coordinate yourselves into an effective management committee. To get straight into this, I'm going to ask you as a group, without me, to work on a task for exactly one hour. After that, we'll have a coffee break and then get together again to review the exercise'. Jim glances at his watch, then goes on: 'The task is this: you are to manage your time for the next sixty minutes in any way you like, providing that what you choose to do is clearly related to why we are here. It's 9. 15 now; the exercise finishes at 10.15'. Having said that, Jim walks over to one of the tables away from the group, and sits down.

The members of the group sit in silence for several seconds, and then Craig says: 'Well you're the boss Geoff, any ideas?'

Geoff sighs and says: 'Well, I suppose we're meant to start by discussing the sorts of things that we could usefully do, since we've been left to it without our leader' (he smiles across the room at Jim). Craig says quickly 'What about we each say what we personally think this committee is supposed to be achieving?'

Kent: 'We'll need a chairperson if we're going to do that sort of thing, otherwise it'll get chaotic – will you take the chair, Geoff?'

Jane cuts in: 'It's not much good starting anything too serious without the other two – how about we just get to know a bit more about each other's division first?'

Kent again: 'We'll still need a chairperson to do that, or it'll get out of hand'.

Geoff: 'Do you all know the brief given to this committee? I'm personally not too happy about the way it's worded'.

Several people indicate that they haven't seen anything official, but the discussion is interrupted by the arrival of Jean, looking rather hot and bothered. She drops her coat and bag on the nearest table, glances at Jim, says 'Sorry about this' to Geoff, and nods to the others, taking a seat between Craig and Geoff.

There is now a pause for a while, and some comments are exchanged with Jean about the evils of militant unionists.

Jane cuts in: 'I suppose we'll just get going again and David will arrive'.

'What's happening?' asks Jean.

Geoff is about to speak when Jane cuts in again and says: 'Oh, we're playing staff development games – fill up the next hour with something useful, you know?'

Her slightly sarcastic tone is not lost on the group, and Kent says: 'We were just discussing getting a bit of order in the proceedings by having a chairperson, but no-one seems very keen'.

'Well why isn't Geoff being it?' asks Jean of no-one in particular.

Geoff replies: 'I'm quite happy to do it if that's what you all want'.

Craig: 'Well maybe we shouldn't have an appointed leader, you know, see if we can act as a democratic group, a leaderless group, you know?' (He looks across the room at Jim).

For some minutes, suggestions follow suggestions, but none is followed through, and the energy of the group gradually seems to ebb away. Several people look across to where Jim is sitting, but he does not respond.

At 9.30 David arrives, and there is a renewed bout of discussing the transport strike, meanwhile David greets everyone, apologises for holding up their work (!), and takes the remaining seat between Jane and Craig. He asks what the group has been doing, and his question is answered with more jokes, topped by Jane's 'We've just been idling our time away waiting till you get here, David, what else?' After Geoff briefly recapitulates what has been happening, David comes out immediately with the suggestion that they divide into two subgroups, each one to work for ten minutes on the question 'What exactly are we here for?', and then come together to compare answers. Peter, Kent and Craig murmur approving noises, but Geoff cuts in and suggests that it might be better to do it in pairs rather than groups of four.

Peter says: 'If we work in pairs, I think it would be best to try and come up first with a definition of what we all mean by this word management'.

'Why work in subgroups at all?' interrupts Jean, 'if we're supposed to be a management team oughtn't we to work as a team rather than splitting up all the time?'.

At this point, Jane, who has been getting increasingly restless, bursts out: 'Oh for God's sake let's do something – two's, fours, having a leader, not having a leader, what's it matter? This is just wasting my time – I could be doing more important things back at my desk'.

Geoff jumps to his feet and says: 'OK, Jane's right – I'd like you to make two groups of four, and each group come up with a definition of management that you're all in agreement with in ten minutes from now - GO!'

Following Geoff's instructions, Peter, Kent and Mandy get to their feet and head for one of the tables. As Peter passes David, he invites him to join them to make a foursome, but at the same time, Jane has followed Mandy, and the five find themselves together.

Geoff says to Craig and Jean 'Well, we seem to be a threesome – never mind, we can stay where we are and use the whiteboard maybe...'

The two subgroups busy themselves for well over ten minutes with the task of defining the term management. There is a lot of noise and laughter from Peter and Kent's group, where arguments revolve around questions of control and power, responsibility and privilege. Jane contributes very little, and sits detached from the other four. Geoff's group is quieter, and Craig has almost filled the whiteboard with doodlings and lists of keywords. Twenty five minutes after they started, Jane goes over to Geoff and points out the time: it is a little after ten o'clock.

The members bring their chairs back to the circle in front of the whiteboard. Geoff invites Kent to show what the group of five came up with, and Kent reads out a list of all the things their group had associated with the word management, but admits they hadn't agreed on a single definition. Jane volunteers her opinion that there was no such thing as a single definition of such an abstract concept, and that she doubted if the time they'd just spent on the task had been worth anything. Geoff quickly turns to Jean and asks her to read out their group's definition, which is 'Management is the effective use of available resources to achieve a desired end.' Geoff looks pleased with this, but then a bit crestfallen when no-one responds.

'Alright, what's our next job, Geoff?' asks David.

Craig cuts in to ask how much time is left for the exercise, and Jane snaps 'Eight minutes!'

There is a long silence.

'What are we going to do with our definitions?' asks Craig.

Another silence.

Craig again: 'We seem to have ground to a halt – maybe we need more direction'.

Further silence.

Jean: 'We don't seem to be managing ourselves very well'.

Jane: 'I've told you before, it's a waste of time sitting around dreaming up odd jobs to fill the time in, we have to have some structure and something useful to do'.

'Like what, for instance?' asks David of Jane.

'Don't ask me', says Jane irritably, 'all I know is that I've got plenty of jobs piling up on my desk downstairs while we sit around here playing games'.

Jean: 'How come we can't make decisions about what to do, when we're all supposed to be the decision-makers back in our own divisions?'

Jane, seeming to support Jean's view, says: 'We still haven't come up with a definition of management, and there's only six minutes left'.

'But that wasn't what Jim asked us to do, Jane, was it?' asks Mandy, speaking in the full group for the first time.

Jane doesn't answer this, and to everyone's obvious surprise, gets up and walks out of the room.

After the door closes behind Jane, nobody seems to know what to say or do for several stunned seconds. It looks like a relief to most of them when Geoff gets up and wanders over to Jim. It seems like a signal for the rest of the group to get up and stretch their legs. Peter, Kent and Mandy stand chatting quietly together, while the others move over to the coffee machine and busy themselves with cups and spoons. Shortly afterwards, Peter, Kent and Mandy join them at the coffee machine. Craig takes his coffee and goes out of the room, followed a few moments later by Jean. It is just 10.15.

A quarter of an hour later, Jim and all the group members are again seated in the circle, including a rather stoney-faced Jane holding a cup of coffee brought to her by Mandy.

Jim looks around the group and says: 'Would anyone like to comment on what happened during that exercise?'

David, Craig and Geoff all start to speak at once, and Jim motions to David to say his piece.

David: 'Well, I have a feeling that we're not really achieving much, it seems a bit of a waste of time to me. I don't think anyone enjoyed that little exercise – what was it all about?'

Craig jumps in as soon as David pauses: 'I think it was about group management, to see how we'd react when we're left to ourselves as a group'.

'Well I certainly felt like a guinea-pig – I can't see the point of this sort of meeting' says Jane, but in a rather more subdued voice than she had used earlier.

'I think it said something about our understanding of management', Geoff started, 'I mean it's interesting that we got a clear definition of management out of it, yet I can't help thinking we didn't manage the session well at all – I'm a bit confused about the whole thing, I think'.

'Why did you leave the room so suddenly Jane?' Mandy asks, quietly. 'I went to the toilet, if you must know' says Jane flatly.

Craig has begun fidgetting about on the edge of his chair, then says: 'Look, we're doing the same thing again, darting about from one thing to the next, totally disorganised. If we're going to learn anything about working together, we have to be directed by someone'.

Jean cuts in: 'I don't agree, I think we have to teach ourselves by learning from our own mistakes, maybe using these types of workshop to do it in'.

'Not more guinea-pigging' groans David.

The discussion goes on in this vein for some minutes, with Jim largely ignored.

Eventually the subject of goals and objectives is brought up by David, who says that one of his problems in his division is that no-one seems to know what the Ministry's goals are, let alone the divisional ones.

David: 'How can we set goals for this committee if we don't know what the organisation's goals are?' 'Goals aren't the problem in my division', says Jane, 'we've had a lot of changes imposed on us over the past six months. Now we're mostly involved in policy, but there's been no matching change in personnel. They're not getting the support they expect, and I'm having problems dealing with a lot of lost people who aren't coping too well with the turmoil'.

Kent: 'I'm fairly new to management, I'd like to know what goal-setting actually entails'.

At this point, Jim summarises by saying: 'I think we could write up a list now of the things people have already mentioned as a problem for them. So far, I've jotted these down (he writes on the whiteboard: the Ministry's goals; the divisional goals; the aims of this committee not clearly known; don't know what goal-setting is; don't know enough about the other divisions; being on this committee takes us away from work in our division; responding to employees experiencing stress in the job; some members want to be led, others to learn by feeling their way). Has anyone got anything that we should add to the list?'

Under Jim's direction now, the group discusses more of their concerns in a cooperative way until close to the end of the session, when Jane asks to be excused as she has to catch her secretary before the lunch hour commences. The others start to wind down the session. The list on the board has eventually developed into two lists – one showing resources, skills or knowledge that the members think are lacking, the other showing some of the things they think this committee ought to be able to achieve if it is to be of any use. As they leave the room, Kent is heard to remark to David: 'Well, maybe that aimless session of Jim's wasn't so aimless after all – I think a few goals were starting to show up on those lists'. As Peter reaches the door, he catches up with the others and says: 'Why don't we all go for lunch together?'

Second meeting

The following Monday morning finds Jim and the eight committee members in their seats at 9.15, chatting casually among themselves. Each has a copy of a memo from Jim which he had circulated a day or two after the previous meeting, in which he has written some notes and observations about the way the meeting went. The memo notes that the group got into the programme with a healthy level of cooperation, encouraged participation, and didn't lack for initiative. On the debit side, the memo also notes that good discussion skills were noticeably lacking, and referred to examples of suggestions not being followed up, people interrupting each other, a lack of focus, ambivalence about leadership, and an almost total ignoring of group process in favour of finding tasks. The memo concluded by saying that this was not unusual in a newly-formed group.

Jim looks around the group and asks: 'Has anyone any comments on my process comments?'

David: 'Well, yes as a matter of fact I have – they're useful and probably quite accurate, but they seem to be a bit more negative than I would have expected. I think we should be more concerned with the details of the daily jobs we're going to be faced with'.

This comment is then discussed at some length, several members disagreeing with David, others supporting him. A polarisation begins to emerge over the question of whether or not it is appropriate for them to focus on their processes (no-one ask what process means, yet all seem to have an understanding of it). Craig speaks up quite strongly in favour of focussing on process, pointing out that Jim's criticisms are useful feedback, and the group needs to get to grips with those sort of things. Others make comments supporting David's view, and eventually references start to be made to 'David's view' and 'Craig's view' of the way they should work.

At last Jane appeals to Jim to make a decision about which they ought to adopt. Without waiting for Jim to reply, Geoff jumps in and suggests that it might be a good idea if the group didn't get into the habit of palming off any further decision-making onto someone outside the committee. He adds that he personally favours working with the sort of approach Jim is offering. This leads to a fresh bout of fairly heated debate, with references to 'Jim's role in all this business' (David), 'What about Geoff's role, too?' (Craig), and 'Last week's fiasco' (Jane). Jim sits back and lets this debate roll on, and it gathers energy for several more minutes. It soon becomes clear that there is a gradual narrowing process under way as the focus shifts almost unnoticed from a discussion of the two competing ways of working to a stand-off between two competing protagonists – David and Geoff. Jim is all but forgotten in the heat of the argument between these two.

Finally, a flushed and angry-looking Geoff almost shouts at David: 'Look here, we're going to run this committee my way, so you'd better get that straight right from the start'.

David looks taken aback by Geoff's abrasive tone of voice, but before he can respond, Jane leans across and says quietly to him: 'I'd be glad if we could all agree to let Geoff run things his way – how about it, David?'

Jane's conciliatory tone seems to have an immediate calming effect on David, who looks a bit uncharacteristically confused.

He says: 'I'm sorry, folks, I don't suppose any of you realised that Geoff and I were in a bit of a battle a few weeks ago over who would get appointed to the chair of this committee. I guess I must have wanted it more than I realised. I'll try and put that aside from now on – how about we take a break? When we come back I'd like to ask Jim if he knows some ways we can cope with that sort of stuff if it crops up again. What do you all reckon?'

The others all nod, and as they break for coffee, Geoff goes over to David and shakes his hand.

After the break, the session is led off by Jim, who hands out written material that he had prepared from the company's recently-compiled Strategy Plan. He has selected material from the 'mission statement' relating to general policy objectives and the functions of each of the divisions. He asks them to read through the handouts, and make notes on their personal reaction to the objectives set out for their own division. This task is completed by the group within half an hour; the rest of the session is chaired by Geoff, who asks each member in turn to speak for no more than five minutes about their own divisional aims and current problems. By the end of the meeting, there is general agreement that the exchange of information and views had been interesting and very helpful.

Third meeting
It is 9.15 on the third Monday morning, and the committee members are getting themselves seated around the whiteboard. Jim is sitting out of the circle at one of the tables.

After a few moments, Geoff says 'I had a talk to Jim last Wednesday about these sessions of ours, and he suggested that to-day we start by having me run the first half of the session while he sits out, then we have our coffee break, and after that we'll let Jim have the floor for a while and he can tell us how he thought we went from the process point of view. Depending on his comments, we'll either carry on working on our committee's goals, or if our processes really upset him, we'll take it on the chin and spend some time having a really good look at what we do that we ought to be doing better! That's a bit garbled, but do you all know what I mean and do you feel reasonably happy about it?'

Geoff looks round at each member in turn, who all nod or motion him to carry on. For about an hour, the group then works cooperatively under Geoff's leadership as he directs the group in a series of activities focussing on the goals of the committee. By a little after 10.15, when they break for coffee, numerous sheets of newsprint have been covered with feltpen scribblings, and on the whiteboard there is a list headed 'We the undersigned hereby declare that these are the goals for the Joint Management Committee'. All of the members have signed their name at the bottom of the list. During the coffee break, the conversation turns to how well they felt they had worked, and it is David who calls them to order after fifteen minutes has elapsed by declaring that he is keen to hear what Jim has to say.

Jim's feedback to the group is entirely positive, and he congratulates them, both on the way they had worked together and on the goal-list they had produced. In response to several requests, he expands on what specific behaviours he thought were most beneficial, and compares these to the sort of things that had been going on at their first meeting only a fortnight ago. At the end of the session, he says he thinks they seem to be off and running as a reasonably effective committee, and suggests that they return to their normal working schedule for the time being, and invites them to let him know at intervals how things go. Geoff brings the session to a close well ahead of time, but no-one seems to be in a hurry to leave. Over further cups of coffee, the subject of further training for team development as well as personal development is discussed enthusiastically, and a profusion of questions keeps Jim and them occupied until well into their lunchtime.

Analysis

With reference to Crawley's model (Figure 1.2), it can be seen that the members did in fact develop an acceptable blend of the task and maintenance realms over the two week period, particularly given their newness as a work group. A further level of understanding can be added by referring to Woodcock's model (Figure 1.4). From this it can be deduced that the group moved rapidly from Stage 1 to Stage 3, but probably still remained well short of being a Stage 4 mature team. With regard to the life-cycle concept, the meetings can be analysed separately or as an overall sequence with a definite beginning and end.

In the pre-group phase prior to the first of the three meetings, there were discussions between Geoff, Jim and senior management personnel concerning the necessity for team-building programmes for the newly-formed Joint Committee. Once the decision was made to run a pilot series of three such sessions, Jim made it his business to seek out each of the members, and spend a while talking informally with them. He gained the impression that each of them was a competent officer with a level of skill in human resource management that could best be described as 'streetwise'. Several of them intimated that they were anxious about the forthcoming involvement in the joint committee, which they saw as an additional burden on their already heavy workload. Recognising their competence, Jim's pre-workshop thinking led him to his decisions to give the group a good measure of autonomy from the start, and to intervene as little as possible with their process. His planning was informed by his conceptual model of group development: he worked on the assumption that the sessions would most likely bring some interpersonal conflicts to the surface fairly soon, and it would be better to allow this to occur so that the group would work their own way through any storming and eventually reach the performing stage. His decision to withdraw his leadership abruptly in the first session was made with this in mind. It would be a test for Geoff and the members, and Jim felt confident they would rise to the occasion. While Jim was doing his planning, the other members would certainly have been preparing themselves for the forthcoming workshop, girding themselves with private thoughts and feelings about it.

Since the members of the Joint Committee were not strangers to Jim or to each other, the forming stage on the first Monday morning consists mostly of arriving in two's and three's, greeting each other, arranging the chairs, delivering messages about the delayed members, and so on. A few moments after Jim's brisk start to the session, Jane indicates her concern that the group is starting with some of the members still absent. This could have been either an inclusion issue for her or one of control. Either way, Jim deals effectively with her question and proceeds with the first exercise. The members acquiesce readily to Jim's initial leadership as it provides the structure and guidance usually desired in the forming stage. They permit him to complete his instructions, but are obviously surprised by his withdrawal immediately afterwards. In Jim's absence, both Craig and Kent then make typical appeals for leadership, but to Geoff rather than to Jim. Jane cuts across this by bringing up her inclusion concern again, at the same time offering a suggestion that they find out a little more about each other. As these are countersuggestions to the two already put forward by Geoff and Craig, Jane may again be seeking control of the task. A further countersuggestion from Geoff supports Craig's earlier one, but Jean arrives at that moment, and the emerging argument is abandoned as the group returns to forming stage behaviours to include Jean.

Jane's rather sarcastic reply to Jean's question about what has been happening indicates some distaste for the task set by Jim, perhaps hostility towards Jim himself. The discussion returns to the subject of leadership (Geoff's chairing of the meeting) with Craig counterproposing that they might be better off without an official chairperson. There is still a desire for direction, but some divergence of opinion about who, in Jim's absence, should provide it. What might have been a storming phase almost slides off into apathy, except that David arrives, and the group returns once again to inclusion behaviours. Conflict is again hinted at in Jane's sarcastic comment to David, but this is eclipsed by the start of a stand-off between Geoff and David about what they should do next. This is taken up by other members, and there are more countersuggestions. This finally prompts Jane's outburst of irritation, which Geoff deals with by an avoidance device: he quickly changes the subject and assertively directs them to work on a specific task. Over the ensuing twenty five minutes the group appears to be performing, but they have not followed Geoff's request that they work in two groups of four, Jane does not participate, and the larger of the two subgroups fails to complete the task even with the extra time. None of this is mentioned when they come together again to discuss the results of their work. As the discussion begins to peter out, their conversation is interspersed with irritable complaints of one sort or another from Jane. The storming phase has been aborted for the time being. An innocent remark by Mandy exposes Jane's apparent misunderstanding of the task Jim set them, and seems to precipitate her dramatic exit. As happened on several earlier occasions when conflict seemed about to erupt, this incident too is smoothed over or ignored; this can be seen as part of the group's norming process.

After the coffee break, they talk about anything except Jane's exit, until Mandy eventually confronts her directly, only to be rebuffed. Craig turns the group's attention back to leadership at this point, but is upstaged by David who focusses their attention on goals. These are then discussed at some length in a more cooperative mood, even by Jane. The group has clearly moved back to the safety of the task, and now performs competently enough. Jim recognises this and returns to the scene to help them summarise the content of their discussion. Jane's early departure in search of her secretary heralds the termination phase of this session. As the others leave, at least some of them seem impressed with what has been achieved. This, and Peter's suggestion that they have lunch together, is also typical of the termination phase, although of course the group is not in the process of disbanding permanently. The meeting has clearly portrayed its own life cycle over its four hour duration, although there was no clear separation between the storming and norming phases. Knowing that the group would need to learn to confront and deal with its control issues in the early part of its life, Jim stays out of all control issues by setting the training task and thereafter holding back his interventions until the group was performing. Jim also recognises that the conflicts that had begun to emerge had not in any sense been confronted or resolved. The theme of anxiety about control would most likely re-surface in subsequent meetings.

In the second meeting, the forming stage is minimal, and David launches the group almost immediately into conflict when he gives his disapproving response to Jim's process notes. The polarisation builds up as the group members align themselves either with 'David's way' or 'Craig's way' of working. There is a side issue as Jane's appeal to Jim for assistance is cut short by Geoff's veiled reprimand and his declaration that he sides with Jim. The scene is set for the main contenders for power and status in the group to make their bids for influence, and the storming phase escalates. Geoff's angry explosion is the catharsis that helps the group (and Jane in particular) to confront and then relinquish their power play through David's open self-disclosure about his dashed hopes for the Chair of the committee. The phase that follows sees the group putting some good communication and leadership skills into practice as they work fairly solidly on the task

The stages of the life-cycle identified over the duration of the second meeting were markedly different, qualitatively as well as quantitatively, from those of the first, although the group theme was the same. The difference was most noticeable in the lengths of time spent on forming, and the quality of the storming phases. In the first meeting the conflicts had been kept suppressed, and it sometimes looked as though it might transform into apathy rather than open confrontation. In the second meeting, the conflict escalated and then erupted into the open and was dealt with swiftly. The resolution of the power theme by means of Geoff's catharsis and David's and Jane's mature response to it then permitted the group to move on unencumbered to a performing stage.

In the third meeting, the forming is again brief and unremarkable. Unlike the expressions of conflict in the first two meetings, there is no discernible hostility or apathy, in fact no storming phase occurs at all. The group stays for most of the meeting in a performing mode, and it is the termination phase that is of special significance. As the group faces the conclusion of Jim's series of three team-building meetings, they are reluctant to leave the room, or even to detach themselves from the trainer. Talk turns to the possibility of further involvement in team-building activities. Since the committee of eight will be continuing to work together, it would seem that the group that they are unwilling to acknowledge as terminated is specifically this group of nine. This is a common phenomenon at the conclusion of a good group experience. In this case, it seems safe to predict that the group of eight-plus-one will soon find themselves together again starting a new cycle as a training group.

In addition to analysing each meeting separately, it is also feasible to look at the development of the group over a cycle lasting the whole of the two-week period that encompassed the three meetings. In this case, it might be said that the cycle had a forming stage that lasted until David arrived, a norming phase which transitioned into the storming that culminated in the stand-off between Geoff and David, and then an extensive norming and performing stage from that point until the very end of the third meeting when Geoff declared the session closed and the termination behaviours began.

If an even broader perspective is adopted, the whole experience could also be regarded as merely the forming stage of a new group still dependent on directive leadership and grappling with definitions of purpose and structure. There may well be a more intensive storming phase to come, which the members will have to work through as deeper issues confront them. Whether a short or long life-span is under consideration, an understanding of group developmental processes is an asset in a number of important ways: (i) it is an indispensable guide to appropriate interventions on the part of the group leader, as it was in this case for Jim the trainer (Figure 7.1 in Key Concept 7 elaborates on this important application); (ii) it can help the group members to become more self-conscious of their own process, which is a necessary first step towards improving effectiveness by involvement in team-building; and (iii) it provides a conceptual backdrop against which to analyse organisational structure and process at any time in the evolution of the group.

Case Study

2

THE RULE MAKERS

This case study describes and analyses structure and process in a learning group undertaking a course in organisational behaviour. The programme focusses on planning and organising, and is nontraditional in that it is based on principles that value student autonomy, self-directed learning, and peer learning. The analysis focusses on the most significant structural and process variables as the students struggle to develop as a group, coping with the task as well as with their transition from dependency to autonomy. The initial programme as presented to them by the staff is a deliberate blend of aspects of traditional as well as nontraditional paradigms of learning. Regulations, individual and group projects, examinations and assessment are interwoven with requirements that they act as teachers for each other, monitor each others' work, and adopt a consensual approach to the task of changing the programme to meet their own learning goals.

The fourteen students (five male, nine female) who embarked on this programme had already completed an earlier course on small-group dynamics in a planning and management context. They were all aged between eighteen and twenty, their sociometric structure was fairly well established, and they were generally an open and cooperative group. They had acquired a working familiarity with the general field of organisational behaviour, although as a planning and decision-making group they were still fairly much at the novice level. Their attitudes to experiential learning ran the gamut from sceptical and mildly resistant to enthusiastic and appreciative. The students knew one of the staff members (Tony) quite well; the other, (Noel) they were meeting for the first time.

The content of the earlier course was quite different from this new one, and was based on a single predominant concept: that all work groups operate in the context of an existing set of rules, a 'constitution' that is in part formal, in part implicit and unwritten. The format of the programme was designed by the two staff members as a set of formal and explicit rules, presented to the students with the clearly-stated objective of getting them to enact the rules and/or change them to accord with the group's implicit norms and priorities. Built in to the design of the programme is the requirement that, in order to do either, they must adopt behavioural norms that encourage cooperative and respectful behaviour towards each other. Such norms would include at least collaboration, assertive challenge and appropriate feedback.

This is the programme as offered by the staff on the first day, embodied in the set of formal rules:

Rules:
1. The field of study in this subject is 'planning and organisation'.
2. Hereinafter, 'the group' shall refer to all currently enrolled students in this subject plus the two staff members.
3. By referring to the literature on organisations, each student in the group is to define a topic for an individual investigation project. This is **Individual Task #1**.
4. Each definition of a topic must be approved unanimously by the group.
5. After receiving approval, each student will explore their selected topic in an existing planning organisation of their choice (other than our own group). This is **Individual Task #2**.
6. Each member of the group will be responsible for writing one examination question which will test the other students' understanding of their topic. Together, the questions will form the three-hour end-of-term examination paper referred to in Rule 10. This is **Individual Task #3**.
7. Each question shall be approved unanimously by the group.
8. Each student shall transmit to the group members what they learnt from Individual Task #2. Deciding when and how the learning will be transmitted is **Individual Task #4**.
9. The scheduled sessions will be reserved for groupwork. Individual Tasks are to be undertaken outside class time.
10. Assessment in this subject will be based on (i) performance in the end-of-term three-hour examination, and (ii) a 3000-word essay comparing the *modus operandi* of this group and the planning organisation chosen for individual study.
11. Both the examination and the essay will be marked by the two staff members. Each item will be worth 50% of the total marks for this subject.

12. Any member of the group may propose a rule change, or an alteration
to the list of rules by addition or deletion.
13. Any change to any of the rules or the rule-list shall only be effected by
a unanimous decision by the group.

First session
The staff members introduced the course by reviewing the earlier group
dynamics course, and explaining that this programme would build on
what they had experienced then. It would introduce further applications of
theory applicable to the larger organisation as well as to small work
groups. The staff talked next about their philosophy of adult education and
its underlying values of self-directedness and student autonomy. They
explained that an important element of training as professional planners
and managers was for the students to come to an understanding of the ten-
sions that arise when individuals have to balance autonomy with commitment to the organisation. The overall aim of the course, they said, was to
improve the students' effectiveness as planners and as organisers of work
teams.

The staff members then went on to say that they had designed the programme with two things in mind: (i) to be a vehicle to enable the students
to visit a 'real world' planning organisation and explore its structures and
processes, and then to compare that organisation with their own group
structure and processes; and (ii) as initial material capable of being adapted
to meet both their individual and group learning styles by progressive modification. As the staff pointed out, such adaptation would require them to
act effectively as individuals as well as collectively. In this way, they were
being offered opportunities for them to practise and evaluate what they had
learnt or wished to learn about working in groups. They concluded their
introduction by saying that they expected the group to change the rules to
accord with its own norms and priorities, in the process designing its own
democratic means of planning and decision-making.

The discussion among the students that followed the lecturers' introduc-
tory remarks was focussed partly on the purpose of the rules, but mostly
on the question of the end-of-term examination. There were many suggestions for alternatives to this, some suggesting a much shorter examination,
others expressing preferences for cumulative assignments, individual projects, longer reports and no formal examination at all, and so on. There
was little understanding apparent of the purpose of the initial rule-set, nor
of its implications. None of the students took time to read the rule-set
carefully enough to discern how it absolutely required them to act cooperatively and not competitively, and as such posed an intentional paradox
with that part of the programme that was competitive and involved them
in assessments to be marked and graded by the staff in the traditional way.

The climate was open and friendly during this session. After some time, Jessica and Julie, who had been voicing similar concerns about the examination and essay combination, put a proposal forward to change Rule 10. They wrote the proposed change on the board as follows:

  (i)   end-of-term exam. to be worth 30%
  (ii) essay to be worth 40%
  (iii) transmission of what is learnt from Task #2 to be worth 20%
  (iv) the exam. question (Task #3) to be worth 10%

Jessica continually interrupted the ensuing lengthy discussion of this proposal to push for it to be put to the vote. Eventually they did so, and it was defeated 11 for, 3 against. No-one noticed that the two staff members abstained. Jessica and Julie withdrew, and the group went on with some further desultory discussion as their energy began to decline. The discussion became more widely scattered, and the topics covered at random included several other ideas for rule changes, complaints about the assessment, queries as to why the lecturers hadn't wanted Individual Tasks 2 and 3 to be assessed, expressions of dislike for consensus decision-making as required by Rules 4, 7 and 13, what was meant by 'groupwork' in Rule 9, and so on.

After nearly twenty minutes of unfocussed talking around all these points, Peter eventually jumped in and suggested that all three rules requiring that decisions be unanimous should be changed to majority vote. Anne asked if he was proposing that as a package rule change, and Peter said he was certainly doing just that. When he put his proposal to the vote, all fourteen students agreed, and they all looked quite pleased with themselves. Then one of the staff members, Tony, commented that it was not a unanimous decision as required under Rule 13, and therefore it was not valid. An argument ensued between Jason and Rob over this point, until they all became clear that Tony's explanation was correct: under Rule 2, 'the group' referred to the students and the two staff members, neither of whom had voted. When asked why they had abstained, both staff members replied that they were going to vote against the proposal, but Peter had not called for the 'no' votes.

The effect of this was a further and somewhat more heated discussion which hovered around two emerging and opposite responses to the rule-set. One group of voices was heard to argue that it was an artificial device obviously intended to create conflict, others argued that it was designed to provide learning opportunities, and that they hadn't yet understood it properly. The proponents of the latter view were, naturally enough, those students who valued and had profitted from experiential learning in the earlier course, and they went to some length to point out that the session had proceeded so far without any intelligent reference to either the detail or the spirit of the exercise as embodied in the rule-set. Some of the students had evidently caught on to the paradoxical aspect of the rule-set, and understood how it required them 'to be effective in order to be effective', and at the same time provided a unique and unusual opportunity to fulfil the aims of the course. Further discussion of this was cut short by the end of the session. Later, Tony made the following process interpretation in his notebook:

> The group was finding its way towards working, relationship-building not being an issue for them at this stage. Much time was spent criticising the concept of the course, and, implicitly, of the staff. They were expressing their very real anxieties about examinations, about their ability to meet the demands of the syllabus and the expectations of the staff. Attempts to reduce the perceived sources of such anxiety naturally enough saw the exam and essay as an immediate focus. This prevented them from studying the rule-set more deeply. Statements about the task being impossible or the group being powerless were balanced by views that the course offered opportunities for meaningful learning. Leadership roles began to emerge and were not rejected; opportunities were made for all members to have their say. There was little awareness of time and no future planning. No-one acted as chairperson or coordinator. Questions were not addressed to specific people, and usually got left unanswered. The students stayed together as a single group, and tended to exclude the lecturers as a separate subgroup, not noticed or consulted much.

Second session
Both staff members but only ten of the fourteen students were present for this session. Cindy started the proceedings by reading out a carefully prepared proposal to amend Rule 10, reducing the three-hour examination to one and a half hours. Put to the vote, it received ten votes for (two of these from the staff members) and two against. Rob pointed out that four members were absent, so no unanimous decision could have been made anyway, so why not discuss the Individual Tasks. He added that he would like to do his investigation on the small business firm where he had a part-time job. This was not a planning organisation, but he was very interested in the firm, knew it well, and could see that decisions and planning were as much a part of their work as any one else's. One or two others said much the same thing, and one of the staff members proposed that when next they have the full group present he'd be happy to propose deleting the word 'planning' from Rule 5. The rest of the time up to the coffee break was mostly devoted to discussions between the staff and four or five of the students about ideas they had for their projects.

After the break, Martin and Steven arrived. A short time later, Martin proposed that Rule 2 be changed so that 'the group' would be re-defined as 'all those persons present at any of the scheduled sessions'. There was a protracted debate about his reasons, and the wisdom of this. Martin argued that it was too much to expect everyone to be there at every session, at the same time insisting on unanimity for all their decisions about rules and tasks. When he put it to the vote, all present, including the staff, voted in favour, and everyone seemed to conclude that it was therefore carried. Again, Tony pointed out that it was not a unanimous decision, as required under Rule 13, but since everyone except two absent members were in favour, they could put it to the vote next time they were all present. This brought on another cycle of heated debate, as it did when the same process occurred in the first session. The same polarisation became evident as before, and the session closed in much the same way. Tony's subsequent process observation was as follows:

> More work was done to-day, specifically on the individual tasks. There was little sign of planning or strategic thinking, and still no regard to time-planning. Apart from the position held by Noel and I, there has been no differentiating of power or status. Leadership roles such as starter, information giver and seeker, harmoniser and process observer were more in evidence. Aimlessness occurred several times, but this was not seen by the students as a problem for them to address. The norms of the group were beginning to be understood as creating a problem for the procedures that had been imposed upon them, but attempts to deal with this were uncoordinated. The members that were present stayed together as a group, and there was more inclusion of the staff members, although they were still treated as an external subgroup.

Third session
All sixteen members of 'the group' were present soon after the start of the session. Martin put his proposal to change Rule 2 to the vote, and it was carried unanimously. The amended rule now read:

Rule 2   Hereinafter, 'the group' shall refer to all those persons present at any of the scheduled sessions.

Jessica asked: 'What if there are only five of us and neither of the lecturers present – can we still make valid decisions?' No-one seems to have thought about the question of a quorum, but as Martin pointed out, the decision had been made and was now law. Jason offered the observation that the lecturers will take great care that at least one of them is present at every session from now on!

Tony put his proposal to delete the word 'planning' from Rule 5, and it was carried unanimously. After this, more students discussed their investigation projects amongst themselves and with the staff. Carol, Vickie and Peter produced written outlines of the projects they intended to undertake, and asked if they could put these to the meeting and get approval. All of these were approved unanimously, and the mood of the group began to border on the convivial. Just before the session closed, Jessica asked about the date when the examination would be held, and the date by which they must have their questions formulated. Jason asked the staff members if they would accept any alternative forms of assessment to an examination, as he and one or two others had been thinking of doing a group assignment culminating in a group report instead of an examination. He pointed out that the departmental handbook (printed eight months before the course commenced) stipulated that assessment would be by a group project and an essay. Tony said that he and Noel would have no objection provided that the relevant rule changes were successfully carried through. People were already beginning to leave the room when Jessica said loudly that she thought it would cause difficulties if some were doing an examination and others were working as a subgroup and just submitting one report between them.

Fourth session

Everyone except Jason and Jessica was present at the start of this session. The lecturers took up the first half of the session with a lengthy review of the group development so far. During the break which followed, while Noel and Tony were having coffee in Tony's room, Jason knocked on the door and asked if they would have a look at a proposed rule change he had drafted and which he wanted to put to the group. Noel said that all Jason needed to do was to read it out to the group, discuss it if necessary, and get them to vote on it. Back in the meeting room, Jason followed their suggestion, but railroaded the vote through with much energy, and with enthusiastic vocal support from Julie, Debra and Christopher. When the vote was taken, they all looked visibly annoyed when the hands were counted as nine for, five against, with Noel abstaining. Jason immediately and aggressively demanded that Rob, one of those who voted against it, explain his reasons. Rob gave a lengthy defence of his action, adding that he and Jessica had talked with a few of the others the evening before, and most of them didn't think it would be equitable to have some of the students doing a group project when the rest wanted an examination. Debra repeated Jason's information that the handbook stipulated a group project as part of the assessment, and this led to an escalation of the argument which had started between Jason and Rob. At this point, Jessica came into the room.

After a few minutes, Rob and then Jason each gave Jessica a resume of what had been happening, each including their own argument justifying their position. Before Jessica could say anything, Noel intervened and asked if those who wanted to work as a subgroup would go and sit together so that he could see clearly who they were. Jason, Julie, Anne, Debra, Carol and Christopher moved their chairs together. Noel asked: 'Does anyone else want to join these investigators, or are the rest of you all happy to do the examination?' No-one responded, and Tony said: 'Looks like we've got two groups here, under one set of rules. Something will have to be negotiated cooperatively to get the rules right for you. I suggest we spend the rest of this session on that – how are you going to deal with this?'

Far from receiving a positive response to his suggestion, Tony was suddenly attacked by Jessica, who accused him of 'engineering this whole conflict so as to give them something to study'. She added that she thought the programme was rubbish, and she'd learn a lot more if the staff set a straightforward project and an ordinary examination. Neither of the staff members got much opportunity to say anything after this, as the issue was immediately jumped on and heatedly debated by Jason and Debra on one side, and Rob and Jessica on the other. At one point, Tony interjected with a reference to 'the residuals' when referring to the students who had elected not to belong to the investigators subgroup. This brought him a further hostile reaction from both Jessica and Rob. Nothing was resolved by the close of the session, and the group disbanded in an aggressive and unhappy mood. The lecturer's notebook read:

> Jason's prior attempt to lobby Noel and I didn't work, and he and his splinter group had to go it alone in the full group meeting. His aggressive manner may have alienated some of the students, but he had already formed a cohesive band around him to support him, and this they did. (The six of them were a strong subgroup last year too). The whole group then polarised quite deeply. It might have been a polarisation into those who are dependent/autonomous, for/against a traditional syllabus, like/dislike exams; whatever it was, Noel had begun to label one group 'the investigators', and I inadvertently called the others 'the residuals'. That must have helped consolidate the division even further. I'd better refer to the residuals as 'the examinees' from here on, or they and I will continue to fight over that. The issue that splits them is still primarily to do with grades and assessment, and making sure that any solution is, above all, fair. It's also partly to do with preferences for different styles of working – some are loners, others prefer to work in a small group.

Fifth session

The session commenced with Tony asking if anyone had any investigation topics to be read out and voted on. Steven read his out, and it received unanimous approval. Jessica then read hers out, and when it was put to the vote eleven of the twelve present voted in favour, but Jason abstained. Another fight broke out over this, with Jason being attacked even by members of The Investigators, as everyone was now calling them. He became very defensive, and stubbornly justified his stance, claiming that he didn't disapprove of Jessica's topic, but since no-one seemed interested in giving

The Investigators' idea any airtime, he didn't feel prepared to be cooperative either. The remainder of the session was spent on this issue of cooperative versus competitive behaviour, with Jessica and Jason as the main antagonists. Gradually, Jason became isolated, as more students began to criticise him for his attitude. Some actually moved across the room, so that after a few minutes, Jason was sitting alone. After many angry exchanges, with Jason taking on the rest, he got up and walked over to join them again, saying: 'Alright, I give up'.

A quieter and more productive mood began to prevail after that, and some of them recalled a similar situation from the previous year, and how a resolution of that had moved the whole group into a more productive phase. Jason remained fairly quiet throughout this period, and it was finally Jessica who proposed that Rule 10 be changed to accommodate The Investigators' idea at the same time retaining the examination for those like herself who wanted to work individually. In her proposal, the essay would remain for all of them as 50% of the assessment. Her proposal was carried unanimously, but Jason could not resist pretending to abstain again before he finally gave his assent. After the session, Tony made the following process notes:

> The structure has now altered radically – there are still two staff members, inside or outside the system depending on the function they are performing; there is a cohesive subgroup now happily calling themselves The Investigators, and working on a group project; and there is an aggregate of more separate students busily engaged on Individual Tasks. Jason and Jessica have exhibited different leadership styles, and Jason seems to have become the undisputed leader of The Investigators. He has let Jessica take a dominant role in the other group, which is still amorphous by comparison. When the conflict broke out over his abstention, it was interesting to see the structure change physically for a brief time as everyone moved away from him, with him rejoining them some moments later. These incidents seem to have had less to do with challenges to the emerging leaders than with developing the sort of structure that would keep them cohesive enough to allow each student to follow their personal learning style. Our structure has not been opposed seriously, and there are signs that they are 'working to rule' and at the same time managing to be autonomous. With all the effort needed for this process of structural change, no wonder they have ignored the fact that the wording and intent of Rules 3, 5 and 11 should have been changed as a result of Jessica's change to Rule 10. They also need to address the question of whether or not The Investigators are still required to complete Individual Task 3. No-one has looked at the effects the rule changes may have on criteria for assessment. The role of 'keeper of the rules' has not yet emerged, and may not be regarded as important.

Sixth session

During the course of this session, the rest of The Examinees finalised their investigation topics, all of which were approved by the group. The Investigators produced a description of their proposed project, but before this received the go-ahead there was considerable discussion of related issues such as assessment. Jessica and Rob were still anxious to ensure that there would be equity. Jason and his group were agitated by the delay in getting their proposal approved. Before that finally happened, the other necessary rule changes had somehow managed to be quickly debated and unanimously approved. The two subgroups had worked cooperatively on the common task.

Seventh and eighth sessions

As the investigation projects got under way, most of the time in the seventh and eighth sessions was spent on discussion and mini-lectures from the staff on different aspects of organisational behaviour pertinent to their projects. The Investigators spent some of the time working together on their project, and this left The Examinees working as another group, temporarily showing signs of cohesion for a change, with the two staff members as they delved further into the subjects of hierarchy and power (!). During the coffee break in the eighth session, most stayed in the room, and listened while Martin and Jason recalled and described differing experiences they had had during the previous vacation in part-time employment. They had both worked in a government department undergoing a massive re-structuring following amalgamation with another but much larger department. Their different views of how other employees dealt with the instability and uncertainty of that time was of great interest to Jessica, who for her project had chosen a small private consulting firm currently proposing to enter into a similar merger with a much larger firm. As the three of them began to talk more animatedly about the different processes that they saw as characterising the re-structuring of these different organisations, they themselves formed a tightly-knit, albeit temporary mini-group surrounded by listeners. Had that specific structure been frozen for an instant, it would have been one fleeting image of a peer learning community at work.

Ninth, tenth and eleventh sessions

These sessions were devoted to further work on the individual and group tasks, and proceeded reasonably smoothly except for one brief incident in the tenth session. The staff reminded the students that they had reserved the latter half of the session, following the coffee break, for their review of the group's development and shifting structures in terms of some of the concepts the students had chosen to explore in their investigation projects. During the coffee break, Jason and The Investigators became engrossed in some problem connected with their group project, and when asked by the staff to rejoin the others for the review, refused to do so. This created a series of increasingly heated exchanges about priorities in view of the rapidly dwindling amount of time left to complete the programme. Eventually, Anne cut across the growing conflict with a fine example of a superordinate goal: she went to the whiteboard and drew a time-line on the board, then skilfully proceeded to develop a schedule that incorporated groupwork sessions, staff review sessions, and fieldwork. She persuaded The Investigators to do their best to hold their subgroup meetings outside the scheduled class times, so that the whole group could use that time for peer-teaching and review sessions. Jason raised some objections at not being allowed to use class time for his group project, since The Examinees could use the time for preparing for their examination. He did not persist with this objection, and Anne's schedule seemed to be happily adopted, and became the basic agenda for the rest of the course.

Twelfth and thirteenth sessions
The group worked on the programme without further serious incident. The examination questions submitted by each student took a considerable amount of time to refine so that they had more substance and validity as instruments of assessment. Several students commented that this task alone taught them a lot about the topic towards which the questions themselves were aimed. They said they had come to realise that to set a valid examination question not only required examiners to know their subject well but also to know the answers well! Each of The Examinees presented their 'transmission', in which they taught to the others what they had learnt during their investigation project. Two representatives of The Investigators then did the same for their group project. The lecturer's process observation notebook included the following comment about structure and process:

> It is interesting to be able to see several structures at once: we work as a total group of sixteen co-workers on the overall programme and course objectives; we work as a group of varying size and membership when unanimous decisions have to be made about topics or rule changes; we work as three distinctive subgroups (the staff, The Investigators, The Examinees); and ultimately we work as two subgroups: staff and students (no-one has any illusions about the basic and on-going difference in status and power between those two subgroups).

> Which structure I see is determined by the task we are performing, by the roles each member plays, by the way members or subgroups are deployed around the space. This classroom, our experiential programme, and our style of leadership favour structures that are in sharp contrast to the examination hall and the lecture theatre. The latter spaces shape a group into visible and implicit structures that constrain the roles and processes that can happen there.

After the course is over, The Investigators and The Examinees will exist in memory only, so that by the time we come to mark their essays, the structure will be different again.

It is also interesting to ponder whether or not The Investigators are independent as a group (possibly counter-dependent), but dependent on Jason for direction and leadership; and whether or not this is in direct contrast to The Examinees, who seem more like independent individuals, who as a collective are (or at least were for a while) dependent on the staff. As for Noel and I, viewed as a team of two, we are (hopefully) interdependent co-teachers and co-learners. Through our programme design and teaching style, we attempt through our interventions to influence the process of the student group towards similar structures and ideology.

To us, structural elements such as size, subgroups, sociometry and cohesion are of lesser importance than the sort of roles, norms and culture that we collectively develop. For the students, the order of priorities may well be the reverse. The challenge of the programme for staff and students alike, is to integrate and benefit from these opposites, and any others that we might find!

Fourteenth (final) session
Most of the time was spent on last-minute refinements of the examination paper, queries concerning the essay and the criteria for assessment, and exchanges of ideas and references for their essays. The final activity was the completion of a course evaluation questionnaire.

Summary

Over the duration of the course there was a covert negotiation between the staff on one hand and the students on the other to modify the initial structure and concept of the course towards a form acceptable to both. Through the processes that took place, the group developed a normative and sociometric structure that enabled this to occur, and were able to get the necessary rule changes made without abandoning the unanimity rule. Statements of what each group ideally would have liked were made; underlying values were partially explored; willingness to make concessions was tested.

In seeking to explain the division of the student body into two distinct subgroups, it is tempting to look for polar opposites such as 'The Investigators were friends, The Examinees were strangers to each other', or perhaps 'The Investigators were radical, The Examinees conservative'. It is more useful, and certainly more constructive, to seek out the common motivation that led them to create that particular structure. In this case, both subgroups took steps towards autonomous learning, so it may well have been the common desire to be self-directed, a phenomenon that is characteristic of people of that particular age group. The structure and process they created enabled them to achieve that goal and thereby 'own' the programme. If the staff had not been prepared to let that happen, they would presumably have played a different role, and the students would have played different roles in response. Everyone would have influenced the process with a quite different set of agendas and interventions, and the structure would have inevitably taken a substantially different form.

Case Study

3

TOPSEED NURSERY

This case study describes a critical situation in the fortunes of Topseed Nursery, a small privately owned country business with a well-founded reputation for supplying high-quality seedlings to an established local market. The analysis of the situation focusses on the interrelatedness of structure, process, communication and leadership. In particular, it shows how the main protagonist, the nursery supervisor, was able to make use of some basic concepts from systems and communication theory in improving both her job satisfaction and the productivity of the business.

Doreen is a friendly woman of 45 who lives and works in a small country town. She is married, and has two teenage daughters, one of whom lives away from home. Doreen's husband Bob is a primary school teacher. For the past five years, Doreen has managed a small plant nursery owned by an elderly local couple, Reg and Ellie, who have always lived in the town and have known Doreen since she was a little girl. Reg and Ellie are now in their late sixties and live in the house on the hill above the nursery. Ellie is a shy woman, and has nothing to do with the running of the nursery. When Reg and Ellie reached retirement age, Reg asked Doreen, who had been their head gardener for a number of years, to take on 'the running of the nursery', as he put it. He wanted to spend more time with Ellie, but would continue to handle promotions and advertising.

At the time when Doreen takes over, the nursery produce is being sold through a number of wholesale outlets, some in the city 50 kilometres distant, but most in the surrounding townships. A regular stream of customers also buys direct from the nursery, which is open seven days a week. Doreen's present responsibility is to supervise the staff of seven.

Most of the time, the business runs fairly smoothly, and Doreen has generally good relations with the employees. She gets on particularly well with the three staff who work on the site, gardeners Anne, Tom and David, and the secretary/book-keeper Eileen, her cousin, also aged 45. Doreen only occasionally has much to do with Alf, the elderly handyman who does routine maintenance and cleaning on a part-time basis. Alf is a distant relative of Reg, who calls him in whenever his services are needed. Of the two delivery-van drivers, middle-aged Ron has been on the payroll for many years, and is Eileen's second husband. Doreen and Ron are not at all close, and tend to relate mainly via Eileen. The other driver is young Mark, and he is fairly new to the job. Although reliable, he has had some difficulty relating to Doreen, and looks up to Ron, whom he considers to be his direct superior.

Over the past six months or so, Doreen has been aware of a growing dissatisfaction with her job as supervisor. She has come to believe that the cause of her problem lies in a particular habit that Reg has always had, and that she has been finding increasingly irritating, particularly since young Mark replaced their previous driver. Reg has always been in the habit of dropping in to the site office to chat about what he calls the 'operations chart' – his term for the wall chart showing the delivery outlets, delivery schedules, and stock holdings. This chart was his own invention for what he called 'maximum smooth running'. While Doreen routinely keeps Reg's public chart updated for him, she in fact runs the business by using her own version, which she keeps in her desk. However, their almost daily ritual of checking on Reg's chart is quite enjoyed by both of them, and they often share a cup of tea while they talk shop. There is one aspect, however, that unfailingly gets under Doreen's skin: every now and again, for example when Reg sees a need for some change in the supply or demand schedules, he gives instructions directly to Ron and Mark concerning variations in the deliveries routine. On several occasions, this has not worked out well, and Doreen has had to come in and sort things out with the drivers, and more recently with a few of the customers too. This situation has been worrying Doreen more and more, but she has not been able to confront Reg, who returns to his house after visiting the site office presumably satisfied that he still has some vestige of a say in the running of the nursery! The outcomes of this once minor interference with Doreen's daily schedule planning have been steadily growing into a problem for her – a nagging sense of frustration at the interference, a growing anxiety preceding the morning chat and coffee session with Reg, and a worsening of her relationship with the drivers, who tend to blame Doreen for messing up their schedules!

At home one evening, Doreen discusses her concern with her husband, Bob, and they agree that the problem needs to be addressed before it gets any worse. They both feel that it revolves around Reg's interference with the drivers' schedules, which Doreen particularly resents because it has little to do with advertising. Neither Bob nor Doreen feels that a successful outcome of a confrontation with Reg would be very likely – on previous occasions when Doreen had attempted to discuss any problem that involved any difficulty with the staff, Reg had been reluctant to discuss the issue, much less deal with it, preferring to 'leave it in Doreen's capable hands'. In one specific case – the dismissal of the driver whom Mark had replaced – it was a control issue. After a succession of relatively minor delivery errors, Doreen one morning had waited until Reg left the office, then called the two drivers into the office and overruled Reg's instructions to vary the delivery route. The younger driver quite rudely said that if he was to have two bosses, and one of them was a woman, he'd take his orders from the male. Ron was standing nearby, but merely smiled and offered no comment.

The incident had upset Doreen considerably, and over the next few days she made several attempts to get Reg to talk about it, but he found a series of excuses each time she tried to pin him down. Eventually, he said 'You're the manager, Doreen, you sort it out'. Doreen was spared the ordeal of having to dismiss the driver, as he came in a few days later and said he was leaving the job anyway. It was about this time that Doreen realised that her appointment as supervisor had never been anything but an informal arrangement when Reg and Ellie retired – at no time had any formal title such as Supervisor or Manager been talked about, much less established.

As Doreen recalls this in her talk with her husband, they both agree that it would be for the better if she had that authority officially, and that it is her due anyway, since she has been successfully running the business now for five years. In touch now with her need for recognition as well as her indignation, Doreen says she is determined to arrange a time to get Reg on one side and broach both the issues with him: her formal appointment as Manager of Topseed Nursery, and the rather more delicate matter of his unwelcome interference with a particular aspect of that management! Bob reminds her that Reg and Ellie are due to leave in two weeks for their annual month's holiday up north. Doreen feels a rush of anxiety at the prospect of what she sees as an impending crisis – at no time has she ever had the confidence to really confront Reg over matters that were important to her. Reg always managed to slide off the subject and evade any direct negotiation, and Doreen always ended up frustrated. Her good relationship with Reg and Ellie on a social level is also important to her, and it is usually this that leads her to be more accepting – or long-suffering – than she really wants to be. Bob suggests that it is time to bring things to a head, and mentions a management course being run the following weekend at an adult education centre in the city. As a teacher, Bob has been on in-service courses of the same type, and assures Doreen that her anxiety might be reduced if she went along to one and explored her problem with the study group. With some relief, Doreen decides to do so before tackling Reg, which she will then be happy to do 'a little later'.

The following weekend, Doreen and ten other participants in the 'Management and Human Behaviour' course are invited by the tutor to write a brief sentence or two describing what aspect of management they most want to explore. She describes her special interest as follows: 'How to cope with conflict in small groups – to handle it without it draining me, especially when caught in the middle between two others'. As the course proceeds, the tutor and the group members focus on each participant's personal interest in turn, exploring it in considerable depth. A high level of cohesion develops among the members, such that towards the end of the second day Doreen feels quite confident when her turn comes to elaborate on her special interest statement. She explains her work situation rather haltingly at first, and the tutor helps by drawing the following picture on the whiteboard to represent his understanding of her work system:

The tutor's view of Doreen's work system.

Doreen and the group members discuss this picture in relation to her verbal statement, and Doreen goes to the board to correct the diagram, placing herself in between the two subsystems of workers and management:

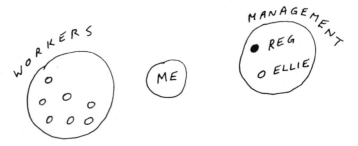

Doreen's amended work system diagram.

This helps her to articulate her problem more clearly – she feels herself caught in the middle between the workers on the one hand and management on the other. Aware that she has not been dealing very effectively either with the disgruntled workers or the interfering manager, Doreen finally points to Reg as the real focus of her growing distress. At this point, the tutor asks her to set out her work system just as she has drawn it, using the other people in the group as role-players. The tutor gets her to coach each role-player to help them get in touch with their character and the attitudes they portray. Doreen then plays herself, and the tutor moves the ensuing role-play through a typical situation in which 'Reg' comes in to the office and alters the drivers' schedule for the day. At the point when this occurs, Doreen shows obvious signs of agitation, but continues to be bright and chatty to 'Reg', who goes back to his house unaware of her concern. At this point the tutor asks her what she was thinking, and she says she was 'beating herself over the head' for not confronting Reg there and then. Some of the other members point out that she is being kind to Reg but unkind to herself in perpetuating this situation.

After some further feedback from the group, Doreen explains that she knows she'll have to pick just the right moment to talk to Reg about it. Pressed for an explanation of what might be 'just the right moment', Doreen seems unclear about it herself, but says that it is certainly not in the site office. After this point, the tutor institutes a full role-training session, in which Doreen explores a number of alternative scenarios that might constitute the conditions most likely to have a successful outcome, both for her and Reg. With the enthusiastic and often humorous assistance of the other members of the group, she tries out several attempts at confronting 'Reg', but it is obvious to all present that both she and Reg are conflict avoiders at heart, and the attempts collapse as he neatly evades her by postponing the discussion or smoothing her over in a way she finds totally disarming. After several more attempts, Doreen again gets in touch with her feelings, first her irritation, then indignation, and finally exasperation.

Role-reversing (changing places with the man playing the role of Reg) enables her to experience how threatened Reg feels whenever Doreen confronts him. The tutor asks 'Reg' (still being played by Doreen) what he thinks of Doreen as a manager, and he (she) gives a glowing tribute to her competence, friendly manner, and thoroughly business-like approach to her job. 'Why then', asks the tutor, 'don't you officially appoint her Manager, and leave everything down at the site office in her capable hands, including all the driving schedules and so on?' 'I'd be relieved to do that, but she's never brought it up, so I suppose she's happy with the way things are' says Doreen-as-Reg. At this point in the role play, the scene seems to have become real for Doreen – reversing roles again, Doreen plays herself and replies to Reg: 'Look, I'm not really happy at all Reg, and while we're both here on our own, I'd like to say that I've reached a point where I'm only prepared to go on running this place if you formally make me the manager, and leave all the day-to-day decisions in my hands. I'm not good at promotions and advertising, and I'd like you to stay in charge of all that side of things. I think you'll agree I'm capable of all the rest. I really have to have the running of the place – and especially the delivery schedules – handled by me alone. That's what you originally invited me to do, if you remember. The staff are having a hard time coping with two of us giving them contradictory orders, and I really don't want that to go on any longer'.

Doreen has been confident and assertive, and has been careful to make sure that 'Reg' hears that she still wants a working relationship with him. At this point, the tutor ends the role-play, and after the role-players have come out of role and returned to being themselves, they share with Doreen their impressions of her performance. Several of them comment on how self-assured she was when, playing Reg, she gave herself a pat on the back for her work at the nursery. The tutor rounds off the session with a brief resume of the main points about roles and leadership in her work organisation, and the communication behaviours that they had all seen to be effective on her part. She is elated with her experience, and for a while discusses with the others how she will go about arranging to set up her talk with Reg before he leaves for his holiday. 'I'll bide my time, be businesslike, be clear, and care for myself as well as Reg' Doreen says.

The following week, Reg calls in to the site office as usual, but with only one day to go before leaving for his holiday his conversation is about everything except the drivers' schedules. Doreen senses that the time is not ripe for a full discussion just at that moment, but is also aware of her own feeling of urgency to start the ball rolling. It is with some surprise that she hears her own very calm and confident voice telling Reg that she would like to have a business meeting with him as soon as he gets back from his holiday. Before Reg has time to ask any questions, Doreen goes on to say that she hopes he and Ellie will have a wonderful trip, then adds that she'd like to walk back up to the house with him to say goodbye to Ellie. As they walk up the hill side by side, Reg is quiet and Doreen chats brightly on about the last holiday she and Bob and the family took three years ago, before their eldest daughter left home. As they are about to go inside the house to find Ellie, Doreen turns to Reg and says 'While you're away, would you give some thought to promoting me officially to Manager? That's what I'd like to talk to you about when you get back. I'm only mentioning it now so that you can have a think about it beforehand and maybe discuss it with Ellie too while you're away. That reminds me, I don't know the date you're planning to be back by, and I'll need to know that in case there are any phone calls about promotions or advertising while you're gone. Now, I'd better go in and say a quick goodbye to Ellie. Have a good holiday Reg, see you when you come back'.

Sequel

Doreen telephoned Reg the day after he and Ellie returned from their holiday. After the customary exchanges and chatting, Doreen asked if he
would come down to the site office the following afternoon for the meeting. Instead, Reg asked her to come to the house there and then, and they
would talk over morning coffee and cakes. For a moment, Doreen felt a
pang of anxiety at the familiar feeling of being caught in a two-way tug of
war, this time tied to the issue of her territory *versus* Reg's. The feeling
went as fast as it came; some sixth sense told her that it was to be a positive meeting and that the 'big house' was the proper place for it. She was
right: Reg and Ellie greeted her with coffee and cakes, and with their decision that not only would she be formally instituted as the Manager of
Topseed Nursery, but she and her family would first be given an all-
expenses-paid fortnight's holiday in recognition of her contribution to the
growth of the business over many years. Doreen has not furnished details
of her reaction at that moment, but subsequently has reported that both her
job satisfaction and the nursery efficiency were 'remarkably better than
they've been for a long time!'

Analysis

Over the past five years or so, the control and leadership structure at
Topseed Nursery has been subject to frequent disturbances caused by
Reg's innocent interference with the schedules. He appears not to be able
to relinquish his former supervisory role to Doreen and stay with promotions and advertising. Instead, he partly performs the earlier role when he
issues instructions to the drivers, and partly abdicates when problems
ensue. Doreen has succumbed to a similar role ambiguity in permitting
this state of affairs to persist over several years. As a consequence, the disruptions are causing an increasing number of problems for her as well as
for some of the customers. There are some complicating factors in her
relationship with Ron and with the younger driver Mark, but the main difficulty seems to be her relationship with Reg, whom she pinpoints as the
cause of her growing dissatisfaction. She is incapable of confronting him
effectively, and there are multiple factors involved in this block to starting
an effective communication. These include low self-esteem, fear of
authority figures and suppression of feelings on Doreen's part, and persistent shifting and some defensiveness on Reg's part. She is, however,
acutely aware of her internal frustration and the sense of being drained by
her position (caught in the middle between management and workers and
feeling loyalty to both).

In the adult education course, it is not until towards the end that Doreen
feels confident enough to take her turn and present her problem. She is as
slow here to build up to the moment of action as she has been at Topseed
Nursery. That she acts at all is possibly due to the learning context being

far safer than the work context. The second of her two diagrams shows her predicament as well as her solution, although at the time it was drawn she would not have been aware of that. It shows her stuck – and being drained by the stress of that – between management and workers, and at the same time portrays her desired state as Manager, through whom the owners would properly channel their interventions into the workplace.

In the role play, Doreen faithfully enacts the recurring situation when Reg comes in to the site office and plays both his social role and his task role, the very behaviour that places Doreen in her dilemma. She cannot make a clear statement to Reg, because she is in a conflicted state of some complexity, which may well have its origins in early childhood patterns to do with self-esteem or relationships with authority figures. Wherever the origins may lie, it is anxiety-provoking, whereas for Reg there is no anxiety arising from playing these two particular roles at once. The clarity and centredness that Doreen needs in order to be able to act effectively could come in a number of ways: through therapy, cognitive learning, role-modelling or experience. The training group was to provide all of this. Without some conceptual understanding of systems, roles and leadership, and a concurrent elevation of her feelings of self-worth, Doreen would remain incapable of successfully communicating either what she wants or what she doesn't want.

During the course of the role-training segment of the session, Doreen's frustration level escalates as she is thwarted again and again by the very appropriately selected group member who played the part of Reg. The role-reversal (when she herself takes the part of Reg) is an opportunity for Doreen to see herself as others see her. More accurately, the technique gives licence for that submerged part of her that really does recognise her worth to speak out. It also gives her some insight into what Reg's thoughts and feelings might be, and in this her perception is likely to be equally trustworthy. The energy underlying her mounting frustration has been rechannelled into self-appreciation, and a new determination to make changes.

Doreen's new understandings and her increased sense of self-worth persist long enough for her to take direct action, and in doing so she intuitively uses clear and effective communication when Reg next appears in the site office. Her sense of timing is impeccable – the meeting she asks for is to be after Reg's return from holiday, and her direct request to be promoted to Manager is made not in the site office face to face across a counter, but on Reg's own territory and after they have walked for a while side by side. Her inner tuning to the nonverbal and environmental contexts serves her well. She is comfortably in command of the situation, and does not allow the issue to be opened into a debate at that point. She creates an opportunity for Ellie to be included in Reg's deliberations, but leaves him free to follow that lead if he feels so inclined. Finally, she terminates the discussion by grounding it back in the business of the nursery, assuring Reg that his responsibilities will be upheld during his absence. Her first move has been made, and she has indeed fulfilled her closing promise made to the training group members a few days earlier.

When Doreen makes her next move, after Reg has returned from his holiday, she again remembers to give him some time and space before they meet, but her anxiety leads her to suggest the site office (her territory). However, she has no hesitation or qualms about accepting Reg's invitation to come up to his house. Her intuition rightly tells her that the news will be good. The confrontation she had been fearing and postponing for so long had been powerfully transformed.

Case Study

4

THE STAFF DEVELOPMENT
TRAINING GROUP

*This case study describes a critical incident in a government
planning and housing authority. The Chief Executive Officer has
given approval for a staff development programme on creative
problem-solving for middle managers in the organisation. Soon
after the start of the programme, some of the managers on the
course complain to the CEO that it is not to their liking. This case
study examines the events leading up to and flowing on from a
brief and informal discussion between the CEO and the two staff
members responsible for running the programme. The analysis
looks at the way the two co-leaders work together as a team to
deal with the situation. The focus is on planning, problem-solving
and conflict management, but the case also illustrates how an
even wider multiplicity of concepts is involved in even the most
routine incidents typical of organisational life.*

The background

Fifteen divisional managers are attending a twelve-week programme entitled 'Management and Creative Problem-solving'. The programme was
approved by the recently-appointed Chief Executive Officer, Dr. Peter
Penn. Two staff consultants are acting as co-leaders to run the twelve sessions at the rate of one per week, each session lasting two hours. In the
first session, co-leaders Dennis and Tim had carried out a brief inventory
of the participants' goals and expectations for the course, and had discov-
ered that very few had attended this type of programme before, and most
were not sure what to expect. No-one had been able to define any specific
personal goals in the topic area, but the mood of the group seemed fairly
relaxed and cooperative. Dennis and Tim gave out some reading material

on creativity, the problem-solving process, and problem-solving techniques. They said that the emphasis in the programme would be on creativity *per se*, since they considered that this type of programme was more than just a grab-bag of techniques to be quickly acquired and then applied indiscriminately. They went on to explain that they also regarded the techniques themselves as something more than mere tools: over and above an awareness and understanding of the mechanics and application of each is the requirement that the user be in 'the creative state' when using them. As Tim pointed out: 'Almost anyone can use a hammer and chisel if they're demolishing a wall, but it's very different if you want to be a sculptor!' Finally, they both made it clear that they wanted their programme to be experiential, so that learning the techniques would be by direct 'hands-on' application to problems that the participants themselves would present.

As the first three sessions progressed, it became clear that this did not suit a number of the managers. Whenever the leaders asked for a problem to be presented, there was a slow response. Some of the participants suggested that it might be safer (*sic*) to use hypothetical problems. Eventually, one or two in turn ventured to offer a problem they were encountering in their work situation, but when these were explored in more detail, it turned out that they were not very problematic at all, and the sessions seemed to lack sparkle and involvement. It became clear in these sessions that most of the participants were experiencing difficulty even with the basic task of how to express a problem. Nevertheless, Dennis and Tim worked intuitively with whatever was presented to them, and in spite of slow responses managed to cover some rational techniques, for instance cognitive mapping, as well as a few of the more innovative ones such as word association and fantasy.

During the fourth session, one participant (Mary) suggested rather aggressively that she would like to know what they were going to be taught (*sic*) each week, as she was finding the programme too random and unstructured. There were murmurs of support for this from several others, and after a few more opinions had been aired James suggested a possible programme outline. This was to divide the remaining time up into the four stages of the traditional problem-solving process (defining, diverging, converging, deciding) and to go through the techniques applicable to each stage one by one. After each stage, there could be a review and discussion session. Tim summarised James's suggestion, adding that it seemed that what the group wanted was a linear and predictable structure for the programme, with himself and Dennis planning the content around problems that they, the leaders, would present. He was about to add that this was something of a contrast to what he and Dennis had originally put to the group, when another participant, Carl, rather heatedly confronted Mary and said he thought her idea and James's programme went quite against the whole point of the programme. Carl spoke passionately about the need to experience spontaneity and unpredictability in order to learn how to cope with it, and said he was intrigued by the leaders' approach because it was making him open up and think for himself. He added that he was finding it useful to have the training environment set up so that it was very much like life in his department, which was definitely not neatly structured and predictable. Mary seemed to be preparing herself for a retort to this, but was cut off by other voices supporting Carl, one of whom in particular expressed an interest in exploring the nature of creativity in some depth before getting down to the mechanics of specific techniques. For some time there was an energetic and sometimes angry debate about these opposing perspectives. The participants seemed to be spread fairly evenly along a continuum from one extreme position to the other. The argument subsided as the end of the session approached, and in closing, Dennis said that he and Tim would try and come back to the next session with a proposal that would attempt to combine the best of both worlds.

During the ensuing week, Dennis and Tim met several times to discuss the programme. Neither of them was feeling happy about moving towards the structured and linear approach, which they both considered to be a limited and simplistic representation. They did recognise that most of the group members were still displaying dependent behaviours, and since this was not advertised as a course on group dynamics it was probably not appropriate that they resist or confront this at this stage. Tim was less inclined than Dennis to go along with a revised structure, and felt that the group might be manipulating them into providing security rather than challenge, which would then keep them in the dependent mode. Both were ambivalent about the wisdom of looking into the 'here-and-now' group dynamics. After further discussion, they agreed that they should go along with the framework suggested by James, but at the same time model the risk-taking and spontaneous behaviours supposed to be the hallmark of creative people by doing a highly innovative activity with the group at the start of each session. They decided to focus next week on divergent thinking, and build on what had been done earlier with word-association and fantasy techniques.

When the fifth session got under way, Dennis told the group that he and Tim had discussed the previous week's comments from the participants, and concluded that since the problem-definition stage had been at least superficially looked at with the cognitive mapping and analogy techniques, they should start to look now at some of the mind-freeing techniques that were readily applicable to the divergent thinking stage. Next week they would do more of the same, and then they would hold a review and feedback session. At a later stage they would move on to converging techniques. The group accepted this without comment, and listened attentively as Dennis talked about goals and some of the conceptual models produced by theorists who saw goals as images of a future. He went on to stress the importance of the imagination in all stages of the problem-solving process, and emphasised that an unbounded imagination is particularly necessary for divergent thinking. Tim then introduced the exercise for the first hour of the evening – a guided meditation to music. There was a rustle of movement in the room as he said that, and several jokes, as people responded to what was evidently an unexpected move on the leaders' part. However, the meditation proceeded uneventfully, and afterwards a number of the participants willingly and sometimes animatedly described some of the images and scenes that the music had evoked. A discussion followed on the relationship between images, goals and planning. This was helpful in bringing the group back to their normal reality, and some members then found it easy to make connections between the points they had been discussing and their work world. A major point of agreement that came out of the discussion was the usefulness of seeing problems as challenges, and how that in itself seemed to alter the mood in which they would be tackled. There seemed to be a positive atmosphere in the group as they began to leave after the session, and several of them stayed behind to discuss the experience with the two leaders in more detail.

Two days later, as he was arriving at work, Peter Penn met Dennis and informed him that he had received some complaints about the course from a few of the participants. Dennis replied at once that they should have a meeting together with Tim to discuss the matter. Peter suggested lunching together informally in his office. Dennis agreed and went off to find Tim. When they all met in Peter's office at lunch-time, they sat in armchairs around a low circular table, Dennis on one side of Peter, Tim on the other. After their preliminary greetings and a few minutes of informal chatting, the following dialogue occurred.

The staff meeting

Peter: 'The reason I asked you to come and talk with me was because I got some feedback about your creative problem-solving course that I'd like to discuss with you. As you know, I have a senior managers' meeting every week, and yesterday quite a few people said they weren't happy with the course. They used words like irrelevant, lack of structure, not well prepared, way-out. I thought I'd better tell you about it'.

Tim: 'That's a bit worrying, I thought the last session went very well, as a matter of fact'.

Dennis: 'Did this come from everyone on the course or just a few?'

Peter: 'Well I'm not sure. They claimed they were representative of the whole group, but not everyone on your course comes to my weekly meetings, so I don't know. Anyway, I thought you'd better know what happened. It would be helpful to me if you would tell me what you are trying to achieve, and how you have structured the course'.

Tim: 'OK, I'll start. It's called creative problem-solving, but its emphasis is really on creativity...

(Tim gives Peter an outline of their approach and rationale, and a resume of the objections they'd received in the fourth session and what changes they'd introduced as a result. He explains how he and Dennis felt they were compromising a bit by adopting the objectors' suggestion for structuring the sessions so tightly, but at the same time they had found a way to keep the spontaneity intact).

Peter: 'I'm fully in support of what you're doing, I think it's very important to introduce these new ideas, that's why I set this programme up in the first place, so don't get me wrong. I'm just wondering whether it's not too much for the group, whether they'd respond better to a bit more structure'.

(Peter gives a double message here; it would appear that he is not fully in support of *everything* they are doing. His own preferences are fairly clear).

Dennis: 'I'm sure they would, most of them, but it's more a question of their structure versus our structure, I think. We see structure enough in the techniques themselves, whereas the context in which most problems exist is usually an absence of structure, or at least an unwanted disruption of an existing structure. For instance brainstorming is a very structured technique with its own set of rules, so is cognitive mapping. What Tim and I wanted to do was to get them to throw in problems that they might have in their work as managers, real problems, and we'd work on those with whatever techniques seem spontaneously right. We don't want to be con- strained by working as if everything we do is set out in some step-by-step guidebook. Linear models are not that realistic, particularly in the creative problem-solving effort. That's fine if you're going to the negotiation table, or drawing up your goal-sets, but it's not fine if you're faced with some- one's problem statement or a crisis and you have to dive in and work on it – that's when you go by intuition, respond to your feelings, draw sponta- neously on your repertoire of skills. Then there's the mood between you and...

Peter: 'OK, OK, slow down – I'm not the ones who are attacking you, I get the message. But I still think that *they* are not where *you* are at. They're not convinced yet that these techniques work, they don't see the point of them...

Tim (interrupting): 'You mean *some* of them don't...

Peter: 'Yes, I suppose we'd better find out a bit more about it. But in the meantime, I've been thinking that you could take one specific management problem, a typical problem, and use that one example all the way through the course to provide some continuity. Then all your techniques could be applied to that problem, some would work, some might not, but you could show them which ones are appropriate, how they work, in practice'.

(Peter moves away from the question of what proportion of the partici-pants are complaining, and precisely what they are complaining about, back to his agenda, which seems to be the same as that of the complainers – more structure, more security, no confrontations or being made to deal with difficult or unpredictable situations).

Dennis: 'We did consider that, but decided we wanted to work on their problems rather than 'typical' problems – no one specific person owns general problems, and I think they're actually less likely to be relevant. However, your idea could certainly provide a good programme, and I sup-pose it would help…I'd be happy to give it a try as from next week. We could build that in, maybe'.

(Dennis has switched from arguing his and Tim's case to agreeing with Peter's plan. However, his ambivalence is showing in the use of words like 'maybe', 'I suppose').

Tim (interrupting again): 'If we want a real problem for them and us to work on, we've got one right here – the problem that some of them like our course and some don't!'

Peter: 'I certainly don't think it would be helpful to get into that'.

(Peter immediately blocks this idea, which serves to make Tim more sure of his intuitive warning signals).

Tim: 'We can't teach creative group techniques if we ignore the fact that groups get into conflict and the conflict is then part of the same process that the use of the technique is. And why can't we teach the techniques just as well by applying them to this very problem arising out of the complaints? It's our problem, it's real, it's certainly a management and planning problem, it's here-and-now – what better way to see if the techniques are any good? If we can work this one out, they'll surely see the relevance and the use of them – then we can get them to feel more inclined to try and apply them to the big ones out there in the management world'.

(Tim has shifted towards a more determined stand for their original programme, recognising Dennis's move to side with Peter, and Peter's determination to get his suggestion adopted. In doing so, he too has left behind the issue about how many participants are dissatisfied. The trigger for Tim's shift of strategy towards coercive persuasion was probably Peter's tone of voice in his attempt to block Tim's move towards looking at the here-and-now group dynamics).

Peter: 'No, I don't think that's the way to do it at all'.

(Peter now shifts to a more overtly authoritarian stand. He and Tim may be about to lock horns).

Dennis: 'No, I agree – I think we'd do better to take a broader man-agement problem first, convince them the methods really work, then we've got them convinced and they'll be more ready and have more con-fidence to apply them to problems within the group'.

(Dennis recognises the boss tone and hurries to placate Peter and bolster his own switch, but his ambivalence is still evident in his words 'No, I agree'. His and Peter's proposal is the reverse of his and Tim's original plan).

Tim, getting more excited: 'Most management problems start at the interpersonal level don't they? How the hell can you expect anyone to learn to lead a brainstorming session if they aren't equipped to deal with resistances, or can't stand being criticised, or...

(Tim is off and running, fired by his own feelings about being criticised and resisted. He has also flipped into his anxiety about the coalition between Peter and Dennis. Tim and Dennis both depend on their long-standing rapport and mutually agreed approach to be able to model effective teamwork as problem-solvers. The situation is now extremely complex, as the three of them are now replicating what has been happening in the group of fifteen doing the course – a polarisation over how to structure the course. Peter's intervention on behalf of some of the participants has now split Dennis and Tim, surfacing their ambivalences that they thought they had resolved when they planned and re-planned the course. It is now Peter and Dennis versus Tim, with each side leaning towards a solution that could work, but resorting to arguing from their fixed positions).

Peter: 'Hang on, hang on. All I'm saying is, I think it would be much better to take a single management problem and keep to that one all through the rest of the course. You have to convince them the methods work in practice, back in the work place'.

Tim, in a rush of words: 'If they don't work or can't even be allowed to be put to the test when the training programme encounters a problem, how can they be expected to believe they'll work in the day-to-day work situation? These training sessions are just as much a work situation as life back in their own departments is!'

Peter: 'It's up to you two to show that they can work in both contexts – I've suggested a way of doing that, and I'll leave it up to you to handle it now'.

(Peter and Tim are both presenting viable arguments, but are in outright conflict over implementation. Peter terminates the discussion abruptly, and his words leave little doubt that he expects the leaders to comply).

Tim, continuing the argument on a fresh issue: 'There's also the question of success – what you're proposing requires that the techniques succeed in producing a solution. Most of them are tools for analysis, clarifying, generating ideas and so on. Pitting them against a huge problem from 'out there' somewhere and expecting an instant solution is asking a bit much. If we could solve unemployment or absenteeism or redundancy in a half-hour brainstorming session we'd be doing the miraculous. I think it's much more likely that we could successfully solve this problem we've got on our hands right now. I think you two are setting us up to fail, and I think the complainers have conned you, Peter. They should have come direct to one or both of us first anyway'.

(Tim has expressed his anger and his thoughts, and risked a stand-off with the boss).

Peter: 'I don't want this to get out of hand. I want you two to sort it out, that's all'.

(Peter backs away from further conflict, and seems unaware of his own part in the scenario. He quickly passes the responsibility back to the two leaders, which is where it belonged anyway, as Tim finally got around to saying).

Tim: 'Well we'll give it a try if you like, but I still would like to know how many of them raised this objection in the first place. I can see it happening now – we'll introduce your revised programme, and the other bunch who've been quite happy with us will object because it's not personal enough, or too structured or something, and we'll still be faced with a problem right on our doorstep of our own doing. Re-structuring content never was a good way to resolve interpersonal problems'.

(Tim is either tired of persisting, having had his say, or prudently recognises the writing on the wall – either way, he capitulates. His parting shot indicates that the conflict, which he has now internalised, is not resolved for him).

At this point, there is a knock on the door, and Carl comes in and hands Peter a file, apologising for the interruption. As he is leaving, Tim asks him what he thinks of the course, as the three of them have been discussing it for a while and would like to hear his opinion.

(Tim's hidden agenda is not hidden from Dennis!)

Carl: 'I thought the last session was terrific, I enjoy them all really. I think it's very important to get into this creativity stuff, and I think we need more of it'.

After Carl goes out, Tim says to Peter: 'Well, there you are – they're not all complaining!'

Peter: 'Let's leave it there for now, and see how the new structure works out. You'd better get some more feedback from the others in the meantime'.

(The cart has now been put before the horse. Tim's last ditch stand to take the problem back into the group is not followed up by any of them: Peter ignores it completely and re-emphasises his wish that they conform to his suggestion, which he clearly regards as a *fait accompli*. It also seems to be of higher priority for him than getting comprehensive feedback from the rest of the participants. He passes this responsibility to Dennis and Tim.)

Dennis, Tim, together: 'OK'.

Analysis

At Peter's weekly admin. meeting, some dissatisfied members of the problem-solving group took the opportunity to register their complaint, presumably in the hopes that he would deal with it on their behalf. Although one or two had from the outset of the course expressed some concerns with the approach, when matters came to a head they chose to avoid a confrontation with the course leaders directly and to appeal to higher authority. Peter, quite properly, brought this information to the notice of the two leaders, but took no steps to verify the extent to which the complainers were representative. Although he made it clear to the co-leaders that he realised the information came from a small number of people, he had meanwhile drawn up a firm proposal of his own to put to the leaders about the sort of change he considered appropriate. He showed little interest during the discussion, even when Carl offered new information, in ascertaining the degree of support there might be either for the programme so far or for the complaints laid before him. Intervening as he did placed him between the dissatisfied group members and the co-leaders, and he thus took upon himself the role of arbiter. Instead of arbitrating, however, he proceeded to join in and contribute strongly to the negotiation of a 'solution' to the 'problem' without the rest of the system present or represented in any way, real or imaginary. No time was spent on problem definition or option generation. This was not modelling good problem-solving behaviours, and in leaping to a solution was merely replicating the way the complainers had handled their problem (which they probably saw as the co-leaders' problem rather than theirs – either way, they succeeded in making it Peter's problem too!).

The coalition between Dennis and Peter was resisted by Tim for a while, who sensed something amiss in the whole scenario. The 'line workers' had bypassed their 'supervisors' and gone straight to the top, the top came down on the middle with a firm fist in a kid glove, and the middle responded by dis-integrating, at least temporarily. Dennis and Peter now formed an unholy alliance, Tim accommodated to Peter and avoided his growing conflict with Dennis, and there was a danger that some of the line workers might end up 'winning'. It would not be long before the other line workers would begin to feel that they have somehow lost, or at least been left out of some important decision-making process. One possible outcome might be that Tim would pick up on this and be tempted to form an equally unholy alliance with them. Thus the polarising will have gone full cycle – Tim and the 'pros' in one camp, Peter, Dennis and the 'antis' in the other.

After the meeting

Dennis and Tim were occupied with other responsibilities after they left Peter's office, and had no time for further discussion. As was usual whenever they were involved in a crisis, each put something in writing to the other by way of conceptualising what was happening and how they were feeling about it. Dennis's memo to Tim contained the following views:

Dear Tim:
1. The conflict between the dissatisfied students and the co-leaders, although legitimate, would best be handled by open confrontation. We have neither the time nor the licence to undertake this. I believe that interpersonal skills and conflict management are of great importance, but I don't think they should form part of this particular programme. A future programme should certainly be drawn up for staff training in these areas.
2. We had hoped that the 'real world' context would be supplied by the participants' own problems, but this is not happening. Peter's solution seems an excellent idea (why didn't we think of it earlier?).
3. One disadvantage of Peter's solution is that it points the course away from the students – the problem owners become the managers 'out there' rather than the participants themselves.
4. The programme must move from a focus on an external (management) problem to a focus on the participants' work problems.
5. The programme should move gradually from being structured (by us) to being unstructured and capable of responding flexibly to the problems and challenges being experienced by the managers in their work situations.
6. The programme should move cumulatively from Problem Definition through Divergent Thinking to Convergent Thinking techniques.

Tim reads Dennis's memo before he has put any of his own thoughts on paper. He notes that Dennis is fully in support of Peter's suggestion, has incorporated much of the students' requests for more linear structure, but still manages to build in aspects of flexibility and spontaneity. Tim's reaction is positive about all of this, but he is disturbed by the first comment about separating out conflict management. He feels a sense of betrayal – neither of them has endorsed that view before, and Tim thinks that Dennis has been 'bought' by Peter. He also notes that Dennis's enthusiasm for Peter's suggestion is qualified in point 5 of his memo to Tim (the course must be 'structured by us') and point 3 ('one disadvantage...'). That night he finally gets the following note to Dennis completed:

Dear Dennis:
I believe Peter's involvement in the system was meant in all honesty to be a helpful intervention, but was based on faulty premises and inadequate information. If it were just this simple, it would still be relatively easy to negotiate an effective solution to the problem. However, nothing is that simple – in this case, Peter's preference for conflict avoidance rather than resolution, my commitment to experiential learning and our original plan in particular, and the complainers' right to have their own learning style

preferences catered for are a few of the givens that place this problem in a much wider context. Issues of basic values are at stake, and if we follow them through, may involve us in time-consuming philosophical questions concerning the nature of education and of human resource management. The three of us may have been collaborating and doing so in a problem-solving mode, but our process was contaminated by all our hidden agendas. I'm sure mine were to do with things like 'challenge the leader', or 'keep the intruders out of our patch'. I think yours had more to do with 'keeping the boss on side no matter what concessions we have to make'. Whatever they are, the storming phase is about to emerge, and we've got it in *our* hands. I think the whole group has to be involved in working through it, not just us.

Here we are with a problem situation that originated from the participants themselves, which is what we wanted to work with, and it presents them with a near-perfect vehicle for the focus of their learning: they own it, and it carries the solution somewhere inside it. We are capable of resolving it – all that is required are our techniques and the 'creative state' – the one without the other would stand little chance of succeeding. The rest of the course could well be the search for those tools and the development of the right state, both individually and collectively speaking. In that way, the initial problem raised at Peter's staff meeting could be transformed into a challenge to be taken on by the group with us starting off in the problem-helper role, and gradually handing that responsibility over to them. If Peter himself would join the group at least for the start of this process, since he's already become a part of the system that the problem is embedded in, and if he'd be prepared to work with all of us in the 'here-and-now', small miracles might happen. The transfer of learning from such a potentially exciting, challenging and creatively produced environment back to the participants' work situations would be greatly facilitated. It is more than likely that it would also be personally meaningful and enduring. What a challenge! I could really get into that – the other plan would work too, but it's nothing like as challenging, and it's not even ours. Let's talk.

Dennis and Tim meet later that day, and discuss each other's memos. It is not very long before their discussion begins to get overheated, as each argues for their own position but deeper feelings begin to surface. Tim in particular reacts angrily to Dennis's insistence that the complaint problem should not be taken as an example to be worked on in the group. He finds fault with everyone in turn, Peter, Dennis, the complainers, the department, the system, and so on. At this point they both stop the fight, and talk about the fact that *they* now have a problem and a storm of their own! As a team of two, they are split over a crucial issue, and both realise that their first priority is to deal with that, before they can start to deal with the split in the training group. They have several hours to spend on this before the next meeting of the group, and they take themselves off with their sandwich lunches to a room where they can do some creative groupwork, as Dennis puts it.

The problem-solving session

Dennis and Tim find themselves, naturally enough, in their own environment – the training room with its whiteboards, butcher's paper, comfortable chairs and so on.

Tim: 'Well, which of our marvellous techniques are we going to use on this one?'

Dennis: 'What's the problem we're dealing with?'

Tim: 'We're split, that's a problem for me. I'd be happy to work on that. You can be the helper!'

Dennis: 'OK, what's the context?'

Tim: 'This programme...no, this room with to-night's class... No that's not right either, it's all of us, never mind the room'.

Tim draws the following picture on the whiteboard:

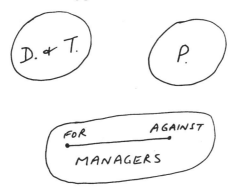

Tim's first system diagram.

Tim: 'There you are – you, me, Peter, the managers. The ones who are for us, and the ones against us. There's probably a continuum there. I'll call them the Antis and the Pros. Now I'll show you what I'm afraid will happen, if it hasn't already'. Tim now re-draws the diagram as follows:

Tim's second system diagram.

Tim: 'See? By not coming to us directly, those (expletive) complainers have split us. They could be out to sabotage the whole programme. I could put them all on one of those empty chairs and tell them what I think of them for telling tales to Daddy'.

Dennis: 'OK, there you go – set out that system right here, and do that'.

(Tim is finding his own way around the problem statement without interruptions from Dennis, who gives him his head until he notes the source of Tim's rising anger. The empty chair idea, which both of them use frequently, is also mentioned by Tim just at that moment, and Dennis moves immediately to get the exploration under way).

Tim: 'OK, there's a chair for the disgruntled ones – I've called them the Antis because they seem to be against everything we want to do. They can go right over in the corner, stare out of the window, have their backs to us. I'll be sitting next to the whiteboard, you next to me, both of us facing the Pros, the ones who are on side and like what we've been doing. That's it'.

Dennis: 'What about Peter, where's he?'

Tim: 'Oh yes, I forgot him. Well he'd be sitting at his desk way over there, half looking at us, half busy with admin. matters and dozens of other people clamouring for his attention. Tim has set out the empty chairs as follows:

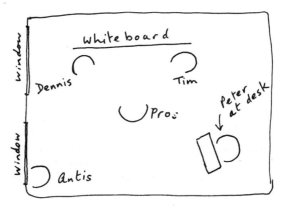

Tim's empty chair system.

Tim: 'Now, I'll be me first'. From this point on, Dennis directs Tim in a series of role reversals in which Tim moves from chair to chair and assumes the character of each person or group of people. In each chair, he starts with a monologue, thinking aloud about the issue and the situation. Switching chairs more rapidly, he develops a series of dialogues between the characters, and as that happens it becomes clear that his anger is largely aimed at the Antis, over in the far corner of the room. Tim gives them a solid harangue, and is able to give full vent to his angry feelings in the safety of the role-play.

For a while after this, Tim sits silently on his own chair. When Dennis asks him what he's thinking, he replies: 'I'm thinking about those Antis. I have to do something about them'. Dennis asks Tim to go over and be Peter again, then asks 'Peter' what Tim should do about the Antis. 'Peter' replies: 'They have every right to be in the circle – Tim's paid to train them, he can't just chuck them out. It's up to him to find a useful role for them to play, and he has to cater for their needs somehow'.

Tim returns to his own chair, thinks for a few moments, then goes over to the Antis' chair, turns it round, and places it back in the circle facing the other three chairs representing himself, Dennis and the Pros, but still at some distance. He returns to his chair and regards the Antis for a while. Then, out of role, he says to Dennis: 'I think the Antis and I really are quite a bit removed from each other, but I feel better having them back in again. I don't feel angry about them any more, maybe they served well as sort of reality testers, or challengers or something. I'll re-label them the Reality Testers, and the Pros can be The Explorers. They could balance each other quite well. (Pause) That feels much better. (Pause). You and I can stay the same. I'm not sure how I feel about Peter out there. I'd like him to stay out there and not interfere again with his plans for our course, but it was a very good one, actually. It's a pity he wasn't really here to see us doing all this – he might have had something nice to say about how we sort out our own management problems!'

Dennis: 'What sort of role do you want Peter to play?'

Tim: 'A boundary role I suppose. Off the top of my head: monitor, adviser, supporter, challenger, I think'.

Tim has now re-defined his system as follows:

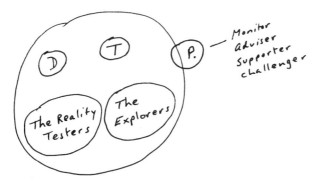

Tim's re-defined system.

Dennis: 'Why don't we invite Peter in to to-night's session by way of rounding things off with all of us present. We'll tell them we've talked to him about the complaints, and have a suggestion for revisions to the rest of the programme. If there's no further problems, he can leave and we'll do what we were planning to do to-night anyway, and implement a revised programme as from next week'.

Tim: 'That's fine with me'.

Analysis of the problem-solving session

The co-leaders have worked through a storming phase in their own relationship rather than taking the issue back to the group. To have done so would have required a lot of time and energy, and it was for this reason rather than any belief that it was inappropriate to do so that led them to work on it alone first. The conflict in the group was still subsurface, and could be managed in advance by the two co-leaders getting themselves re-integrated as a functioning team. Wholeness in the leadership team would provide legitimate security for the group; a mere restructuring of the programme would not. In this way, Tim's internal conflicts would not be projected into the group situation to complicate matters further. Peter's perspective might also have been based on similar reasoning, or on intuition alone.

Since the whole situation had seemed to be more significant for Tim than for Dennis, it is not surprising that it was he who provided the process of resolving the splits that had occurred or were likely to occur. His own internal ambivalence about the training process was revealed in his rejection of the traditional models whenever they threatened to disrupt the spontaneity of the approach he personally preferred. Far from not valuing structure and linear models, both he and Dennis made frequent and conscious use of them. The issue for him was one of control, which he saw as interference. This was further exaggerated by his anxiety about the disintegration that then threatened his working relationship with Dennis, until eventually his rising frustration and anger found a focus in those he saw as culprits. (He had not regarded them as such when he wrote earlier in his memo to Dennis that they had a right to have their learning style preferences catered for).

The role reversals gave Tim an opportunity to surface and discharge his anger, which otherwise would have contaminated his relationships with some of the participants, and probably with Dennis and Peter too. The reversals then gave him chance to re-integrate his own split values, and through that his split from Dennis, although this was never a serious one. He achieved this re-integration by a re-labelling of the role that the former 'culprits' had played, and symbolically bringing them back into the class.

Both he and Dennis recognised the value of an input from reality testers in an otherwise very exploratory programme. At the end, Tim also clarified his expectations concerning the roles he would like Peter to play.

The role system as set out and explored by Tim is ostensibly his interpersonal work system at a given moment. It is also a reflection of his *intrap-ersonal* system, for the other people carry Tim's projections of his own psychodramatic roles. He too is teacher, learner, explorer, reality-tester, monitor, adviser, challenger and supporter. Those people who surround him in the work situation present no problem for him as long as they perform these projected roles in a way that conforms to his set of sent roles. When a reality tester seems to Tim to be behaving more like a saboteur, or an adviser seems more like an interrupting parent, his expectations will not be met. Consequently, his interactions with these people will be contaminated. This applies regardless of whether his perceptions of their behaviour and motives are valid or not. A role exploration helps to bring both the existing system and the inappropriate reactions to the problem-solver's awareness so that remedial action based on understanding can be taken. The alternative might have been punitive or rebellious behaviour based on unawareness, stemming from a conflicted and uncentred person. All that remains after using this type of technique is to transform the learning into effective action.

Sequel

That evening, Peter sat in on the group meeting. Dennis gave the participants a resume of the events described above, but with minimal reference to their use of a role reversal technique, as this had not yet been covered in the syllabus. Peter spoke briefly about how he valued Dennis and Tim's approach, and how he had had direct experience of many of the methods, including some that he thought at first were rather 'way out' ones, before taking up his new position here. He described his own proposal for re-structuring the course as a suggestion for them and the leaders to consider. Dennis and Tim also spoke in favour of Peter's ideas, and Tim was firm in his request that they complete the 'mind-freeing' section they were already embarked on before implementing any changes. Dennis, having put the revised programme on the whiteboard, asked if there were any comments. One participant said that she was not aware of anyone being entitled to represent her views about the course to the Chief Executive Officer, and she was quite happy with the course the way it had been. She added that she had no objections to the proposed changes either. One other participant said that he was of the same opinion, but asked what would happen to the things they had promised to explore (!) in the earlier version. Tim said they would be incorporated in the revised programme and anchored to the specific real-world problem they would be studying. Dennis then put the proposal to the vote, and it was accepted unanimously.

After this, Peter excused himself and left, and the remainder of the session was devoted to an amicable discussion about the type of problem to be selected for study.

Footnote

The three leaders attended the above meeting as an integrated unit, and this sense of authority must have contributed to the climate of acceptance they received from the participants. Tim and Dennis both felt centred in themselves, back together as a team, and confident about the advantages of their version of the revised programme. Peter's original suggestion was built in to this, and those who originally complained would have seen that action satisfactory to them had been taken. Dennis and Tim were pleased that Peter had heard some balancing comments from group members who were happy with their performance. The revised programme enabled Dennis and Tim to keep Peter on side, at the same time retaining those features that were important to both of them. The integrity of the group-as-a-whole was preserved, as the attitudes and language identify a culture based on cooperation rather than competition. As Tim said to Dennis later that evening – 'Dare we call that a Win-Win-Win-Win solution?'!

Appendix

SEATING PATTERNS

The familiar rectangular seating pattern serves for all types of small group meetings (Figure A.1a and b). The 'X' at the top of the table represents the chairperson or team leader, since this is the position most often associated with that role. This end of the table thus provides some sort of 'up front' control, although the seats at the opposite end also have some power.

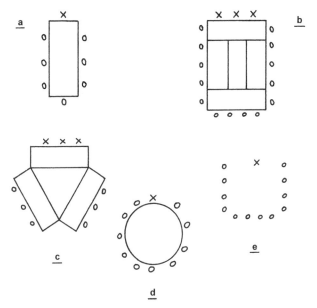

Figure A.1   Seating patterns for small-group meetings.

The wider the table, the more formal the interactions will tend to be. A square arrangement reduces the concentration of power at either end, but retention of the four-sided shape does little to increase the sense of unity. The triangular arrangement (Figure A.1c) produces a more even distribution of power, but limits the direction of interactions, and may favour sub-grouping. Circular arrangements (Figure A.1d) distribute power even more equally, and the interactions between members will be more random than in straight-line seating.The circle, an age-old symbol of wholeness, helps to emphasise unity and equality. Informal meetings and experiential learning situations, particularly those involving activity, favour seating without the hindrance or concealment of tables. Seating may be set out evenly (Figure A.1e), or 'shotgun fashion', in which case members may tend to move the chairs into more regular arrangements to suit themselves.

In small group meetings, seating arrangements and seating choice is in the first instance influenced by cultural as well as organisational norms, and then is further affected by individual perceptions of status and power differentials. The purpose of the meeting will also have a direct bearing on who sits where: informal discussion, hard competitive bargaining, and co-operative problem-solving will each dictate a different seating pattern. So too will hidden agendas, anticipated pleasure or anxiety, and the existence of cliques and coalitions. In informal group meetings, the third dimension may also be significant: the one who chooses to sit perched a little higher than the rest – on the back of a chair or on a window-ledge for example – may nonverbally be indicating a wish to attract attention, dominate the discussion, or make a bid for leadership or power over the other members.

For meetings involving predominantly one-way communication, as in skill instruction or an address by invited speakers, open table arrangements clustered around the instructor/speakers are favoured (Figure A.2). These should afford members an uninterrupted view of the speaker and of each other.

Figure A.2   Seating patterns for listening and watching.

Arrangements of seating or work stations for groups and teams engaged in technical operations (such as assembly lines, secretarial pools, and so on) have an endless variety. These usually result from a combination of a number of variables: the nature of the task, the technology, the room shape and size, the desired or established patterns of communication or status, the organisational culture, and so on.

For detailed reading on seating, see Malandro and Barker, 1983, pp.192–207; Sommer, 1969; Russo, 1967; Hare and Bales, 1963; Howells and Becker, 1962.

Appendix

B

TEAMWORK EVALUATION METHODS

In team-building, feedback about group health and effectiveness can be obtained by the following methods:

Scanning: during a session, we can be alert to verbal clues indicating frustration, boredom, excitement, discovery, complaint, disappointment etc. We can also be alert to nonverbal cues: dulled or sparkling eyes, slumped body postures, laughter, window-gazing, absenteeism, lively interactions, etc.

Questions: it is useful to ask for views and feedback from time to time during a session or in the breaks.

Reflection: everyone leaves a session with a feeling about 'how it went'. We can put that to positive use by reflecting on it, and maybe making a few written notes.

Discussion: we can chat to others about a work session, discuss different viewpoints, etc. More formally, we could select particular individuals with whom to discuss specific aspects of the group's functioning.

Observation: an observer can be invited to 'sit in' and subsequently give a report or feedback on how the meeting went.

Questionnaires: these vary greatly in length, type of questions (open/ closed, rating/ranking etc.), frequency of use, timing, depth of probing. Unless carefully designed, they can give biased or invalid information, and considerable thought should be given to their construction. Questions should be constructed with the sort of information desired in mind. Avoid ambiguity, asking two questions in one, 'leading' questions etc. Two examples of questionnaires are given below. The first consists of open-ended questions, the second requires respondents to select the most appropriate answer on a rating scale. The information elicited by these types of questionnaires should be openly shared with the group members as a basis for remedial action. Either of these examples would be suitable for use by a group wishing to embark on an examination of its own effectiveness, a safe first step into team-building.

Open-ended questionnaire (Jenkins, 1974)

Meeting date: _____

A. Direction and orientation
1. How far did we get?
2. To what extent did we understand what we are trying to do?
3. To what extent did we understand how we are trying to do it?
4. To what extent were we stymied by lack of information?

B. Motivation and unity
1. Were all of us equally interested in what we are trying to do?
2. Was interest maintained or did it lag?
3. To what extent did the group feel united by a common purpose?
4. To what extent were we able to subordinate individual interests to the common goal?

C. Atmosphere
1. Formal or informal?
2. Permissive or inhibited?
3. Co-operative or competitive?
4. Friendly or hostile?

D. Contributions of members
1. Was participation general or lop-sided?
2. Were contributions 'on the beam' or off at a tangent?
3. Did contributions indicate that those who made them were listening carefully to what others in the group had to say?
4. Were contributions factual and problem-centred or were the contributors unable to rise above their preconceived notions and emotionally-held points of view?

E. Contributions of special members
How well did special members serve the group?
1. Leader:
2. Recorder:
3. Resource person:
4. (Other):

F. Any other observations
1. How did you feel about this meeting?
2. What were the weaknesses?
3. What were the strengths?
4. What improvements would you suggest?

Rating scale questionnaire (Napier and Gershenfeld, 1983, pp. 218–9)

The following questionnaire asks group members to consider several common dimensions in groups and to rate their group with respect to these dimensions. Members are asked to tick the place on the scale that fits their view.

1. **Productivity:**   Given the time the group has been together, and given the nature of the task it is supposed to be working on, do you believe that your group has been

1	2	3	4	5
very productive	above average in productivity	about average in productivity	below average in productivity	very unproductive

2. **Cohesiveness:**   Given the time the group has been together, and given the nature of the task, do you believe that your group has been

1	2	3	4	5
very cohesive	above average in cohesiveness	about average in cohesiveness	below average in cohesiveness	not at all cohesive

3. **Emotional climate:**   Given the time your group has been together, and given the nature of the task, do you believe your group has been

1	2	3	4	5
very tense	above average in emotional tension	about average in emotional tension	below average in emotional tension	not tense at all

4. **Task v. Group solidarity:**   As a group do you believe your group has been

1	2	3	4	5
primarily interested in accomplishing the task	more interested in accomplishing the task than in maintaining solidarity	about equally concerned with accomplishing the task and maintaining solidarity	more interested in maintaining solidarity than in accomplishing the task	primarily interested in maintaining solidarity

5. **Personal satisfaction:**   How satisfied are you with your experience in this group?

1	2	3	4	5
very satisfied	satisfied	somewhat satisfied	dissatisfied	very dissatisfied

Appendix

C

CREATIVE PROBLEM-SOLVING

TECHNIQUES

The techniques outlined first in the following list are the easiest to adopt. Some of the later ones may require special expertise from whoever directs the session, and a few will only be feasible in a group that has developed trust to a level where the members are comfortable with the informality, novelty or risk-taking behaviour demanded by the method. The selection of the appropriate technique from the repertoire at the disposal of the group calls for a degree of skill that can only come from familiarity and experience. This should not, however, deter group members from trying out new ones to see if they are productive. A shift of medium or of viewpoint can quickly open up new paths.

Listing: Newsprint (butcher's paper) and feltpens are indispensable for creating lists that can be displayed and then retained for later reference. Lists may be created with headings such as 'for' and 'against', 'strengths' and 'weaknesses', 'resources needed', 'action steps' and so on. An important one to compile is a list of suggestions to come back to at a later stage – this lets members see that their contributions are noticed and valued. Listing provides a readily accessible 'group memory', and it is helpful to have them typed up and photocopies provided if there is to be a subsequent meeting.

Doing rounds: This is a disciplined way of quickly canvassing opinions, ideas or information held by each member of the group, at the same time giving an opportunity for the less vocal members to get a word in. Going round the group in strict order, each person is invited to contribute, and the round must be completed before any discussion is allowed. It is important that everyone knows a round has been called for, and that everyone knows exactly what the question or instruction is. Responses should be restricted to a very few words, if possible even to a single word. Members who try to launch into lengthy preambles or discourse should be gagged until the round has finished! Anyone who is unready or unwilling to speak may choose to say 'pass'. It is helpful to have someone tally or list the responses. A round should not be permitted to veer off into debate part way through, leaving no time to complete it.

Giving mandates: When the group begins to skitter or gets bogged down with too many Chiefs and not enough Indians, it is helpful to call a halt and give one member a mandate to lead and focus the discussion on his or her own ideas. This is done for a limited time only, although that may be extended if good progress is being made. If nothing satisfactory emerges, a different person may be given a mandate for a similarly limited time. A more formal and extended version of this technique is the 'rotating chairperson', although that has as its aim the distribution of power rather than the channelling of the members' problem-solving discussion.

Buzz groups: Members divide off into smaller groups of two to five, work for a short time on the problem, and then re-convene to share their findings. The topic for discussion should be concisely expressed so that the group can cope with it in the short time allotted. Each group must be allowed to complete its report-back before general discussion is resumed. This technique is particularly useful when the size of the total group is such that it begins to suffer some of the problems typical of large groups.

Snowball groups: These are similar to buzz groups, but members form pairs in the first instance. After a time, two pairs join up as a group of four, share their findings and do further work as necessary. Then two sets of four join together and so on until the total group is re-formed.

The Nominal Group Technique: As a break from the interactive process, members work independently and in silence on some aspect of the problem for a while. The group then re-convenes, and each member has their contribution recorded on a list visible to everyone. These ideas are then discussed one at a time, and may subsequently be ranked in order of importance. A variation can be introduced whereby members write their ideas on cards which are passed on to the person next to them. Each person comments on or adds to the original idea and again passes the card on. The Nominal Group Technique is quick and effective, and assures fairly equal participation. It can be applied without the members meeting at all – contributions from each member can be collected, summarised, and distributed to all members for further consideration whenever they choose to meet again.

The Delphi method: This is a special case of a Nominal Group Technique. The expertise, experience and critical judgement of a panel of experts are brought to bear on a problem without them ever meeting together as a real group. The problem is commented on and solutions are suggested by each expert, and their written contributions are then compiled and reproduced at a central location, then distributed back to each of them. Each then comments on the contributions of all the others, and sends back new ideas and feedback that is again collated and distributed. This cycle is repeated as often as necessary until a satisfactory consensus is reached. This method taps the resources of a range of people who might not otherwise be able to meet face to face, or who might not be skilled in group interaction. It can, however, be a cumbersome and time-consuming exercise.

Force Field Analysis: In most problem situations that involve change it is possible to identify two opposing sets of forces. There are the *driving forces* which assist and favour change or action, and the *restraining forces* which oppose change or action. A group may experience being at an impasse when these two sets of forces are approximately equal. At this time an analysis of the various forces will be helpful. Lists are made of all the driving and restraining forces which affect the situation (Figure C.1).

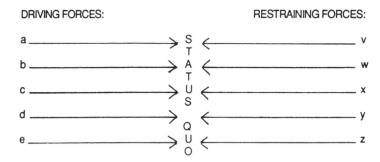

Figure C.1   A force field (Lewin, 1951).

The individual forces are then ranked according to importance and assessed in terms of what may be done about them. Next, and assuming that the group desires the change, action steps are listed that may help to increase the effect of the driving forces, and reduce the effect of the restraining forces. Force Field Analysis is based on the work of Kurt Lewin (1951).

Morphological Analysis: Also referred to as the checkerboard method or the morphological box, this entails the construction of a matrix for the display of alternative elements covering the largest possible field of solutions. The matrix shows as many elements as possible without any censorship at this stage, the intention being to encourage divergent thinking and minimise prejudice. The problem is first broken down into sub-problems, and each is given one horizontal line of the matrix. The possible solutions for each sub-problem are set out along each line as shown below:

	1	2	3	4	5	.	.
A	A1	A2	A3	A4	A5	.	.
B	B1	B2	B3	B4	B5	.	.
C	C1	C2	C3	C4	C5	.	.

etc.

A range of possible solutions, ranked in order of feasibility, can next be extracted from the matrix by tracing paths from top to bottom. In complex cases, some of the paths may not be feasible at all. In the simple example below, all the *nine hundred* possible paths generated by the $6 \times 5 \times 5 \times 6$ matrix certainly are:

Problem: How to design a children's outdoor play space.

Plan	square	rectangular	oval	L-shape	D-shape	triangular	etc.
Contours	flat	sloping	terraced	mounded	hollowed		etc.
Surface	grass	asphalt	bricks	tanbark	wood-blocks		etc.
Roofing	tin	timber	tile	shingles	slate	none	etc.

An even greater number of possibilities can be extracted by combining some elements, for example having an area partly grassed and partly bricked. If all the elements in the example above are equally viable, a timber-roofed, terraced, D-shaped area of tanbark is as feasible as an oval mound of grass without roofing. If the elements are differentially weighted (for example by cost, durability, aesthetics etc.) then non-preferred solutions can be progressively eliminated. Matrices should not be made too large – as the number of lines and columns increases, the number of possibilities increases in a 'combinatorial explosion'. For instance, 6 lines each of 6 elements would give over 46,000 possibilities! Morphological Analysis is based on the work of Zwicky (1969).

Sentence completion: The first word that springs to mind when asked to complete a given sentence is usually revealing, authentic and – regrettably – censored. An instantaneous response can be very illuminating or evocative. For example, each member of a group which has met to deal with the problem of an ailing After-Sales Department could be asked to complete the sentence *'Our after-sales service ought to be...'*

The responses might include the following:
- well-advertised
- expanded

- impressive
- in *my* department
- computerised
- scrapped
- free

Each of these responses opens up a different or unexpected avenue for further discussion. Sometimes, long-suppressed attitudes and feelings are helped to surface, especially if the responses are written anonymously on cards which can then be shuffled and put up on display. Members should be urged to capture the very first word or thought which flashes into their mind, without censoring or moderating it. Responses should be very brief, preferably a single word.

Word-play: Roget's Thesaurus is an obvious source of synonyms that could help to expand or crystallise thinking about specific keywords in the problem statement. Word-association ('free-associating') is a useful technique for divergent thinking and 'springboarding' of ideas, and is an essential element in brainstorming (see below). A checklist of transformations can also be a catalyst for changing words or concepts into new and potentially rewarding ideas. Such a list might include:

magnify	rotate	distort
minify	invert	flatten
multiply	elevate	squeeze
rearrange	repeat	stretch
reverse	add	soften
combine	subtract	harden
separate	subdivide	fade

Brainstorming: Love it or hate it, brainstorming is a powerful technique for encouraging lateral thinking and variety generation. It is basically a group activity – participants are asked to come up with as many ideas as possible, calling them out to be listed on a whiteboard by a 'scribe'. The session leader has the task of keeping the free flow of ideas going, and seeing that the following rules are observed:

1. Quantity rather than quality – the greater the number of contributions, the better the chance of a useful solution.
2. No discussion – evaluation of ideas will take place at a later stage.
3. No criticising, ridiculing or blocking of ideas.
4. No subgrouping – the energy of all participants is directed to the board rather than siphoned off into private conversations or cliques.
5. Free-wheeling to be encouraged – the wilder the idea the better.
6. Springboarding to be encouraged – jumping off from an earlier idea, or combining ideas.

The flow of ideas may be slow at first, but will then most likely speed up dramatically. The activity should not be stopped at the first sign of a slow-down – it usually picks up again for a second or third 'wave' of ideas even richer than the first. When the generation of ideas phase clearly seems to reach a natural end point, there is a number of things that can be done with the listed ideas. One would be to apply a checklist of transformations (see 'Word-play' above) to the more promising-looking ideas or combinations of ideas. The following verbatim extract from a session held by the Public Relations Office of a large company shows how they brainstormed a publicity gimmick for one of their presentations at an international trade exhibition; it clearly illustrates word-association, springboarding, slowing and surging. The session leader started by asking for ideas about how they might show off their product:

slides
films
video
mixed media
mime
play
sing
song
opera
operetta
theme song
team song
team spirit
game
show
gaming
board game
boardroom
monologue
speech
speechifying
petrifying
Dungeons and Dragons
    (pause)
cartoons
balloons
sculptures
mazes
amazes
computers
computer games
computer programme

commuter programme
entertainment
slide show
puppet show
lecture
sermon
tablets of stone
flagstone
stone floor
    (pause)
floorshow
male striptease
female striptease
staff striptease
braintease
brainwash
    (pause)
review
pantomime
fairy story
circus
fiasco
triumph
summit conference
talkfest
picnic
meeting
bunfight
barbecue
    etc.

The list continued far beyond this point, but it was the eventual combination of several ideas (barbecue, dungeon, and puppet) that eventually blossomed into a stunning presentation of the company's product. An alternative to moving straight into transformations and combinations might be to do nothing for a period of time, but simply let the ideas incubate for a while. Meanwhile the list can be transcribed, photocopied and distributed to the participants. Some ideas may lend themselves immediately to further brainstorming, while others may better be followed through using graphics or analogies (see below). Brainstorming is best suited to single-concept problems, so it is necessary to break complex problems down into simpler parts. Although it is not suited to a group consisting of rigid, hierarchical or self-conscious individuals, it can often help to transcend such barriers if it is skilfully conducted and seen to be both enjoyable and productive. Brainstorming is based on the work of Osborn (1963).

Graphics: Most groups are reluctant to move out of the talk mode, yet almost everyone doodles. The conscious use of freehand sketching may need to be introduced with the assurance that artistry is *not* what is being sought, just the idea that comes across via the image. Groups that regularly make use of newsprint, whiteboards, flipcharts and the like soon come to realise that they have added a whole new dimension to their communication and problem-solving repertoire. For example, a cognitive map (see Eden, Jones and Sims, 1983) can be a great help in clarifying the jumble of thoughts going on in someone's head concerning a proposed action:

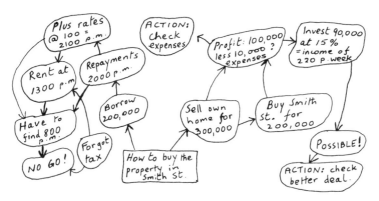

Figure C.2   A cognitive map.

Members of an ailing committee asked simply to 'draw a picture of the group' may be surprised as well as helped by the array of responses. One such committee of six managers produced images that included a dead tree whose roots had withered from lack of water; a passenger liner that had run aground, had six Captains on the bridge, and no passengers; and a tug-o'-war contest with the three male members competing against the three female members.

Visual brainstorming: Traditional brainstorming is constrained by the limitations of the spoken and written word. In visual brainstorming, the members meet in a workshop setting with a wide selection of communication aids and art materials, from which their responses are fashioned. Drawings, models, sculptures, overlays and so forth are produced by individuals in response to the problem statement. These are then developed either in concrete or conceptual form as a group activity, using springboarding, transformations, analogies, and so on. Visual brainstorming is based on the work of McKim (1972).

Analogies: Divergent thinking is further opened up by seeking a Direct Analogy for some aspect of a problem, drawing on nature, the arts, technology, history, etc. A parking problem might be compared with storage of books in a library, goods in a supermarket, data on a hard disk. A new type of glue might be analogous to resin, sap, tar or wax. In a Personal Analogy, members identify with the aspect of the problem or with an object, imagining how they (as the object) would be feeling, what they would be thinking, doing or wanting. A Symbolic Analogy is abstract, such as a mathematical equation or a poetic or linguistic concept that describes the essence of the aspect being explored. A Fantasy Analogy involves a free flight of imagination, such as might occur in response to a *'What if we could...'* or *'Wouldn't it be fantastic if...'* type of question. All these types of analogic thinking are also at the core of the technique known as Synectics (see below).

Active imagination: Participants are asked to close their eyes, relax, switch off from the outside world, and simply focus on the problem or object under discussion. They should allow their mind to free-associate, wander, fantasise at will around the problem focus. Silent soliloquies or dialogues (see below) should be followed through. After some time (generally a few minutes will suffice) they are asked to open their eyes and briefly share their thoughts, conversations, or images. It helps to use graphics or some other medium for the purpose of concretising the imagery, rather than slipping back into lengthy verbal descriptions. The group then explores the images and, particularly, looks for any connections that can be made between them.

Guided fantasy: Considerable sensitivity and experience is required of anyone attempting to conduct a guided fantasy, as the images evoked can often bring with them an emotional response of surprising depth. Fairly superficial ones, however, can open up a range of new possibilities, particularly if the imagery is subsequently captured in the form of notes or sketches. The technique is basically the same as active imagination, but with a guide or facilitator to give direction and focus from time to time. The group members are asked to close their eyes, relax, and focus on their breathing. The guide then quietly leads them on an imaginary journey to some place, or around or through the problem situation or its components. Guides' instructions should not contain references to things that they themselves imagine are to be seen on the journey, and should be interspersed with long pauses to allow the participants time to explore their images fully before being 'moved on'. The guide should return the participants to reality by verbally leading them back to the room where they now are. When everyone has 'arrived', they should be invited to share what they experienced on their journey, preferably in graphic form such as annotated sketches.

Future projection: This is a special case of a guided fantasy, in which the participants are led to imagine a future scenario, one in which the problem has been solved or in which the product is being put to use.

Soliloquy: Musing aloud about the problem, or perhaps placing it on an empty chair and addressing it directly as if it were another person can often generate a totally new viewpoint.

Dialogue: This is a natural extension of a soliloquy. The speaker changes places with the problem, object or person they addressed and responds to what they said to them. The dialogue could be extended into a sequence of such role reversals. Alternatively, another participant may take the role of the problem and carry on a dialogue with one or several other people.

Tableaux: The elements of a problem situation, or of the problem itself, can be set out as a 'still life' using objects or people. When the problem involves a social group such as a family or work organisation, it is revealing to have the presenter set out the relevant parts of the system and of its environment in a way that indicates the essential features of the problem scenario. Tableaux often take the form of quite sophisticated socio-sculptures which then lend themselves to being further explored in movement and dialogue. The system can first be expanded, and eventually fully mobilised and moved towards a role-play with the problem presenter as director, participant or observer. The acting-out of a problem involving intergroup relations is termed a sociodrama.

Role-play: All forms of role-play, from brief role-reversals to simulation games which may last for several days can be applied to problem-solving. They are mostly used to gain increased understanding of complex situations as they exist, and to test the outcomes of alternative solutions. Action methods require the involvement of the whole person – thinking, feeling, doing – and a level of interaction with others that can be emotionally as well as intellectually demanding. Anyone attempting to direct such an activity should be alert to the signs of stress that even a light-hearted role-play can induce. A trained director is essential for the safe and productive use of any serious action methods. This is particularly true for the more sophisticated methods such as sociodrama and psychodrama (Zeleny, 1948; Moreno, 1953, 1964; Blatner, 1973; Yablonsky, 1976). A fuller treatment of these techniques is thus beyond the scope of this appendix, but certainly simple role-reversal dialogues and extended tableaux can be attempted by any group.

Synectics: A Synectics group is normally specially commissioned to deal with a specific problem, usually in the field of design or in product improvement. It is a rigorous process that requires a trained and experienced director working with a group of people having a wide range of backgrounds and knowledge, and a similar degree of experience of the method. A typical session goes through the following stages:

1. A statement of the 'Problem As Given' (PAG): the leader or client describes the problem in his or her own words, provides the background information, and outlines what has been done so far to try to solve it.
2. Problem analysis: the PAG is discussed at length, together with the main difficulties that seem to prevent a solution. Different interpretations are given by various group members until eventually a refined statement of the problem is arrived at: the 'Problem As Understood' (PAU).
3. The PAU is now explored metaphorically and analogically using Direct, Personal, Symbolic and Fantasy Analogies (see above). Under the leader's direction, the group explores these exhaustively (not necessarily in sequence), until a promising connection is made between one of them and the PAU.
4. The analogy and the problem are subjected to a 'force fit' between them, paving the way for a new viewpoint, from which a promising solution may emerge.

Where brainstorming encourages people to begin with the answers, Synectics allows the problem to be more thoroughly dissected before moving on to consider solutions. Its main disadvantage is the length of time taken to gain the required levels of competence and creativity, particularly on the part of the leader/director. Synectics is based on the work of Gordon (1961) and Prince (1970).

For detailed reading on creative problem-solving, see Adams, 1987; Rawlinson, 1986; Eitington, 1984; Popper, 1979; Stein, 1975; McKim, 1972; de Bono, 1968, 1977.

Appendix

D

TROUBLESHOOTING

Conflict

If: – every suggestion seems impossible for some reason,
 – members are impatient with each other,
 – everyone seems pushed for time,
 – members insist the group doesn't have the know-how,

Then:
the group may have been given an impossible task, and members are frustrated because they feel unable to meet the demands made of them,
or
the task is not clear, or is disturbing to the group.

If: – ideas are attacked before they are completely expressed,
 – members take sides and refuse to compromise,
 – there is no progress towards a solution,
 – members subtly attack one another on a personal level,
 – there are subtle attacks on the leadership,
 – there is much clique formation,

Then:
the main concern of members may be to find status in the group; the main interest is not really in the problem – the problem is being used as a vehicle for expressing interpersonal concerns.

If: – the goal is stated in very general, non-operational terms,
 – members take sides and refuse to compromise,
 – each member pushes his or her own plan,

– members don't listen to one another,
– members disagree on plans or suggestions,

Then:

each member may be operating from an individual unique point of view, perhaps because of loyalty to outside groups with conflicting interests.

If: – there is a goal which members understand and agree on,
   – most comments are relevant to the problem,
   – members express disagreements and make comments with vehemence,
   – there is some warmth, and some movement towards the group goal,

Then:

the fight being expressed is constructive rather than destructive, and reflects real interest on the part of the members – they feel involved and are working hard on the task.

Apathy

If: – questions like *'what do they want us to do?'* or *'what's our job?'* are raised,
   – confused or irrelevant statements are left unchallenged,
   – members fail to follow through on decisions,
   – suggestions are made that the group work on something different,
   – members are inattentive, restless, bored, absent or frequently late,
   – members won't volunteer for extra work,

Then:

the group goal may be unimportant to the members.

If: – there are long delays in getting started,
   – the group is reluctant or embarrassed to discuss the task,
   – members are over-tentative, make suggestions apologetically, worry about the imagined dire consequences of making a wrong decision,
   – proposals are attacked as unrealistic,
   – there are calls for others (or the leader alone) to make decisions,

Then:

the members probably fear working towards the group goal.

If: – no-one is able to suggest the first step,
   – members can't stay on track,
   – members over-talk each other, misunderstand each other,
   – the same points are made over and over again,
   – little attention is given to fact-finding or use of resources,
   – subgroups continually form round the table with private discussions off to one side,
   – complaints are made that the task is impossible,

Then:
the group may have inadequate problem-solving skills and procedures.

If: – members call for someone else with more power to be present,
  – there is suggestion that the decision doesn't really matter because the boss/leader isn't going to listen to what the group says,
  – reaching consensus is less important than getting the leader to hear,
  – discussion is oriented towards power relations in or outside the group,
  – members feel they have good ideas that they just can't get across,

Then:
members feel powerless about influencing final decisions.

If: – two or three members dominate all discussion, but never agree,
  – regardless of what is discussed, conflict between strong members predominates,
  – dominant members appeal to others for support, but make all the decisions,

Then:
conflict among a few is unresolved and creates the apathy in the others.

Indecision

If: – the group swings between making too rapid decisions and having difficulty in deciding anything,
  – the group almost makes a decision but at the last minute retreats,
  – group members call for definition and redefinition of minor points,
  – the discussion wanders into abstraction,

Then:
there has been premature calling for a decision, or the decision is too difficult, or the group is low in cohesiveness and lacks faith in itself.

If: – the group has lack of clarity as to what the decision is,
  – group members refuse responsibility,
  – there is continued effort to leave decision-making to leader, sub-group or outside source,

Then:
the decision area may be threatening to the group, either because of unclear consequences, fear of reaction of other groups, or fear of failure for the individuals.

Source: Bradford, Stock and Horwitz, (1978).

REFERENCES

Ackerman, L. S. (1984) 'The transformational manager: facilitating the flow state'. *The 1984 Annual: Developing Human Resources.* San Diego, Ca.: Pfeiffer and Co.

Adair, J. (1990) *Understanding motivation.* Guildford, Surrey: Talbot Adair Press.

Adair, J. (1984) *The skills of leadership.* Aldershot: Gower.

Adair, J. (1983) *Effective leadership – a self-development manual.* Aldershot, UK: Gower.

Adams, H. (1993) *The search for wholeness.* Springwood, NSW: The Gestalt Institute of Australia.

Adams, J. L. (1987) *Conceptual blockbusting.* 3rd edn. Harmondsworth: Penguin.

Adler, N. J. (1986) 'Cultural synergy: managing the impact of cultural diversity'. *The 1986 Annual: Developing Human Resources.* San Diego, Ca.: Pfeiffer and Company, 145–56.

Albano, C. (1974) *Transactional Analysis on the job.* New York: American Management Associations.

Alderfer, C. P. (1969) 'An empirical test of a new theory of human needs'. *Organizational Behaviour and Human Performance.* May, 142–75.

Alexander, M. (1977) 'Organizational norms'. In J.W. Pfeiffer and J.E. Jones (eds) *The 1977 Annual handbook for group facilitators.* La Jolla, Ca.: University Associates, 123–25.

Allcorn, S. (1989) 'Understanding groups at work'. *Personnel* 66:8, 28–36.

Argyle, M. (1983) *The psychology of interpersonal behaviour.* 4th edn. Harmondsworth: Penguin.

Argyle, M. (1975) *Bodily communication.* London: Methuen.

Argyris, C. (1983) *Increasing leadership effectiveness.* Malabar, Florida: Krieger.

Argyris, C. (1970) *Intervention theory and method.* Reading, Mass.: Addison-Wesley.

Argyris, C. and Schon, D. A. (1978) *Organizational learning – a theory of action perspective*. Reading, Mass.: Addison-Wesley.

Argyris, C. and Schon, D.A. (1974) *Theory in practice: increasing professional effectiveness*. San Francisco: Jossey-Bass.

Bales, R. F. (1952) 'Some uniformities of behavior in small social systems'. In G. E. Swanson, T. M. Newcomb and E. L. Hartley (eds) *Readings in social psychology*. New York: Holt, 146–59.

Bales, R. F. (1950) *Interaction Process Analysis: a method for the study of small groups*. Cambridge, Mass.: Addison-Wesley.

Bales, R. F. and Strodtbeck, F. L. (1951) 'Phases in group problem-solving'. *Journal of Abnormal and Social Psychology* 46, 485–95.

Balgopal, P. R. and Vassil, T. V. (1983) *Groups in social work: an ecological perspective*. New York: Macmillan.

Bandler, R. and Grinder, J. (1975) *The structure of magic*. Volume I. Palo Alto, Ca.: Science and Behavior Books.

Banet, A. G. (1976) 'Yin/Yang: a perspective on theories of group development'. *The 1976 Annual Handbook for Group Facilitators*. La Jolla, Ca.: University Associates, 193–214.

Barry, D. (1991) 'Managing the bossless team: lessons in distributed leadership'. *Organizational Dynamics*, June, 31–47.

Batros, J. G. (1996) 'Buber's "I-Thou": more than a language game?' Paper presented at the 5th World Congress on Narrative, University of Kentucky, Lexington, November.

Batros, J. G. (1991) 'Process consultation: a Gestalt approach'. *Proceedings of the First World Congress on Action Research and Process Management, Vol. 1*. L. Collins and P. Chippendale, (eds). Queensland: Acorn Publications.

Belbin, R. M. (1993) *Team roles at work*. Oxford: Butterworth-Heinemann.

Benne, K. D. and Sheats, P. (1948) 'Functional roles of group members'. *Journal of Social Issues* 4, 41–9.

Berne, E. (1972) *What do you say after you say hello?* New York: Grove Press.

Berne, E. (1964) *Games people play*. New York: Grove Press.

Berne, E. (1961) *TA – Transactional Analysis in psychotherapy*. New York: Ballantine.

Bertcher, H. J. (1979) *Group participation: techniques for leaders and members*. Beverly Hills, Ca.: Sage.

Biddle, B. J. and Thomas, E. J. (1979) *Role theory: concepts and research*. New York: Krieger.

Bierstedt, R. (1970) *The social order*. 3rd edn. New York: McGraw-Hill.

Bion, W. R. (1961) *Experiences in groups*. London: Tavistock Publications.

Birch, H. G. (1945) 'The role of motivational factors in insightful problem-solving'. *Journal of Comaparative Psychology* 38, 295–317.

Blake, R. R. and Mouton, J. S. (1984) *Solving costly organizational conflicts: achieving intergroup trust, cooperation, and teamwork*. San Francisco: Jossey- Bass.

Blake, R. R. and Mouton, J. S. (1978) *The new managerial grid*. Houston: Gulf Publishing.

Blake, R. R. and Mouton, J. S. (1964) *The managerial grid.* Houston: Gulf Publishing.

Blake, R. R., Mouton, J. S. and Allen, R. L. (1987) *Spectacular teamwork: how to develop the leadership skills for team success.* New York: Wiley.

Blatner, H. A. (1973) *Acting-in: practical applications of psychodramatic methods.* New York: Springer Publishing.

Boas, P. (1982) *Truth and lies.* Kew, Victoria: Magic Mouse Publishing.

Bolman, L. G. and Deal, T. E. (1991) *Reframing organizations.* San Francisco: Jossey-Bass.

Boud, D., Cohen, R. and Walker, D. (eds) (1993) *Using experience for learning.* Buckingham, UK: Open University Press.

Boud, D., Keogh, R. and Walker, D. (1985) *Reflection: turning experience into learning.* London: Kogan Page.

Bradford, L. P., Stock, D. and Horwitz, M. (1978) 'How to diagnose group problems'. In L.P.Bradford (ed.) *Group development.* 2nd edn. La Jolla, Ca.: University Associates. 62–78.

Brown, A. (1995) *Organisational culture.* London: Pitman.

Brown, F. G. (1980) 'Three types of experiential learning: a nontrivial distinction'. *New Directions for Experiential Learning* 8, 47–56.

Buber, M. (1958) *I and Thou.* 2nd edn. Southampton: Camelot Press.

Burton, R. L. (1982) 'Group process demystified'. *The 1982 Annual for Facilitators, Trainers, and Consultants.* San Diego, Ca.: Pfeiffer and Co.

Carnevale, A. P. and Kogod, S. K. (1996) *Tools and activities for a diverse workforce.* New York: McGraw-Hill.

Cartwright, D. and Zander, A. (eds) (1968) *Group dynamics: research and theory.* 3rd edn. New York: Harper and Row.

Charrier, G. O. (1972) 'Cog's ladder: a model of group development'. *The 1972 Annual Handbook for Group Facilitators.* San Diego, Ca.: Pfeiffer & Co.

Chartier, M. R. (1974) 'Five components contributing to effective interpersonal communications'. *The 1974 Annual handbook for group facilitators.* La Jolla, Ca.: University Associates, 125–28.

Chemers, M. M., Oskamp, S. and Costanzo, M. A. (1995) *Diversity in organizations.* Thousand Oaks, Ca.: Sage.

Clarkson, P. (1995) *Change in Organisations.* London: Whurr Publishers.

Clarkson, P. and Mackewn, J. (1993) *Fritz Perls.* London: Sage.

Clayton, G. M. (1993) *Living pictures of the self.* Caulfield, Victoria: ICA Press.

Cohen, A. M. and Smith, R. D. (1976) *The critical incident in growth groups: theory and techniques.* La Jolla, Ca.: University Associates.

Cohen, A. R., Fink, S. L., Gadon, H. and Willits, R. D. (1992) *Effective behavior in organizations.* Homewood, Il.: Irwin.

Cohen, M. D., March, J. G. and Olsen, J. P. (1972) 'A garbage can model of organizational choice'. *Administrative Science Quarterly* Vol. 17, 1–25.

Colman, A. D. and Geller, M. H. (eds) (1985) *Group relations reader 2.* New York: A. K. Rice Institute.

Colman, A. D. and Bexton, W. H. (eds) (1975) *Group relations reader 1.* New York: A. K. Rice Institute.

Condliffe, P. (1991) *Conflict management – a practical guide.* Collingwood, Victoria: TAFE Publications.

Corey, M. S. and Corey, G. (1987) *Groups: process and practice.* 3rd edn. Monterey, Ca.: Brooks/Cole.

Cornelius, H. and Faire, S. (1989) *Everyone can win: how to resolve conflict.* Brookvale, NSW: Simon & Schuster.

Crawley, J. (1979) 'The nature of leadership in small groups'. *Small Groups Newsletter (Australia)* 2(3), 28–31.

Crawley, J. (1978) 'The life cycle of the group'. *Small Groups Newsletter (Australia)* 1(2), 39–44.

Csikszentmihalyi, M. (1975) 'Play and intrinsic rewards'. *Journal of Humanistic Psychology* 15:3, 41–63.

Daft, R. L. (1994) *Management.* 3rd edn. Fort Worth: Harcourt Brace.

de Board, R. (1978) *The psychoanalysis of organisations: a psychoanalytic approach to behaviour in groups and organisations.* London: Tavistock Publications.

De Bono, E. (1977) *Lateral thinking.* Harmondsworth: Pelican.

De Bono, E. (1968) *The 5–day course in thinking.* Harmondsworth: Penguin.

Deutsch, M. (1954) 'Field theory in social psychology'. In G. Lindzey *Handbook of social psychology* Vol. 1. Cambridge, Mass.: Addison-Wesley, 181–222.

DeVito, J. A. (1995) *The interpersonal communication book.* 7th edn. New York: HarperCollins College Publishers.

Dewey, J. (1933) *How we think.* Boston: Heath.

Douglas, T. (1995) *Scapegoats: transferring blame.* London: Routledge.

Drucker, P. F. (1977) *Management.* London: Pan Books.

Duncan, W. J. (1985) 'The superiority theory of humor at work: joking relationships as indicators of formal and informal status patterns in small, task- oriented groups'. *Small Group Behavior* 16:4, November, 556–64.

Duncan, W. J. (1984) 'Perceived humor and social network patterns in a sample of task-oriented groups: a re-examination of prior research'. *Human Relations* 37:11, November, 895–907.

Duncan, W. J. and Feisal, J. P. (1989) 'No laughing matter: patterns of humor in the workplace'. *Organizational Dynamics* 17, 118–30.

Dunphy, D. C. (1981) *Organizational change by choice.* Sydney: McGraw-Hill.

Dyer, W. G. (1995) *Team building: current issues and new alternatives.* 3rd edn. Reading, Mass.: Addison-Wesley.

Eden, C., Jones, S. and Sims, D. (1983) *Messing about in problems.* Oxford: Pergamon Press.

Egan, G. (1988) *Change-agent skills A: assessing and designing excellence.* San Diego, Ca.: University Associates.

Egan, G. (1970) *Encounter: group processes for interpersonal growth.* Belmont, Ca.: Brooks/Cole.

Eitington, J. E. (1984) *The winning trainer.* Houston, Texas: Gulf Publishing.

Emery, F. E. (ed.) (1981) *Systems thinking.* Volumes 1 & 2. Harmondsworth: Penguin.

Emery, F. E. and Trist, E. L. (1969) 'Sociotechnical systems'. In F. E. Emery (ed.) *Systems thinking: selected readings.* London: Penguin.

Erikson, E. H. (1963) Childhood and society. 2nd edn. New York: Norton.

Eunson, B. (1994) *Communicating for team building.* Milton, Qld.: Wiley.

Farace, R. V., Monge, P. R. and Russell, H. M. (1977) *Communicating and organizing*. Reading, Mass.: Addison-Wesley.

Feldman, D. C. (1985a) 'A taxonomy of intergroup conflict-resolution strategies'. *The 1985 Annual: Developing Human Resources*. San Diego, Ca.: Pfeiffer and Co., 169–75.

Feldman, D. C. (1985b) 'Diagnosing and changing group norms'. *The 1985 Annual: Developing Human Resources*. San Diego, Ca.: Pfeiffer and Co., 159–68.

Fessler, D. R. (1976) *Facilitating community change: a basic guide*. La Jolla, Ca.: University Associates.

Fiedler, F. E. (1967) *A theory of leadership effectiveness*. New York: McGraw-Hill.

Fiedler, F. E. (1978) 'The contingency model and the dynamics of the leadership process'. In L.Berkowitz (ed.) *Advances in experimental social psychology*. Volume 11. New York: Academic Press. 59–112.

Field, L. and Ford, B. (1995) *Managing organisational learning*. Melbourne: Longman.

Fisher, B. A. (1980) *Small group decision making*. 2nd edn. New York: McGraw- Hill.

Fisher, K. (1993) *Leading self-directed work teams*. New York: McGraw-Hill.

Fisher, R., Ury, W. and Patton, B. (1991) *Getting to yes: negotiating agreement without giving in*. Boston: Houghton Mifflin.

Francis, D. and Young, D. (1992) *Improving work groups – a practical manual for team building*. 2nd edn. Sydney: Pfeiffer and Co.

Francis, D. and Young, D. (1979) *Improving work groups – a practical manual for team building*. San Diego, Ca.: University Associates.

French, R. and Bazalgette, J. (1996) 'From "Learning Organization" to "Teaching-Learning Organization"?' *Management Learning* 27:1, 113–28.

French, R. P. and Raven, B. H. (1959) 'The bases of social power'. In D. Cartwright (ed.) *Studies in social power*. Ann Arbor: University of Michigan Press, 150–67.

Freud, A. (1946) *The ego and the mechanisms of defense*. London: Hogarth Press.

Freud, S. (1923) *The ego and the id*. Standard edition, Volume 19.

Freud, S. (1922) *Group psychology and the analysis of the ego*. International Psychoanalytic Press.

Gardner, H. (1995) *Leading minds: an anatomy of leadership*. New York: Basic Books.

Garrett, B. (1992) 'Creating the culture of the learning organisation: the challenge for learning leaders'. In M. Syrett and C. Hogg (eds) *Frontiers of leadership*. Oxford: Blackwell.

Gentile, M. C. (ed.) (1994) *Differences that work – organizational excellence through diversity*. Boston, Ma.: Harvard Business School Publishing Corporation.

Gersick, C. J. G. (1988) 'Time and transition in work teams: towards a new model of group development.' *Academy of Management Journal* 31:1, 9–41.

Ghoshal, S. and Bartlett, C. A. (1995) 'Changing the role of top management: beyond structure to process'. *Harvard Business Review,* Jan-Feb, 86–96.

Gibb, J. R. (1984) 'Defensive communication'. In D. A. Kolb, I. M. Rubin and J. M. McIntyre *Organizational psychology: readings on human behavior in organizations.* 4th edn. Englewood Cliffs, NJ: Prentice-Hall, 279–84.

Gilmore, T. N. and Krantz, J. (1985) 'Projective identification in the consulting relationship: exploring the unconscious dimensions of a client system'. *Human Relations* 38:12, 1159–77.

Gordon, J. R. (1993) *A diagnostic approach to organizational behavior.* Boston: Allyn and Bacon.

Gordon, W. J. J. (1961) *Synectics: the development of creative capacity.* New York: Harper and Row.

Gould, L. J. (1989) 'Exploring the origins of personal authority'. Paper prepared for the 9th Scientific Meeting of the A. K. Rice Institute, New York.

Gould, L. J. (1993) 'Contemporary perspectives on personal and organizational authority: the self in a system of work relationships'. In L. Hirschhorn and C. K. Barnett (eds) *The psychodynamics of organizations.* Philadelphia: Temple University Press, 49–63.

Hale, A. E. (1981) *Conducting clinical sociometric explorations.* 1601 Memorial Avenue, Roanoke, Virginia: published by the author.

Hall, J. (1971) *Toward group effectiveness.* Conroe, Texas: Teleometrics International.

Hames, R. D. (1994) *The management myth: exploring the essence of future organisations.* Chatswood, NSW: Business & Professional Publishing.

Hampden-Turner, C. (1992) *Creating corporate culture – from discord to harmony.* Reading, Mass.: Addison-Wesley.

Handy, C. B. (1976) *Understanding organizations.* Harmondsworth, Middlesex: Penguin.

Hare, A.P. (1976) *Handbook of small group research.* 2nd edn. New York: The Free Press.

Hare, A. P. and Bales, R. F. (1963) 'Seating position and small group interaction'. *Sociometry* 26, 480–86.

Harrison, R. and Stokes, H. (1992) *Diagnosing organizational culture.* San Diego, Ca.: Pfeiffer & Co.

Hartford, M. E. (1972) *Groups in social work.* New York: Columbia University Press.

Hastings, C., Bixby, P. and Chaudhry-Lawton, R. (1986) *The superteam solution.* Aldershot: Gower.

Heap, K. (1977) *Group theory for social workers.* Oxford: Pergamon.

Heider, J. (1985) *The Tao of leadership.* New York: Bantam Books.

Herman, S. M. (1974) 'The shadow of organization development'. *The 1974 Annual Handbook for Group Facilitators.* La Jolla, Ca.: University Associates, 239–45.

Herman, S. M. & Korenich, M. (1977) *Authentic management: a Gestalt approach to organisations and their development.* Reading, Mass.: Addison-Wesley.

Heron, J. (1975) *Six category intervention analysis.* Guildford: University of Surrey, Centre for Adult Education, Human Potential Research Project.

Hersey, P. and Blanchard, K. H. (1977) *Management of organisational behaviour.* 3rd edn. Englewood Cliffs, NJ: Prentice-Hall.

Herzberg, F. (1974) *Work and the nature of man.* St. Albans, Herts.: Granada Publishing.

Higgin, G. and Bridger, H. (1965) *The psychodynamics of an intergroup experience.* Pamphlet No.10, Tavistock Institute, London. Reprinted in shortened form (1990) in E. L. Trist and H. Murray (eds) *The social engagement of social science, Vol. I: The socio-psychological perspective.* London: Free Association Books, 199–220.

Hirschhorn, L. (1991) *Managing in the new team environment.* Reading, Mass.: Addison-Wesley.

Hirschhorn, L. (1990) *The workplace within: psychodynamics of organizational life.* Cambridge, Mass.: The MIT Press.

Hirschhorn, L. (1983) 'Managing rumors'. In L. Hirschhorn (ed.) *Cutting back.* San Francisco: Jossey-Bass, 49–52.

Hirschhorn, L. and Barnett, C. K. (1993) *The psychodynamics of organizations.* Philadelphia: Temple University Press.

Hogg, M. A. (1992) *The social psychology of group cohesiveness.* Hemel Hempstead, Herts.: Harvester Wheatsheaf.

Hollander, E. P. (1978) *Leadership dynamics: a practical guide to effective relationships.* New York: The Free Press.

Horwitz, L. (1985) 'Projective identification in dyads and groups'. In A. D. Colman and M. H. Geller (eds) *Group relations reader 2.* New York: A. K. Rice Institute, 21–35.

Howells, L. and Becker, S. (1962) 'Seating arrangement and leadership emergence'. *Journal of Personality and Social Psychology* 64, 148–50.

Huber, G. P. (1991) 'Organizational learning: the contributing processes and the literature'. *Organization Science,* February.

Ivancevich, J., Olekalns, M. and Matteson, M. (1997) *Organisational behaviour and management.* Sydney: McGraw-Hill/Irwin.

Jackson, S. (1992) *Diversity in the workplace: human resources initiatives.* New York: The Guildford Press.

Jacobson, A. (1985) *Women in charge.* New York: Van Nostrand Reinhold.

Janis, I. L. (1982) *Groupthink.* 2nd edn. Boston: Houghton Mifflin.

Janis, I. L (1971) 'Groupthink'. *Psychology To-day* 5(6).

Janis, I. L. and Mann, L. (1977) *Decision making.* New York: The Free Press.

Jenkins, D. H. (1974) 'Feedback and group self-evaluation'. In L. P. Bradford (ed.) *Group development.* La Jolla, Ca.: University Associates, 81–9.

Johnson, B. M. (1977) *Communication: the process of organising.* Boston: Allyn and Bacon.

Johnson, D. W. (1986) *Reaching out: interpersonal effectiveness and self- actualization.* Englewood Cliffs, NJ: Prentice-Hall.

Johnson, D. W. and Johnson F. P. (1994) *Joining together: group theory and group skills.* 5th edn. Boston: Allyn and Bacon.

Jones, J. E. (1972) 'Communication modes: an experiential lecture'. *The 1972 Annual handbook for group facilitators.* La Jolla, Ca.: University Associates, 173–77.

Kahn, R. L. and Boulding, E. (eds) (1964) *Power and conflict in organizations.* New York: Basic Books.

Karp, H. B. (1988) 'A positive approach to resistance'. *The 1988 Annual Handbook for Group Facilitators.* La Jolla, Ca.: University Associates, 143–6.

Karp, H. B. (1980) 'Team building from a Gestalt perspective'. *The 1980 Annual Handbook for Group Facilitators.* La Jolla, Ca.: University Associates.

Karp, H. B. (1976) 'A Gestalt approach to collaboration in organizations'. *The 1976 Annual Handbook for Group Facilitators.* La Jolla, Ca.: University Associates, 203–9.

Katz, D. and Kahn, R. L. (1978) *The social psychology of organizations.* 2nd edn. New York: Wiley.

Katzenbach, J. R. and Smith, D. K. (1993) *The wisdom of teams: creating the high-performance organization.* Boston, Mass.: Harvard Business School Press.

Kellerman, H. (ed.) (1981) *Group cohesion: theoretical and clinical perspectives.* New York: Grune and Stratton.

Kelley, R. E. (1988) 'In praise of followers'. *Harvard Business Review,* November-December, 142–8.

Kiechel, W. (1985) 'In praise of office gossip'. *Fortune* 19 August , 253–6.

Kilmann, R. H. (1996) 'Management Learning Organizations: enhancing business education for the 21st century'. *Management Learning* 27:2, 203–37.

Kim, D. H. (1993) 'The link between individual and organizational learning'. *Sloan Management Review* Fall, 37–50.

Klein, M. (1975) *Envy and gratitude and other works, 1946–1963.* New York: Delacorte Press.

Klein, M. (1959) 'Our adult world and its roots in infancy'. *Human Relations* 12, 291–303. Also in A. D. Colman and M. H. Geller (eds) (1985) *Group relations reader 2.* New York: A. K. Rice Institute, 5–19.

Klein, M. (1948) *Contributions to psycho-analysis 1921–1945.* London: Hogarth Press.

Klein, M. (1946) 'Notes on some schizoid mechanisms'. *International Journal of psycho-analysis* 27, 99–110.

Klein, S.B. (1982) *Motivation: biosocial approaches.* New York: McGraw-Hill.

Kleinmuntz, B. (1974) *Essentials of abnormal psychology.* New York: Harper and Row.

Koffka, K. (1925) *The growth of the mind.* New York: Harcourt Brace Jovanovich.

Koffka, K. (1922) 'Perception: an introduction to Gestalt theory'. *Psychological Bulletin* 19, 531–85.

Kogod, S. K. (1992) 'Managing diversity in the workplace'. *The 1992 Annual: Developing Human Resources.* San Diego, Ca.: Pfeiffer and Company, 243–51.

Kohler, W. (1929) *Gestalt psychology* New York: Liveright.

Kohler, W. (1925) *The mentality of apes.* New York: Harcourt Brace Jovanovich.

Kolb, D. A. (1984) *Experiential learning: experience as the source of learning and development.* Englewood Cliffs, NJ: Prentice-Hall.

Kolb, D. A. and Fry, R. (1975) 'Towards an applied theory of experiential learning'. In C. L. Cooper (ed.) *Theories of group processes.* London: Wiley.

Koontz, H., O'Donnell, C. and Weirich, H. (1980) *Management.* 7th edn. NewYork: McGraw-Hill.

Kormanski, C. (1985) 'A situational leadership approach to groups using the Tuckman model of group development'. *The 1985 Annual: Developing Human Resources.* San Diego, Ca.: Pfeiffer & Co.

Kormanski, C. and Mozenter, A. (1987) 'A new model of team building: a technology for to-day and tomorrow'. *The 1987 Annual Handbook for Group Facilitators.* San Diego, Ca.: University Associates, 255–68.

Kotter, J. P. (1978) *Organizational dynamics: diagnosis and intervention.* Reading, Mass.: Addison-Wesley.

Krantz, J. and Gilmore, T. N. (1990) 'The splitting of leadership and management as a social defense'. *Human Relations* 43:2, 183–204.

Kurtz, R. R. and Jones, J. E. (1973) 'Confrontation: types, conditions, and outcomes'. *The 1973 Annual handbook for group facilitators.* La Jolla, Ca.: University Associates, 135–8.

Laborde, G. (1983) *Influencing with integrity.* Palo Alto, Ca.: Syntony Publishing.

Lacoursiere, R. B. (1980) *The life-cycle of groups.* New York: Human Sciences Press.

Lankton, S. (1980) *Practical magic.* Cupertino, Ca.: Meta Publications.

Lawrence, W. G., Bain, A. and Gould, L. (1996) 'The fifth basic assumption'. *Free Associations* Vol. 6, Part I (No. 37), 28–55.

Le Bon, G. (1920) *The crowd: a study of the popular mind.* 1st edn. 1920, 2nd edn. 1987, London: Fisher Unwin.

Le Grew, D., Watson, D., Crawshaw, B., Itami, R., and Seddon, G. (1980) *Creative problem-solving and environmental management.* Melbourne, Victoria: Centre for Environmental Studies, The University of Melbourne.

Levinson, D. J. (1978) *The seasons of a man's life.* New York: Ballantyne Books.

Lewin, K. (1951) *Field theory in social science.* New York: Harper.

Lewin, K. (1948) *Resolving social conflicts.* New York: Harper.

Lewin, K. (1947) 'Frontiers in group dynamics'. *Human Relations* 1, 2–38.

Lewin, K. (1944) 'Dynamics of group action'. *Educational Newsletter* 1, 195–200.

Lewin, K., Lippitt, R. and White, R. K. (1939) 'Patterns of aggressive behavior in experimentally created "social climates"'. *Journal of Social Psychology* 10, 271–99.

Likert, R. (1984) 'The nature of highly effective groups'. In D. A. Kolb, I. M. Rubin and J. M. McIntyre *Organizational psychology: readings on human behavior in organizations.* 4th edn. Englewood Cliffs, NJ: Prentice-Hall, 153–66.

Likert, R. (1967) *The human organization.* New York: McGraw-Hill.

Likert, R. (1961) *New patterns of management.* New York: McGraw-Hill.

Limerick, D. C. and Cunnington, B. (1993) *Managing the new organisation: a blueprint for networks and strategic alliances.* Chatswood, NSW: Business & Professional Publishing.

Long, S. (1992) *A structural analysis of small groups.* London: Routledge.

Luft, J. (1984) *Group processes.* 3rd edn. Palo Alto, Ca.: Mayfield Publishing Co.

Luthans, F. (1985) *Organizational behavior.* 4th edn. New York: McGraw-Hill.

Mahl, G. F. (1971) *Psychological conflict and defense.* New York: Harcourt, Brace, Jovanovich.

Maier, N.R.F. (1970) *Problem solving and creativity in individuals and groups.* Belmont, Ca.: Brooks/Cole.

Main, T. (1985) 'Some psychodynamics of large groups'. In A. D. Colman and M. H. Geller (eds) *Group relations reader 2.* New York: A. K. Rice Institute, 49–69.

Malandro, L.A. and Barker, L.L. (1983) *Nonverbal communication.* Reading, Mass.: Addison-Wesley.

Maslow, A. (1987) *Motivation and personality.* 3rd edn. New York: Harper and Row.

Maslow, A. (1968) *Toward a psychology of being.* 2nd edn. New York: Van Nostrand Reinhold.

Maslow, A. (1954) *Motivation and personality.* New York: Harper and Row.

McClelland, D.C. (1961) *The achieving society.* New York: Van Nostrand Reinhold.

McCollom, M. (1990) 'Group formation: boundaries, leadership, and culture'. In J. Gillette and M. McCollom (eds) *Groups in context: a new perspective on group dynamics.* Reading, Mass.: Addison-Wesley, 35–48.

McCroskey, J.C., Richmond, V.P. and Stewart, R.A. (1986) *One on one: the foundations of interpersonal communication.* Englewood Cliffs, NJ: Prentice- Hall.

McDonald, A. (1972) 'Conflict at the summit: a deadly game'. *Harvard Business Review* No.72210.

McDougall, W. (1920) *The group mind.* Cambridge: Cambridge University Press.

McGregor, D.M. (1960) *The human side of enterprise.* New York: McGraw-Hill.

McKim, R.H. (1972) *Experiences in visual thinking.* Monterey, Ca.: Brooks/Cole.

Mehrabian, A. (1981) *Silent messages: implicit communication of emotions and attitudes.* 2nd edn. Belmont, Ca.: Wadsworth.

Merry, U. and Brown, G. I. (1987) *The neurotic behaviour of organizations.* New York: Gestalt Institute of Cleveland Press.

Milgram, S. (1974) *Obedience to authority.* London: Tavistock.

Miller, E. J. (ed.) (1976) *Task and organisation.* London: Wiley.

Miller, E. J. and Rice, A. K. (1967) *Systems of organization.* London: Tavistock Publications.

Mindell, A. (1993) *The leader as martial artist.* San Francisco, Ca.: Harper.

Mintzberg, H. (1983) *Power in and around organizations.* Englewood Cliffs, NJ: Prentice-Hall.

Mintzberg, H. (1979) *The structuring of organizations*. Englewood Cliffs, NJ: Prentice-Hall.

Moore, C. W. (1996) *The mediation process: practical strategies for resolving conflict*. 2nd edn. San Francisco: Jossey-Bass.

Moreno, J. L. (1964) *Psychodrama*. Volume I. Revised edn. New York: Beacon House.

Moreno, J. L. (ed.) (1956) *Sociometry and the science of man*. New York: Beacon House.

Moreno, J. L. (1953) 'Sociodrama'. In J. L. Moreno *Who shall survive?* New York: Beacon House, 87–9.

Moreno, J. L. and Jennings, H. H. (1960) *The sociometry reader*. The Free Press of Glencoe.

Morgan, G. (1997) *Images of organization* 2nd edn. Thousand Oaks, Ca.: Sage.

Mullins, L. J. (1996) *Management and organisational behaviour*. 4th edn. London: Pitman

Napier, R. W. and Gershenfeld, M. K. (1993) *Groups: theory and experience*. 5th edn. Boston: Houghton Mifflin.

Napier, R. W. and Gershenfeld, M. K. (1985) *Groups: theory and experience*. 3rd edn. Boston: Houghton Mifflin.

Napier, R. W. and Gershenfeld, M. K. (1983) *Making groups work*. Boston: Houghton Mifflin.

Neck, C. P. and Manz, C. C. (1994) 'From groupthink to teamthink: toward the creation of constructive thought patterns in self-managing work teams'. *Human Relations* 47:8, 929–52.

Neilson, E. H. (1978) 'Applying a group development model to managing a class'. In L. P. Bradford (ed.) (1978) *Group development*. 2nd edn. La Jolla, Ca.: University Associates, 117–31.

Nevis, E. C. (1987) *Organizational consulting – a Gestalt approach*. New York: GIC Press.

Newstrom, J. W., Monczka, R. E. and Reif, W. E. (1974) 'Perceptions of the grapevine: its value and influence'. *Journal of Business Communication*, Spring, 12–20.

Northen, H. (1969) *Social work with groups*. New York: Columbia University Press.

Northway, M. L. (1952) *A primer of sociometry*. University of Toronto Press.

Nuttin, J. (1984) *Motivation, planning, and action*. Leuven University Press.

Obholzer, A. and Roberts, V. Z. (eds) (1994) *The unconscious at work*. London: Routledge.

Ogden, T. H. (1991) *Projective identification and psychotherapeutic technique*. Northvale, N.J.: Jason Aronson Inc.

Oldham, J., Key, T. and Starak, I. Y. (1978) *Risking being alive* Bundoora, Vic.: Phillip Institute of Technology Press.

Osborn, A.F. (1963) *Applied imagination: principles and procedures of creative thinking*. 3rd revised edn. New York: Charles Scribner's Sons.

Oshry, B. (1995) *Seeing systems: unlocking the mysteries of organizational life*. San Francisco: Berrett-Koehler.

Oshry, B. (1977) *Power and position.* Boston, Mass.: Power and Systems Training, Inc.

Pasmore, W. A. and Sherwood, J. J. (1978) *Sociotechnical systems: a source book.* San Diego, Ca.: Pfeiffer and Co.

Passons, W. R. (1975) *Gestalt approaches in counseling.* New York: Holt, Rinehart and Winston.

Pease, A. (1985) *Body language.* North Sydney: Camel Publishing.

Perls, F. S. (1973) *The Gestalt approach & Eye witness to therapy.* New York: Bantam Books.

Perls, F. S. (1969) *Gestalt therapy verbatim.* New York: Bantam Books.

Perls, F. S., Hefferline, R. and Goodman, P. (1951) *Gestalt therapy.* New York: Dell Publishing.

Peters, T. and Austin, N. (1985) *A passion for excellence: the leadership difference.* London: Collins.

Pfeffer, J. (1992) *Managing with power: politics and influence in organizations.* Boston: Harvard Business School Press.

Pfeiffer, J. W. (ed.) (1994) *Pfeiffer and Company Library of Presentation and Discussion Resources.* Vols 1–3 (Individual development); Vols.4–6 (Communication); Vols. 7–9 (Problem solving); Vols. 10,12,13 (Groups); Vols. 11,12,13 (Teams); Vols. 14–16 (Consulting and organization development); Vols. 14,15,17 (Facilitating); Vols. 18–20 (Leadership); Vols. 21–23 (Training technologies); Vols. 24–27 (Theories and models in Applied Behavioural Science); Vol. 28 (Guide and Index). San Diego, Ca.: Pfeiffer & Company (formerly University Associates).

Pfeiffer, J. W. (1973) 'Conditions which hinder effective communication'. *The 1973 handbook for group facilitators.* La Jolla, Ca.: University Associates, 120–23.

Pfeiffer, J. W. and Jones, J. E. (1974) ' "Don't you think that...?" : an experiential lecture on indirect and direct communication'. *The 1974 Annual handbook for group facilitators.* La Jolla, Ca.: University Associates, 203–8.

Pfeiffer, J. W. and Jones, J. E. (1972) 'Openness, collusion and feedback'. *The 1972 handbook for group facilitators.* La Jolla, Ca.: University Associates, 197–201.

Philippson, P. and Harris, J. (1992) *Gestalt: working with groups.* Manchester: Manchester Gestalt Centre.

Pondy, L. R., Frost, P. J., Morgan, G. and Dandridge, T. C. (1983) *Organizational symbolism.* London: JAI Press.

Popper, K.R. (1979) *Objective knowledge: an evolutionary approach.* Revised edn. Oxford: Clarendon Press.

Prince, G. M. (1970) *The practice of creativity.* New York: Harper and Row.

Privette, G. (1983) 'Peak experience, peak performance, and flow: a comparative analysis of positive human experiences'. *Journal of Personality and Social Psychology* 45:6, 1361–68.

Rawlinson, J. (1986) *Creative thinking and brainstorming.* Aldershot: Wildwood House.

Raz, J. (ed.) (1990) *Authority.* New York: New York University Press.

Rendero, T. (ed.) (1974) *Communicating with subordinates.* New York: American Management Associations.

Rice, A. K. (1969) 'Individual, group and intergroup processes'. *Human Relations* 22:6, 565–85.

Rice, A. K. (1965) *Learning for leadership.* London: Tavistock Publications.

Rice, A. K. (1958) *Productivity and social organization: the Ahmedabad experiment.* London: Tavistock Publications. Reissued 1987, New York: Garland.

Rioch, M. J. (1975a) 'The work of Wifred Bion on groups'. In A. D. Colman and W. H. Bexton (eds) *Group relations reader 1.* New York: A. K. Rice Institute, 21–33.

Rioch, M. J. (1975b) ' "All we like sheep—" [Isaiah 53:6]: Followers and leaders'. In A. D. Colman and W. H. Bexton (eds) *Group relations reader 1.* New York: A. K. Rice Institute, 159–77.

Robbins, S. P. (1979) *Organizational behavior: concepts and controversies.* Englewood Cliffs, NJ: Prentice-Hall.

Robbins, S. P., Waters-Marsh, T., Cacioppe, R. and Millett, B. (1994) *Organisational behaviour: concepts, controversies and applications, Australia and New Zealand.* Sydney: Prentice-Hall.

Rogers, C. R. (1977) *On personal power.* New York: Dell Publishing Company.

Rogers, C. R. (1969) *Freedom to learn.* Columbus, Ohio: Merrill.

Rogers, C. R. and Farson, R. E. (1984) 'Active listening'. In D. A. Kolb, I. M. Rubin and J. M. McIntyre *Organizational psychology: readings on human behavior in organizations.* 4th edn. Englewood Cliffs, NJ: Prentice-Hall, 255–67.

Rosener, J. B. 'Ways women lead'. *Harvard Business Review,* Nov-Dec, 119–25.

Rubin, I. M., Plovnick, M. S. and Fry, R. E. (1978) *Task-oriented team development.* New York: McGraw-Hill.

Russo, N. (1967) 'Connotation of seating arrangements'. *Cornell Journal of Social Relations* 2, 37–44.

Sanford, J. A. (1982) *Between people.* New York: Paulist Press.

Satir, V. (1972) *Peoplemaking.* Palo Alto, Ca.: Science & Behavior Books.

Scheidel, T. M. and Crowell, L. (1964) 'Idea development in small discussion groups'. *Quarterly Journal of Speech* 50, 140–5.

Schein, E. H. (1993) 'How can organizations learn faster? The challenge of entering the Green Room'. *Sloan Management Review,* Winter, 85–92.

Schein, E. H. (1992) *Organizational culture and leadership.* 2nd edn. San Francisco: Jossey-Bass.

Schein, E. H. (1990) 'Organizational culture'. *American Psychologist* 45:2, 109–19.

Schein, E. H. (1987) *Process consultation – lessons for managers and consultants.* Vol. 2. Reading, Mass.: Addison-Wesley.

Schutz, W. C. (1972) *Here comes everybody.* New York: Harrow Books.

Senge, P. M. (1990) *The fifth discipline: the art and practice of the learning organisation.* New York: Doubleday.

Sennett, R. (1993) *Authority.* London: Faber & Faber.

Shaw, M. E. (1981) *Group dynamics*. 3rd edn. New York: McGraw-Hill.

Shaw, M. E. (1964) 'Communication networks'. In L. Berkowitz (ed.) *Advances in experimental social psychology*. Volume I. New York: Academic Press, 111–47.

Sherwood, J. J. and Glidewell, J. C. (1973) 'Planned renegotiation: a norm-setting OD intervention'. *The 1973 Annual handbook for group facilitators*. La Jolla, Ca.: University Associates, 195–202.

Simon, H. A. (1960) *The new science of management decision*. New York: Harper.

Simon, H. A. (1957) *Administrative behavior*. 2nd edn. New York: Macmillan.

Smith, K. K. (1982) *Groups in conflict – prisons in disguise*. Dubuque, Iowa: Kendall/Hunt.

Smith, K. K. (1977) 'An intergroup perspective on individual behavior'. In J. R. Hackman, E. E. Lawler and L. W. Porter (eds) *Perspectives on behavior in organizations*. New York: McGraw-Hill.

Smith, K. K. and Crandell, S. D. (1984) 'Exploring collective emotion'. *American Behavioral Scientist* 27:6, 813–28.

Sofer, C. (1961) *The organization from within*. London: Tavistock Publications.

Sommer, R. (1969) *Personal space: the behavioral basis of design*. Englewood Cliffs, NJ: Prentice-Hall.

Spencer, B. A. (1995) 'Identifying cultural norms in the management classroom'. *Journal of Management Education* 19:4, 503–7.

Stace, D. and Dunphy, D. (1996) *Beyond the boundaries – leading and re- creating the successful enterprise*. Roseville, NSW: McGraw-Hill.

Stanford, G. and Roark, A. E. (1974) *Human interaction in education*. Boston: Allyn and Bacon.

Stead, B. A. (1985) *Women in management*. Englewood Cliffs, NJ: Prentice-Hall.

Steele, F. I. (1973) *Physical settings and organisation development*. Reading, Mass.: Addison-Wesley.

Stein, M. I. (1975) *Stimulating creativity, Volume 2: Group processes*. New York: Academic Press.

Steiner, I. D. (1972) *Group process and productivity*. New York: Academic Press.

Stogdill, R. M. (1974) *Handbook of leadership*. New York: The Free Press.

Stott, K. and Walker, A. (1994) *Teams, teamwork and teambuilding*. Sydney: Prentice Hall.

Sun Tzu, trans. by T. Cleary (1988) *The art of war*. Boston: Shambhala Publications.

Susskind, L. and Cruikshank, J. (1987) *Breaking the impasse*. New York: Basic Books.

Sutton, H. and Porter, L. W. (1968) 'A study of the grapevine in a governmental organization'. *Personnel Psychology* Summer 1968, 223–30.

Sweiringa, J. and Wierdsma, A. (1991) *Becoming a learning organization: beyond the learning curve*. Reading, Mass.: Addison-Wesley.

Tajfel, H. and Fraser, C. (eds) (1978) *Introducing social psychology*. Harmondsworth: Penguin.

Tannenbaum, R. and Schmidt, W. H. (1958) 'How to choose a leadership pattern'. *Harvard Business Review* 36, 95–101.

Taylor, R. (1993) 'How much power will you give the new team?'. *HRMonthly*, September, 16–17.

Tead, O. (1935) *The art of leadership*. New York: McGraw-Hill.

Thiederman, S. (1993) 'Managing and motivating the culturally diverse work force'. *The 1993 Annual: Developing Human Resources*. San Diego, Ca.: Pfeiffer and Company, 253–64.

Thomas, R. R. (1990) 'From affirmative action to affirming diversity'. *Harvard Business Review*, March-April, 107–117.

Thomas, K. W. and Kilmann, R. H. (1974) *Thomas-Kilmann conflict mode instrument*. New York: Xicom Inc.

Tichy, N. M. and Devanna, M. A. (1990) *The transformational leader*. New York: Wiley.

Tjosvold, D. and Tjosvold, M. M. (1995) *Psychology for leaders*. New York: Wiley.

Trist, E. L. (1981) 'The sociotechnical perspective'. In A. H. Van De Ven and W. F. Joyce (eds) *Perspectives on organization design and behavior*. New York: Wiley, 19–75.

Trist, E. L. and Murray, H. (eds) (1990) *The social engagement of social science, Vol. I: The socio-psychological perspective*. London: Free Association Books.

Trist, E. L. and Sofer, C. (1959) *Exploration in group relations*. Leicester: Leicester University Press.

Trist, E. L., Higgins, G. W., Murray, H. and Pollock, A. B. (1963) *Organisational choice*. London: Tavistock Publications.

Tuckman, B. W. (1965) 'Developmental sequence in small groups'. *Psychological Bulletin* 63:6, 384–99.

Tuckman, B. W. and Jensen, M. A. (1977) 'Stages of small group development revisited'. *Group and Organization Studies* 2:4, 419–27.

Turquet, P. M. (1975) 'Threats to identity in the large group'. In L. Kreeger (ed.) *The large group: therapy and dynamics*. London: Constable.

Turquet, P. M. (1974) 'Leadership: the individual and the group'. In G. S. Gibbard, J. J. Hartman and R. D. Mann (eds) *Analysis of groups*. San Francisco: Jossey-Bass. Republished (1985) in A. D. Colman and M. H. Geller (eds) *Group relations reader 2*. New York: A. K. Rice Institute, 71–87.

Tyson, B. T. and Low, N. P. (1987) 'Experiential learning in planning education'. *Journal of Planning Education and Research* 7:1, 15–27.

Vaverek, K. A. (1987) *The nature of semi-autonomous work group structure: an integration of the sociotechnical systems approach and group development theory*. University of Florida Ph.D. dissertation. Ann Arbor, Mich.: University Microfilms International.

Vecchio, R. P., Hearn, G. and Southey, G. (1996) *Organisational behaviour*. 2nd edn. Sydney: Harcourt Brace.

Von Bertalanffy, L. (1968) *General systems theory: foundations, development, applications*. New York: George Braziller.

Vroom, V. H. and Deci, E. L. (eds) (1979) *Management and motivation.* Harmondsworth: Penguin.

Vroom, V. H. and Yetton, P. W. (1973) *Leadership and decision-making.* Pittsburgh: University of Pittsburgh Press.

Wagner, F. R. and Goldsmith, H. M. (1981) 'The value of humor in teaching OB'. *Exchange: The Organizational Behavior Teaching Journal,* 6:3, 12–17.

Wardman, K. T. (1994) *Reflections on creating learning organizations.* Cambridge, Ma.: Pegasus Communications.

Watt, E. D. (1982) *Authority.* London: Croom Helm.

Wellins, R. and George, J. (1991) 'The key to self-directed teams'. *Training and Development Journal* April, 26–31.

Wells, L. (1990) 'The group as a whole: a systemic socioanalytic perspective on interpersonal and group relations'. In J. Gillette and M. McCollom (eds) *Groups in context: a new perspective on group dynamics.* Reading, Mass.: Addison-Wesley, 50–85.

Wertheimer, M. (1945) *Productive thinking.* New York: Harper and Row.

Westcott, J. M. (1988) 'Humor and the effective work group'. *The 1988 Annual: Developing Human Resources.* San Diego, Ca.: University Associates, 139–42.

Whitaker, D. S. and Lieberman, M. A. (1964) *Psychotherapy through the group process.* New York: Atherton Press.

Wilson, G. (1995) *Self-managed teamworking.* London: Pitman.

Wilson, G. L. and Hanna, M. S. (1986) *Groups in context.* New York: Random House.

Wing, R. L. (1986) *The Tao of power.* New York: Doubleday.

Woodcock, M. (1989) *Team development manual.* 2nd edn. Brookfield, Vermont: Gower.

Woodcock, M. (1979) *Team development manual.* Aldershot: Gower.

Woodcock, M. and Francis, D. (1981) *Organisation development through team-building.* Aldershot: Gower.

Wyatt, R. G. (1989) *Intelligent planning.* London: Unwin Hyman.

Yablonsky, L. (1976) *Psychodrama: resolving personal problems through role-playing.* New York: Basic Books.

Yukl, G. A. (1994) *Leadership in organizations.* 3rd edn. London: Prentice-Hall.

Zander, A. (1994) *Making groups effective.* 2nd edn. San Francisco: Jossey-Bass.

Zeleny, L. D. (1948) 'Sociodrama as a means of studying controversial issues'. *Southern California Social Science Review,* October.

Zobrist, A. and Enggist, R. E. (1984) 'Sociotechnical systems thinking in management consulting: a holistic concept for organization development'. *The 1984 Annual: Developing Human Resources.* San Diego, Ca.: Pfeiffer and Co.

Zwicky, F. (1969) *Discovery, invention, research through the morphological approach.* London: Macmillan.

INDEX